WOMAN

IN THE

PAST, PRESENT, AND FUTURE

AMS PRESS

NEW YORK

International Library of Social Science.

VOL. I.

WOMAN

IN THE

PAST, PRESENT, AND FUTURE,

BY

AUGUST BEBEL,

TRANSLATED FROM THE GERMAN BY

H. B. Adams Walther.

———◆———

1885.

—

LONDON: THE MODERN PRESS,
13, PATERNOSTER ROW, E.C.

Library of Congress Cataloging in Publication Data

Bebel, August, 1840-1913.
    Woman in the past, present, and future.

    Translation of Die Frau und der Sozialismus.
    Reprint of the 1885 ed. published by Modern Press,
London, which was issued as v. 1 of International
library of social science.
    1. Women and socialism. I. Title. II. Series:
International library of social sciences; v. 1.
HX546.B35   1976   335.43'8'301412   72-9616
ISBN 0-404-57409-2

Reprinted from an original copy in the collections
of the University of Indiana Library

From the edition of 1885, London
First AMS edition published in 1976
Manufactured in the United States of America

AMS PRESS INC.
NEW YORK, N. Y. 10003

CONTENTS.

* *
*
*

INTRODUCTION.

During the last decades of our social development a certain excitement and perturbation of mind has been making itself more and more apparent throughout all classes of the community. Many questions have arisen, for and against which we are contending. One of the most important of these is indisputably the so-called women's question.

The question as to what position in our social organism will enable woman to become a useful member of the community, will put her in possession of the same rights as its other members enjoy, and ensure the full development of her powers and faculties in every direction, coincides with the question as to the form and organisation which the entire community must receive, if oppression, exploitation, want and misery in a hundred shapes are to be replaced by a free humanity, by a society which is physically and organically sound. The so-called women's question is therefore only one side of the whole social question, which is at the present hour agitating all minds ; only in connection with each other can the two questions reach their final solution.

The fact that those whom the women's question chiefly concerns—the women themselves—represent, at any rate in Europe—the larger half of society, is in itself sufficient justification for a special treatment of the subject. It is one well worth " the sweat of the noble."

In the women's question, just as in the general social question, there are naturally various parties, who deal with it from their own particular social and political standpoint, from which they pass their verdict upon it, and propose measures for its settlement. Some maintain, as in the social question, in which the working classes play the principal part, that there really is no women's question at all, inasmuch as the position which woman occupies in the present and will occupy in the future is circumscribed by her " natural calling," which destines her to become a wife and mother and restricts her to the family circle. What goes on outside her four walls or does not stand in the closest and most visible relation to her housewifely duties does not concern her at all.

The adherents of this view have, as we see, a recipe ready to hand and imagine that they have therewith settled the question. These wise men are not troubled by the consideration that millions of women are unable to fulfil their "natural calling" of housewives and child-bearers, for reasons that will be given in detail further on, and that other millions have in great measure missed this calling, because the marriage tie means subjection and slavery to them, or because they have to support an existence of misery and want. The wise men close eyes and ears to these unwelcome facts, as energetically as to the needs of the people, conforting themselves and others with the reflection that "it has always been so and will always remain so." They absolutely refuse to listen to the argument that woman has a right to share in the results of civilisation, to make use of these results for the alleviation and improvement of her position, and to develop and apply her mental and physical faculties to her own advantage in the same degree as man. If we go still further and claim pecuniary independence for woman, as the only means of ensuring her physical and mental independence and freeing her from subjection to the "goodwill" and "grace" of the opposite sex, they lose patience altogether, their temper is roused, and a volley of angry accusations and invectives against the "madness of the times," and the "arrant folly of women's rights" closes the scene.

These are the Philistines of both sexes, who cannot find their way out of the narrow circle of prejudice. They belong to the race of night birds that are always to be found in the twilight, and flutter in alarm when a ray of light crosses the darkness which is their proper element.

Then there are others again, less successful in closing eyes and ears to patent facts; they acknowledge that at no other period of history has the position of women in comparison with the general advance of civilization been so bad as at present, and that it is therefore necessary to enquire what can be done to help them, and what they must do to help themselves. For those who have reached the haven of marriage the question is supposed to be already solved.

Accordingly they demand that all fields of labour for which the strength and faculties of woman qualify her shall be thrown open, and that nothing shall stand in the way of her free competition with man. The more advanced among them condemn the restriction of this competition to the lower employments and trades, and demand its extension to the higher professions, to art and science. They demand the admission of women to all higher training schools and academies, and especially to the Universities, which have hitherto been closed. They direct their attention principally to the various branches of instruction, to the medical profession, and to appointments in the Civil Service (Post Office, Telegraph, Railway), which they consider especially suitable to women, chiefly on account of the practical results obtained in the United States by the employment of women in these branches. A small minority among them go so far as to demand political rights for women. A woman, they say, is just as much a human being and a citizen of the State as a man ; the exclusive male legislation which has been practised hitherto proves that men, while keeping women in a state of tutelage, have made use of their privileges only to their own advantage.

It is characteristic of all the suggestions which we have here cursorily summed up, that they do not exceed the limits of the present framework of society. No one asks whether these propositions, if realised, would suffice to essentially ameliorate the position of women. No one recognises that the goal, at least with regard to the admission of women to the various branches of trade and industry, is already practically reached ; although under existing social conditions, this admission only results in a competitive struggle between the workers, fiercer than any that ever raged before, and the consequent inevitable lowering of the wages and salaries earned by both sexes in all posts open to their competition.

This want of thoroughness and clearness as to the aims to be attained is explained by the fact that the women's question has so far been almost exclusively taken in hand by women of the upper classes, whose attention was engrossed by the limited circle in which they lived, and for whose benefit their claims were chiefly made. But the position of women in general will remain entirely unaltered, whether or not some hundred or some thousand women of the needy middle classes force their way into the ranks of schoolmasters, doctors, or officials, and there secure more or less lucrative posts. The subjection of the sex under men, the pecuniary dependence of the enormous majority and the consequent sexual slavery which finds its expression in modern marriage and in prostitution, will still remain untouched. Moreover, a fragmentary solution such as this will fail to rouse any enthusiasm among the majority of women ; small aims cannot warm or stir the mass. And still less will such a solution appeal to that influential class of men who regard the encroachment of women on well remunerated and honourable posts only as a highly undesirable form of competition for themselves and their sons. They will oppose this encroachment by every means in their power, and, as experience has shown, their opposition will not always respect the limits of either fairness or decency. It is true that these same influential men have not the slightest objection to make when women inundate every department of so-called inferior employment; on the contrary, they consider it perfectly justifiable and encourage it, on the ground that it cheapens labour. But women must not intrude on man's higher social and official domain ; the attempt to do so is viewed in a very different light.

Neither is it probable that the modern State, to judge by recent experience, will in the future show itself disposed to appoint women to posts in the Civil Service, and least of all to higher posts, however well qualified the women may be to fill them.

The State and the upper classes have broken down every barrier to competition in trade and among the working classes, but with regard to the higher callings they are endeavouring to raise up fresh barriers. It makes a singular impression on the impartial spectator, to observe the energy with which scholars and higher officials, doctors and lawyers " defend their rights," when an outsider ventures to overstep the traditional limits. And in these circles women are regarded as outsiders *par excellence ;* these professional persons are of opinion that they have been specially favoured by God, inasmuch as the powers of comprehension with which they imagine themselves endowed, are, according to them, altogether very exceptional, and quite beyond the reach of ordinary mortals, more particularly of women.

It is clear that if this book had no other object than to prove the necessity of placing men and women on a footing of equality in society as it is, it would better have remained unwritten. The attempt would be mere patchwork, and would fail to point the way to any complete solution of the question. By a complete solution I understand not only the equality of men and women before the law, but their economic freedom and material independence, and, so far as possible, equality in mental development. *This complete solution of the*

Women's Question is as unattainable as the solution of the Labour Question under the existing social and political institutions.

My fellow Socialists will agree with the last proposition, but I am not at present in a position to affirm that they will agree to the manner in which I foresee its realisation. I must therefore request readers, and especially opponents, to regard the following statements as the expression of my personal opinions, and to direct any attacks they think fit to make against me alone. I trust that any such attacks will be honest ones, that my words will not be purposely misconstrued and that calumny will be avoided. The majority of my readers will imagine that this is a matter of course, but the experience of many years has taught me what to think of the honesty of some of my opponents. Indeed I have every reason to believe that my explicit request will be disregarded by a certain number of them. They must be left to the promptings of their own hearts. In the following argument I shall not hesitate to draw such conclusions as are demanded by results based on the examination of facts.

THE POSITION OF WOMAN IN THE PAST.

From the beginning of time oppression has been the common lot of woman and the labouring man. In spite of all changes in form this oppression has remained the same. Only at rare intervals during the long course of history has either woman or the labourer become alive to the consciousness of servitude, woman even more rarely than the labourer, because her position was even lower than his, and even by him was she regarded and treated as an inferior, and continues to be so to this day. Servitude which lasts for hundreds of generations ends by becoming a habit. Inheritance and education teach both parties to regard it as the natural state. Consequently woman accepts her subordinate position so entirely as a matter of course, that it costs no little trouble to convince her of its degradation and to rouse in her the aspiration to become a member of society enjoying the same rights as man and in every respect his peer.

The statement that from the beginning of time oppression was the common lot of woman and the labourer must be emphasized even more forcibly with regard to woman. *Woman was the first human being that tasted bondage. Woman was a slave before the slave existed.*

The basis of all oppression is economic dependence on the oppressor. This has been the condition of woman in the past and it still is so.

On the threshold of the past we find the horde as the first human community. In the horde, as in the cattle herd, sexual impulses were gratified without order or separation according to pairs. We have no grounds for assuming that in this primitive state men were physically or mentally superior to women.* Not only is such an assumption *a*

---

* Tacitus, for instance, states distinctly that among the Germans, who, in his time, had already reached a higher degree of civilization than the one under discussion, the women were by no means inferior to the men, either in size or strength.

priori improbable, the observations afforded us by savage races at the present day tend to prove the contrary. Among all such races the size and weight of the brain differs far less according to sex than is the case among civilised nations, while in regard to bodily strength, little or no inferiority exists on the side of the women. Indeed, certain tribes in the interior of Africa are governed by women instead of men, owing to the superior strength of the former.* In one Afghan tribe the women carry on war and hunt, while the men attend to the household. The King of Ashantee in West Africa, and the King of Dahomey in Central Africa have female body-guards, and regiments entirely recruited from and officered by women, which distinguish themselves from the male troops by greater courage and bloodthirstiness. ("Da werden Weiber zu Hyänen." Then women become hyænas. Schiller, Lied von der Glocke).

The so-called Amazon States which are supposed to have existed in ancient times on the shores of the Black Sea and in Asia, and which were composed entirely of women, can only be explained on the grounds of physical superiority. There are said to have been remnants of these States as late as the reign of Alexander the Great, as Diodorus tells us, that a Queen of the Amazons, named Thalestris, came into Alexander's camp, in order to become a mother through him.

If these Amazon States were really historical communities, their existence could only have been possible by the strict exclusion of men. Accordingly they are said to have satisfied their sexual impulses, and to have provided for the propaga-tion of the race by uniting themselves on certain days of the year with the men of neighbouring States.

But such conditions are always exceptional, and their un-tenableness is proved by the fact that they no longer exist.

The bondage of women in primæval times, the continuation of this bondage through the centuries that followed, and the consequent differentiation of bodily and mental powers which resulted therefrom, and thus became the secondary cause of severer bondage still, have their foundation in the peculiarities of women as sexual beings. Primæval woman, although the equal of man in bodily and mental power, nevertheless became his inferior *when periods of pregnancy, birth and lactation forced her to look to him for assistance, support and protection.* This

---

* L. Büchner: Die Frau ; ihre natürliche Stellung und gesellschaftliche Bestimmung. (Woman, Her Natural Position and Social Destiny.) "Neue Gesellschaft," vols. 1879 and 1880.

occasional helplessness of woman at a time when physical strength alone was held in respect, and the struggle for existence appeared in its most brutal and savage form, was the origin of many acts of violence towards the female sex, of the destruction of female children, and of rape.

As long as the single hordes, and later on the tribes (clans) were in a state of constant warfare, and before agriculture or the breeding of cattle had been introduced, and dearth was consequently no rare occurrence, it was a matter of primary importance for the horde or tribe to free itself from every appendage that required care, that was an impediment in battle or flight, and that promised small future return for the trouble incurred. This applied especially to female children, who were consequently put out of the way as soon as possible after birth. A few only of the strongest were allowed to live for the necessary purposes of propagation. This is the simple explanation of the practice which still exists among many savage races of Further Asia and Africa, of killing female infants immediately after birth, a practice which has also been erroneously ascribed to the modern Chinese. The same fate was shared by all male children who came crippled or misshapen into the world, and therefore threatened to become a burden to the tribe. They too were put out of the way. As is well known, the same custom prevailed in several Greek States, *e.g.*, in Sparta.

A further reason for destroying female children was the loss of life which an endless state of warfare occasioned among the males, who thus sought to avoid a disproportionate increase of women. Moreover, it was a far simpler plan to capture women by force than to bring them up from infancy.

At first and for a considerable length of time no lasting union existed between man and wife; unrestricted intercourse (promiscuity) prevailed; the women were the property of the horde or tribe, without the right of choice or refusal. They were made use of just like any other common belonging. The existence of the mother's right of property in the child (gynecocracy), long maintained among certain races, for instance in Strabo's time, among the Lydians and Socrians, and up to the present day on the island of Java, among the Huronian Indians, and Irokees, and many tribes of central Africa, clearly proves this promiscuity of sexual intercourse. According to this law the children were the property of the mother, as the multiplicity of males excluded paternal research. The question of paternity is, as Goethe puts into the mouth of Friedrich in the " Wanderjahre," at best only a question of good faith. The maternal right was preserved as a custom among some races, even after they had reached a higher stage of civilisation, after private property had begun to exist, and a distinct system of inheritance had been introduced. Its result was validity of succession in the female line alone. The existence of this maternal right was doubtless the cause that among some nations, even in early times, women became rulers. We are not likely to go far wrong in assuming that there was from the beginning a difference of rank between captured women and those born in the tribe, and that, after the leadership had by degrees become hereditary in certain families, and a male heir was wanting, a capable woman, if such there were, was invested with supreme authority. When this had once occurred it would easily become a matter of habit, until at length the right of women to succeed to the chieftainship was as much recognised as that of men.

Woman must further have obtained an ascendancy in all places in which her sex was in the minority, and in which consequently instead of polygamy, polyandry prevailed. This is the present condition in Ceylon, in the Sandwich and Marquesas Isles, in the Congo and Loango territories. It was moreover the privilege of kings' daughters among the Incas in Peru to possess several husbands. It appears to be a natural law of communities in which polyandry exists, that the number of males born is considerably larger than that of females, a circumstance which tends to perpetuate the previous condition.

With the exception of these examples which must be regarded as abnormities, man has everywhere arrogated the supreme power to himself. This must certainly have been the case from the moment in which a lasting connection between a single man and a single woman commenced, a connection which was probably brought about by the man. It was doubtless a scarcity of women, or admiration of one particular woman, that first roused in him the desire for permanent possession. Male egotism awoke. One man took possession of a woman with or without the consent of the other men, who then followed his example. He obliged the woman to receive only his caresses, taking in return the obligation upon himself to regard her as his wife and to protect and bring up her children as his own. This relationship appeared more advantageous to the woman than her former condition on account of its greater security. Thus marriage arose.*

The foundations of private property, of the family, tribe and state, were thus laid.

The possession of wife and children taught primæval man to regard a fixed abode as desirable. Hitherto he had ranged through the woods, sleeping by night on trees or in caves, when not driven away by wild beasts. Now he built himself a hut, to which he returned after hunting and fishing. The division of labour began. The man hunted, fished and fought, the woman did the housework, if the expression may be applied to this primitive age. The uncertain returns of the chase, the inclemency of the seasons, forced the family, when it increased in numbers, to tame animals and use their milk and flesh for nourishment. The hunter became a herdsman. The children grew up, intermarried (the conception of incest belongs to a very much later period), and thus gave rise successively to the patriarchal family, the village community, the tribe.† The tribe became divided into many smaller tribes, which, when their numbers increased, quarrelled with each other about pasture land. This quarrel for pasture land, the desire to remain in a fruitful and

---

* Of course I do not mean to say by this that any individual "discovered" marriage, or created it, as "God the Father created the first man Adam." New ideas are never the property of one individual, they are the product of an abstraction obtained by the co-operation of many individuals. The way is long between grasping an idea, formulating it, and realising it in practice. On this road many meet. This is the reason why one so frequently recognises the ideas of another as one's own and *vice versâ*. When ideas fall on ground that is ready for them, in other words, when they are the expression of a generally felt need, they are quickly accepted. We are justified in assuming that this applies to the institution of marriage. Although no one man was the author of marriage, there must have been one man who made the beginning and whose example was soon followed by all.

† Max Stirner, in "Der Einzige und Sein Eigenthum." (The Individual and His Property) expresses his indignation at this change in opinion concerning incest, which, he says, is a question which every one has to settle with his own conscience. Some are impelled to anathematise the act by zeal for a "Holy God," others by zeal for "Sacred Right." The condemnation of incest is embarrassing for believers in the Bible. After God had created the first pair of human beings, and their son Cain had killed Abel, the propagation of the race was only possible by a repetition of the creative act or by Cain's union with a sister. But he possessed no sister, as, according to the Bible story, the first pair of human beings were Malthusians or adherents of the Two-children System. So Cain went and took a wife. But where did she come from? And this fratricide, the only survivor of Adam, became the ancestor of the whole human race.

pleasant district, in spite of a thickening population, was the origin of agriculture.

Woman had her own part to play in all these phases of development. She was man's chief servant, she not only attended to the children and to the household, but also made the clothing, built the hut or tent, took it to pieces again, and carried it, when the family left one spot to settle in another. After the introduction of agriculture, and the invention of the plough, woman was the first beast of draught; she too mostly gathered in the harvest.

Man meanwhile played the part of lord; the nature of his employments tended more to rouse thought and awaken reflection. Accordingly he advanced in bodily and mental development, while woman, under the weight of her double yoke, slavery and the treatment befitting a slave, was compelled to overtax her physical strength and remain stunted in mind.

Man, having grown accustomed to rule, enforced her total estrangement from other men, she was obliged to retire from their presence and to confine herself to the space assigned to her in the hut, and finally, to avoid putting temptation in the way of a covetous neighbour, to veil her face and person. In the East, where, owing to the climate, sexual desires have always been strongest and least restricted, this seclusion of woman from the sight of a stranger naturally reached its highest pitch. The relationship of master and servant between man and wife led to the following results.

Woman was no longer a mere object of sexual enjoyment and a means of propagation, as in the horde; she was the bearer of heirs through whom the man continued to possess his property after his death, and thus, as it were, immortalized himself, and she was also a valuable servant. She began to represent a definite worth and became a much sought article of exchange, which man obtained by bargain from its possessor, the father of the young woman, and in return for which he gave other articles of exchange, cattle, game, arms, or fruits of the field. Up to the present day among all uncivilized nations we still find the virgin exchanged for some other object of value; consequently she becomes as much the property of the man as any other possession, which he can dispose of at his pleasure, which he can retain or cast off, ill treat or protect. A further consequence was that the virgin, in leaving her father's house, broke off all connection with it; her life was divided as it were into **two** entirely separate parts, the first in the parental home, the second in that of her husband and master. This absolute separation was symbolically expressed among the old Greeks by burning the decorated two-wheeled carriage, which conveyed the virgin and her dowry to her husband, before the door of his house.

At a higher stage of civilization the purchase-money took the shape of a gift, which, however, was no longer received by the parent but by the bride, as compensation for her surrender, a custom, which as we know is still preserved as a symbol in all modern states.

If the possession of a wife was desirable, people were not particular in uncivilized times as to the manner in which she was obtained. It was cheaper to carry her away by force than to buy, and rape was inevitable when there was a scarcity of women among young tribes or peoples. The classical example of rape on a large scale is related in the story of the Rape of the Sabines by the Romans. Rape has been continued symbolically up to the present day, *e. g.*, among the Araucanian Indians in South Chili. While friends of the bridegroom are bargaining with the father, the former steals with his horse into the neighbourhood of the house, captures the bride, flings her on to the horse's back and escapes with her into the nearest wood. Men, women and children endeavour to hinder the flight, by cries and screams. As soon as bride and bridegroom have reached the wood, the marriage is regarded as concluded, even in cases in which the elopement took place against the will of the parents. The virgin forest is the bridal chamber, entrance into which completes the wedding ceremony.

As the greatest possible fertility is an innate natural impulse implanted in every living being, and fertility becomes easy and unrestricted in proportion to the excess of fertile soil, as further woman was always a desired object of enjoyment to man, which he was ready to change as often as possible, and as her powers of work as well as those of her offspring served to increase the riches and importance of her husband, there was every inducement to polygamy. But as women are naturally hardly more numerous than men—as will be shewn later on—the only resource was to buy them from foreign tribes or nations, or, better still, to capture them. Women became the most valuable booty in war.

Among all peoples at a certain stage of civilization land was possessed in common, with the modification that, while wood, meadow and water belonged to all, the part assigned to agriculture was separated into lots and divided among the fathers of families according to the size of the latter. This institution gave rise to a new distinction between the sexes, which clearly shews that woman was regarded as a second rate being.

As a rule the daughters were entirely excluded from participation in the lots; only the sons received their share, and it is evident that under such circumstances the father would from the first regard the birth of a son with other eyes than that of a daughter. Only among the Incas* and a few other nations, the daughter received half a lot. In harmony with the conception of the inferiority of woman was the exclusion of daughters from the rights of inheritance among ancient races, among some still living races in a low state of civilization. On the other hand there existed among monogamous nations like the Germans an institution which led to the most injurious results. It was customary for the sons to receive their lot from the community on marriage. This frequently induced the fathers to marry their sons at the age of ten or twelve to mature virgins. A consummation of the marriage being therefore impossible, the father abused his paternal power and took the place of his son as husband.† The consequent degeneration of family relationships may be readily imagined. The marriage chastity of our ancestors, like so many admirable traits of these ancient times, is a beautiful fable.

As long as the daughter remained in her father's house she had to earn her bread by hard work; if she forsook his house to become a wife, she relinquished all claims and became a stranger to the community. This was the condition of things everywhere, in India, Egypt, Greece, Rome, Germany, England, in the Aztec and Inca kingdoms. And it exists to-day in the Caucasus and in many districts of Russia and India. If a man died without son or nephew, his landed property reverted to the community. Not till much later were the daughters permitted to inherit household utensils or cattle, or to receive a dowry on marriage, and it was later still before they enforced their claim to the inheritance of landed property.

Another form in which the man obtained possession of

---

* Laveleye: " Primitive Property."

† Laveleye: " Primitive Property."

woman is mentioned in the Bible, in the story of Jacob, who earns first Leah, and then Rachel, by service. A number of years spent in the service of Laban was the price, a bargain in which the cunning Laban outwitted Jacob by giving him Leah instead of Rachel and so forcing him to serve another seven years for the second sister. We here see two sisters at once as the wives of one man—according to our modern notions an incestuous relationship. Jacob is moreover promised a part of the next young flock as marriage portion ; selfish Laban decides that he is to have the spotted sheep, which are known by experience to be the least numerous. Laban himself is to have the unspotted. But this time Jacob was the cleverer. As he had cheated his brother Esau of his birthright, he now cheated Laban of his lambs. He had studied Darwinism long before Darwin ; as the Bible tells us, he cut spotted rods which he put up at the ponds and salt-pits resorted to by the sheep. The constant sight of these rods had such an effect on the mother sheep that most of their young were spotted. Thus was Israel saved by the cunning of one of his earliest ancestors.

Another consequence of the supremacy of man over woman and which makes itself felt to-day more intensely than ever before, is Prostitution. Although among all the civilized nations of the earth man has demanded from his wife the strictest sexual reserve with regard to other men, and has frequently chastised transgression of this law by the cruellest forms of punishment—hls wife was his property and his slave over whose life and death he was arbiter—in spite of all this he was by no means inclined to subject himself to a similar restraint. He could buy two wives, or as victor in battle, capture them from the conquered, but this was of no avail if he were unable to support them permanently. In later times after the distribution of property had become extremely un-equal, only a small minority were in a position to do this, and the limited number of beautiful women heightened their price. But the man was often absent in war or on a journey, and even when at home he desired variety in his amorous enjoy-ment. To meet this desire, unmarried women, widows, cast off wives or the wives of the poor, offered themselves as prostitutes who were paid for the temporary gratification they afforded.

For a long period of time, at any rate in the East, un-married women were not forced to practise the rigid reserve im-posed on married women. Virginal chastity was not exacted by men until much later ; the claim represents a higher stage of refinement. Prostitution was not only permitted in the case of unmarried women, it was demanded of them as the fulfilment of a religious act, in Babylon, Phœnicia, Lydia and other places. The origin of the custom was evidently the promiscuity of intercourse in primæval times, which had been retained in the shape of a religious sacrifice of virginity to any one who paid the price asked by the priests. Similar customs still exist, as Bachofen relates, among various tribes of Further India, in Southern Arabia, in Madagascar and New Zealand, where the bride is surrendered to the whole tribe before her marriage. In Malabar the bridegroom rewards the man who deflorates his bride. " Many Caimars hire Patamars to deprive their wives of their virginity," consequently men of this class are regarded with great respect and are accustomed to settle the price of their services beforehand. It is the function of the High Priest (Namburi) to perform this service for the king (Zamorin) at his marriage, for which the priest receives fifty pieces of gold.* Such institutions and customs were doubly to the advantage of a lascivious priesthood and were consequently upheld by it and by a male community as lascivious as itself. In the same way the prostitution of unmarried women was made into a law of religious duty. The public sacrifice of virginity symbolized the fructification and fertility of Mother Earth, and was consummated in honour of the Goddess of Fruitfulness, revered by the peoples of the ancient world under the names of Aschera-Astarte, Mylitta, Aphrodite, Venus and Kybele. For her worship special temples were erected, surrounded by chambers of many kinds, in which sacrifice of the nature described was offered. The price paid by the men found its way into the sacerdotal purse. When Jesus drove out the dealers and money-changers for desecrating the Temple at Jerusalem, those same chambers existed there, in which sacrifices were offered to the Goddess of Love.

When, according to our notions, such a scandalous exposure of the most intimate though most natural relations between the sexes was possible, we cannot wonder that the prostitution of women appeared neither immoral nor indecent to the men of the times, who then as now were the sole representatives

---

* K. Kantsky : "Die Entstehung der Ehe und Familie." Kosmos, 1883. (The Origin of Marriage and the Family).

of "public opinion." A considerable number of women preferred the greater freedom which they enjoyed as Hetæræ to marriage, and carried on the trade of prostitution as a means of livelihood. In unrestrained intercourse with men, the more intelligent of the Hetæræ, who were doubtless often of good birth, acquired a far greater degree of versatility and culture than that possessed by the majority of married women, living in a state of enforced ignorance and bondage. This invested the Hetæræ with a greater charm for the men, in addition to the arts which they employed in the special exercise of their profession. This explains the fact that many of them enjoyed the esteem of some of the most distinguished and eminent men of Greece, to whom they stood in a relationship of influential intimacy, a position held by no legitimate wife. The names of these Hetæræ are famous to the present day, while one enquires in vain after the names of the legitimate wives.

Under such conditions the position of woman in the ancient world was one of extreme oppression. She was physically restrained and repressed, and mentally even more so. In the household she was only one degree better than the servants, her own sons were her masters, to whom she owed obedience. This relationship is well described in the Odyssey. Telemachus, feeling that he has reached man's estate, enters the ranks of the suitors, and commands his mother, Penelope, to retire to her own apartments, an order which she obeys in silence. Telemachus also promises the suitors to marry his mother to one of them within a year, if his father does not return before that time has elapsed, and the suitors regard the promise as perfectly natural. The position of woman in cultured Greece is also placed clearly before us in "Iphigenia in Tauris." Iphigenia laments: "The condition of women is worse than that of all human beings. If man is favoured by fortune he becomes a ruler, and wins fame on the battle-field, and if the gods have ordained him misfortune, he is the first to die a fair death among his people. But the joys of woman are narrowly compassed; she is given unasked, in marriage, by others, often to strangers, and when destruction falls upon her house, she is dragged away by the victor, through the smoking ruins, through the corpses of her dear ones."

After all this we need not wonder that among many nations and at many differents times, the question was seriously discussed, as to whether women were human beings and

c

possessed a soul. The Chinese and Indians deny the human equality of women, and at the Council of Mâcon in the sixth century, A.D., the question of the soul and humanity of women was gravely weighed and answered in the affirmative by a small majority. Woman is not a subject, she is an object, which man uses and abuses, as a thing is used and abused. There was therefore no reason why Roman Catholic casuists should not whet their wit on the question. After all this it is easy to understand why woman has been kept in a state of dependance until now, and that although the forms of her oppression have varied, the oppression has always remained the same.

What the forms and gradual changes of this oppression were will be shown in the sequel.

Subject to man in all social relationships, woman was especially so where his sexual desires were concerned. These desires increase in violence, in proportion to the warmth of the climate, which makes the blood flow hotter and faster, while at the same time the fertility of the soil makes the struggle for existence easy. For this reason, the East has from time immemorial been the nursery of all sexual vices and excesses, to which the richest and poorest, the wisest and most ignorant, alike gave themselves up. For this reason, too, the public prostitution of women was introduced into all civilized eastern countries at a very early date.

In Babylon, the powerful capital of the Babylonian empire, regulations existed, requiring every virgin to make at least one pilgrimage to the Temple of the goddess Mylitta, and there to surrender herself in honour of the deity to the free choice of the men who flocked in crowds to the place.

In Armenia, the goddess Anaitis was worshipped in the same manner. A similar organisation of the sexual cult existed in Egypt, Syria, Phœnicia, Cyprus, Carthage, and even in Greece and Rome. Not even the Jews were strangers to the prostitution of women as part of a religious ceremony, as is abundantly shown by Old Testament evidence. *e.g.*, to Pharaoh, who rewarded him richly. The forefather of the Jews and ancestor of Jesus saw nothing objectionable in a bargain, which was, according to our ideas, in the highest degree sordid and indecent. It is certainly strange that our children are still taught at school to regard this man with the greatest veneration. Jacob had, as we know, two sisters, Leah and Rachel as wives, who gave him their maids as concubines.   David, Solomon and others possessed whole harems, without falling into disfavour with Jehovah on that account.   It was customary (moral) and the women made no objection.

In Lydia, Carthage and Cyprus, young girls were permitted to earn their marriage portion by prostitution.   It is asserted that Cheops, King of Egypt, covered the cost of building a pyramid with the sums earned by the prostitution of his daughter.   King Rhampsinit, who lived about 2,000 years B.C., is said, on the discovery of a dexterous theft in his treasury, in order to trace the thief, to have issued a proclamation to the effect that his daughter would surrender herself to every man who could tell her a particularly interesting story.   The thief, we are told, appeared among the suitors. After he had related his tale and received his reward, the king's daughter tried to hold him fast.   But instead of his hand, she found the hand of a corpse in her own.   This clever trick caused the king to declare publicly that he would inflict no punishment on him but give him the hand of his daughter in marriage if he would come forward and make himself known, which he accordingly did.

Owing to this state of affairs, the custom was preserved, for instance among the Lydians, of tracing the descent of children through the mother.   Another habit which existed among many ancient races, according to J. Scherr, among the ancient Germans, was that of showing hospitality to a guest by giving him wife or daughter for the night.

In Greece public brothels were universally established at an early date.   Solon introduced them as State institutions into Athens, about 594 B.C., which caused a contemporary to sing his praise in the following manner : " Solon be extolled ! for thou hast bought public women for the safety of the town, for the morals of a town filled with strong young men, who, but for thy wise institution, would have given themselves up to the annoyance and pursuit of women of the upper classes."   Thus did a law of the state recognise as the natural right of men an act which, when committed by women, was regarded as degrading and criminal.   This same Solon decreed in this same Athens that "a woman who had intercourse with a lover must atone for the enormity by loss of freedom or life."   Her husband might sell her as a slave. And this unequal meting out of justice exists as much to-day as then.

In Athens a sumptuous temple was dedicated to the goddess

Hetæra. In the time of Plato, 400 years B.C., there were no
less than one thousand prostitutes (Hierodulae) in the Temple
of Aphrodite in Corinth, which was celebrated for its luxury
throughout all Greece. Corinth enjoyed the same reputation
among the male Greek population of that age as Hamburg
enjoyed among the Germans in the middle of the nineteenth
century. Hetæræ, famous at once for their beauty and
intellect, such as Phryne, Lais of Corinth, Gnathœna, and
Aspasia, afterwards the wife of the renowned Perikles, were
objects of universal admiration among the most distinguished
Greeks. They were admitted to their assemblies and ban-
quets, while the " honest " women of Greece were without
exception confined to the house. The " honest " woman was
allowed to appear nowhere in public, she always wore a veil
in the streets, and was dressed with the greatest simplicity.
Her culture was of the lowest order, for her instruction was
intentionally neglected ; she spoke badly, and possessed
neither refinement nor grace. How many men are there
among ourselves who prefer the society of a fair sinner
to that of their legitimate wife, belonging to the " Props
of the State," the " Pillars of Order," and whose function
it is to watch over the sanctity of married and family
life.

Demosthenes, the great orator, defined the sexual relations
of the Athenians shortly as follows : " We marry in order to
obtain legitimate children and a faithful warder of the house ;
we keep concubines as servants for our daily attendance, but
we seek the Hetæræ for love's delight." Thus the wife was
a mere apparatus for bearing children, a faithful dog that
watched the house. The master of the house lived according
to his own good pleasure. The ideas on women and the sexual
relationship which Plato develops in his " state " are, judged
by our standard, crude in the extreme. He demands community
of wives and the regulation of generation by selection.
Aristotle is more of a bourgeois. In his " Politica " woman
is free although inferior to man, but he vindicates her right
of " giving good advice." Thukydides expresses an opinion
which will meet with the approval of all modern Philistines.
He says : " The wife who deserves the highest praise is
she of whom one hears neither good nor evil outside her own
house."   He therefore expects women to lead a kind of
passive, vegetable existence, which at no point crosses the
circle of man.

Most of the Greek States were towns with but little ad-

joining land; the Greeks lived by their slaves.* Too great
an increase of the ruling class would therefore have endangered the continuance of the accustomed manner of life.
Accordingly Aristotle advised abstinence from women, and
preached sodomy in the place of natural love. Socrates
regarded sodomy as the privilege and sign of higher culture.
The male Greeks shared this view and lived in harmony with
it. There were just as many houses with male as with female
prostitutes. In such a social atmosphere as this, Thukydides
was able to exclaim, " Woman is more evil than the storm-
tossed waves, than the heat of fire, than the fall of the wild
cataract; if it was a god who created woman, wherever he
may be, let him know, that he is the unhappy author of the
greatest ills."†

During the first centuries after the foundation of Rome, the
Roman woman possessed no rights at all. Her position was
as abject as in Greece. It was not until the State had grown
large and powerful, and the Roman patrician had accumu-
lated vast riches that her condition gradually changed, and
that she obtained at any rate greater social, though not
greater legal freedom. This occasioned the elder Cato to
complain, that if every father of a family followed the example
of his ancestors and endeavoured to keep his wife in the
proper state of servility, the sex would cease to give so much
public annoyance.‡

Under the Empire woman acquired the right of inheritance,
but she herself remained a minor, and could dispose of
nothing without the consent of her guardian. The father
was guardian as long as he lived, even though the daughter
were married, unless he appointed another as guardian in his
stead. After his death he was replaced by the nearest male
relative, even though the latter, being an agnate, was himself
incapable of inheriting. The new guardian also possessed
the right of transferring his functions at will to any third
person. By Roman Law, the man was the proprietor of the
woman, who had no will of her own. The right of divorce
was possessed only by the man.

With the growing power and wealth of Rome, its former

---

* " He who works for one person is a slave; he who works for the
public is an artificer or day labourer." Aristotle, " Politica."

† Lèon Richer : " La Femme libre." Free Woman.)

‡ Karl Heinzen : " Ueber die Rechte und Stellung der Frauen." (The
Rights and Position of Women).

austere morality disappeared and made way to vices and excesses. Rome became the centre of debauchery and sensual refinements. The number of public brothels increased, while at the same time Greek pederasty grew more and more common among men. Celibacy and childlessness became more frequent in the ruling class, and Roman ladies avenged themselves by having their names registered in the lists of the Ædiles, whose duty it was to superintend prostitution, as a means of avoiding the heavy punishments of adultery.

Owing to the rapid decrease in the number of Roman citizens and patricians that went hand in hand with the decrease in the number of marriages and children, caused by the system of large landed estates, and the civil wars to which this system gave rise, Augustus issued the so-called Julian law, in the year 16 B.C., providing for the reward of paternity and for the punishment of celibacy. The fathers of children took rank before unmarried or childless men. Celibates might inherit from none but their nearest relatives. Childless men might only receive the half of legacies, the other half reverted to the State. This caused Plutarch to observe: "The Romans do not marry to obtain heirs but to inherit."

Later on the Julian law was made still more severe. Tiberius decreed that no woman might prostitute herself whose grandfather, father or husband had been a Roman knight. Married women who had themselves registered as prostitutes were to be treated as adultresses and banished from Italy. Naturally no such punishments were inflicted on the men.

There were various forms of the marriage ceremony under the Empire. The most solemn was performed by the High Priest in the presence of at least ten witnesses. The bridal pair partook together of a cake made of flour, salt and water, as a sign of union. The second form was "entering into possession," which was regarded as accomplished after the woman, with the consent of her father or guardian, had lived for one year with the man under the same roof. The third form was a kind of mutual purchase; gold coins and the marriage promise were given on both sides.

Among the Jews marriage became a religious act at an early date. Nevertheless, the wife had no right of choice, the bridegroom was appointed by her father. The Talmud writes: "When thy daughter has reached maturity, set one of thy slaves free and betroth her unto him." Marriage was regarded as a duty by the Jews. "Be fruitful and multiply." And the Jewish race obeyed the command and multiplied abundantly, in spite of all persecution and oppression. The Jews are the sworn enemies of Malthusianism.

Tacitus says of them. " They hold obstinately together and are generous to each other, but they hate all other men as their foes. They neither eat nor drink with strangers, and although of extremely sensual temperament, they refrain from cohabiting with women of another race. . . . But they seek to increase their numbers. They regard it as a sin to kill one of their offspring, and they believe that the souls of all who die in battle or by execution are immortal. Hence their desire to propagate the race, and their contempt of death."

Tacitus hates and detests the Jews because they disregard the (heathen) religion of their fathers, and accumulate gifts and treasures. He calls them the worst of men, an abominable nation.*

While the Jews, under the dominion of the Romans, were driven to attach themselves more and more to each other and thus to develop that intimate family life which characterised them during the long period of tribulation that was their lot almost throughout the Christian Middle Ages, and which is regarded as a model of virtue by the bourgeois world of to-day, the process of dissolution was reaching its climax in Roman Society. On the one hand debauchery that bordered on madness, on the other the sternest abstinence. Asceticism began to assume a religious form, as licentiousness had done before, and was preached with extravagant fanaticism. The riotous luxury that knew no limits stood in glaring contrast to the want and misery of millions and millions that conquering Rome had dragged from all parts of the known world to slavery in Italy. Among these were innumerable women who, torn from home and children, and separated from their husbands, felt their condition more acutely than any, and yearned for deliverance. Among the Roman women many were in a hardly better condition, and shared the feelings of the others. Moreover, the conquest of Jerusalem and of the Jewish kingdom by the Romans, and the annihilation of all national independence, had raised up among the ascetic sects of that country fanatics who proclaimed the advent of a new empire that was to bring happiness and freedom to all.

Christianity arose. Its misanthropic doctrines advocated

---

* Tacitus. History. 5th Book.

abstinence, the mortification of the flesh. Its ambiguous phraseology, applicable alike to a heavenly or to an earthly kingdom, found a fruitful soil in the morass of the Roman Empire. Women, hoping, like all the wretched, for redemption and deliverance from their present state, became eager and zealous adherents. No movement of great importance has ever taken place in the world, in the past or present, in which women have not played a prominent part as combatants and martyrs. Those who extol Christianity as a great achievement in civilisation, should not forget that to women a large portion of its success was due. Their missionary zeal made itself felt as a powerful agent in the early days of Christianity, as well as among barbarous nations in the Middle Ages, and men of high rank were converted by them. Among others we are told of Chlotilda, who induced Chlodwig, King of the Franks to accept Christianity; of Bertha, Queen of Kent, and of Gisela, Queen of Hungary, who introduced Christianity into their countries. It was a woman's influence too that effected the conversion of the Duke of Poland, of the Czar Jarislaw, and of many other kings and nobles.

But Christianity requited her ill. Its dogmas contain the same contempt of women as all the ancient religions of the East; it degrades her to the rank of the humble servant of man, and forces her to pledge her obedience to her husband before the altar to this day.

Let us see in what tone the Bible and Christianity speak of woman and marriage.

At the creation woman is commanded to be subject unto man. The ten commandments of the Old Testament are as a matter of fact addressed only to man, for the tenth commandment names woman along with the servants and the domestic animals. In truth, woman was a piece of property, which man obtained for a price or for a corresponding service on his part. Jesus, who belonged to a sect that imposed the strictest asceticism, especially in sexual matters, on its members, looked with contempt on marriage, and preached: " Some there be that are eunuchs from their mother's womb, and some there be that are made eunuchs of men, and *some there be that are eunuchs for the kingdom of heaven's sake.*" When his mother humbly sought his assistance at the marriage feast at Cana, he replied: " Woman, what have I to do with thee."

And Paul, who must be regarded even more than Jesus as the founder of Christianity, Paul, who was the first to give the doctrine an international character and rescue it from the

fetters of narrow Jewish sectarianism, preached as follows :
" It is good for a man not to touch a woman." " He that
giveth her (the virgin) in marriage doeth well, but he that
giveth her not in marriage doeth better." " Walk in the Spirit
and fulfil not the lust of the flesh, for the flesh lusteth against
the Spirit and the Spirit against the flesh." " They that
are Christ's have crucified the flesh, with the affections and
lusts." He followed his own teaching and remained unmarried. This hatred of the flesh is hatred of woman, who
is represented as the seducer of man. Compare the scene in
Paradise, which becomes significant when viewed in this
light. The same spirit inspired the preaching of the Apostles
and of the Fathers of the Church, the same spirit dictated
the course pursued by the Church throughout the whole
Middle Ages, the same spirit called cloisters into existence,
and the same spirit is still active to-day.

According to Christianity, woman is the unclean one, the
seducer, who brought sin into the world and caused the fall
of man. Consequently all apostles and fathers of the Church
have regarded marriage merely as an inevitable evil, just as
prostitution is regarded to-day. For instance Tertullian
exclaims : " Woman ! thou oughtest always to walk in
mourning and rags, thine eyes filled with tears of repentance,
to make men forget that thou hast been the destruction of the
race. Woman ! thou art the gate of Hell." Jerome says :
" Marriage is at the best a vice, all that we can do is to excuse
and purify it." Accordingly it was made a sacrament of the
Church. Origen declares : " Marriage is unholy and unclean,
a means of sensual lust," and he therefore castrated himself
to avoid temptation. Tertullian says : " Celibacy must be
chosen, though the human race perish in consequence ; "
Augustine, " Celibates will shine in heaven like dazzling
stars, while the parents who begot them resemble stars
without light." Both Eusebius and Jerome agree that the
Bible utterance : " Be fruitful and multiply," was out of
harmony with the times and did not concern Christians.
Hundreds of quotations might be made from the most
eminent fathers of the church, all teaching the same doctrine,
the continual accentuation of which has spread abroad these
unnatural ideas about sex and sexual intercourse, *notwithstanding
that the latter is a law of nature and its fulfilment one of the most serious
duties of life.* Modern society still suffers heavily from the effects
of this teaching, and is but slowly recovering from them.

Peter tells women emphatically : " Be obedient unto your

husbands." Paul writes to the Ephesians : " For the husband is the head of the wife, even as Christ is the head of the Church," and to the Corinthians : "The head of every man is Christ, and the head of the woman is the man." According to this theory, any simpleton of a man may consider himself better than the cleverest woman, and practically he does so.

Paul also raises his influential voice against the higher education and culture of women, when he says : " *Let the woman learn in silence with all subjection, but I suffer not a woman to teach, nor to usurp authority over the man, but to be in silence.*"

It is true that such doctrines were not peculiar to Christianity. Christianity was a mixture of Judaism and Greek philosophy, and the latter had its origin in the older civilizations of Egypt, Babylon, and India. The inferior position which Christianity assigns to woman was common to the entire ancient world. And this inferior position has been more completely preserved among the undeveloped nations of the East than in Christendom. The cause of its gradual improvement in the so-called Christian world was not Christianity, but the *advancing civilization of the West, acting in spite of Christianity.*

It is therefore not the merit of Christianity if the position of woman to-day is a better one than at the time of its introduction. It has merely denied its true attitude with regard to woman, and that reluctantly and under pressure. Fanatics who imagine that it was the mission of Christianity to liberate mankind, think differently on this as on many other points. They assert with confidence that Christianity freed woman from her former state of dependence, and seek to prove their assertion by pointing to the worship of Mary, the mother of God, which they regard as a veneration of the female sex in her person. We suspect that the Catholic Church which has cultivated this worship up to the present day, would energetically protest against such a view of the case. The saints and fathers already quoted, whose numbers might be easily increased, including the greatest and most distinguished, are unanimous in their enmity to woman. Neither does the Council of Maçon, mentioned above, which, in the sixth century discussed whether woman possessed a soul or not, seem to have been inspired by much of the veneration in question. The introduction of celibacy by Gregory VII.,*

---

* A step against which the clergy of the diocese of Mainz protested as follows: "You bishops and abbots possess great riches, a regal table, luxurious equipages for the chase ; we poor simple priests have only a wife

the raging of the Reformers, especially Calvin, against the "lusts of the flesh," and above all the Bible, in its numerous misanthropic and misogynic passages prove the contrary.

It was a shrewd calculation that impelled the Catholic Church, when it introduced the worship of Mary, to substitute for the heathen goddesses revered in all lands over which Christianity was spreading, a deity of its own. Mary, spiritually idealised by Christianity, took the place of the Kybele, Mylitta, Aphrodite, Venus, &c., of the southern nations, of the Edda, Freya, &c., of the German races.

The powerful, uncultured, but also unsophisticated races, abounding in physical strength, which in the first centuries of the Christian era, inundated and overflowed the enervated Roman Empire in which Christianity had by degrees established itself, from east and west like gigantic waves, opposed with all their might the ascetic teachings of Christian priests, who found themselves compelled to reckon with these healthy natures, whether they liked it or not. The Romans saw with amazement that the morals of these races were totally different to their own. Tacitus expresses his recognition of this fact in the following words: "Their marriages are very strict, and none of their customs is more worthy of praise than this, for they are almost the only barbarians who content themselves with one wife. One rarely hears of adultery among this populous nation; when it occurs it is punished on the spot by the husbands themselves. The man chases the adulterous woman, shorn and naked, in the presence of the relations out of the village, for an offence against decency can hope for no indulgence. Neither beauty, nor youth, nor riches can procure such a woman a husband. No one laughs at vice, nor is seduction regarded as a sign of good breeding. The young men marry late, and so preserve their strength, neither are the young women married in haste, and they possess the same bodily size. They marry equal in years and health, and the strength of the parents is transmitted to the children."

We must not forget that Tacitus, anxious to present a model to the Romans, painted the marriage relationship of the old Germans, with which he was himself insufficiently acquainted, in somewhat rosy colours. Though it was true that an adulterous woman was severely punished, this did not

---

to comfort us. Abstinence may be a fair virtue, but it is in truth severe and hard." Yves Guyot; "Les Théories Sociales du Christianisme." Second edition. Paris. (The Social Theories of Christianity.

apply to an adulterous man. The German wife was absolutely subjected to her husband; he was her lord; she performed the hardest tasks, and attended to all the household duties, while the man fought or hunted, drank or gambled, or lay on his bearskin, dreaming away the day.

Among the old Germans as among all ancient nations, the patriarchal family was the first form of society. From it was developed the community, the clan and race. The head of the family was the born lord of the community; after him came the male members. Wives, daughters and daughters-in-law were excluded from council and leadership.

It occasionally happened that, favoured by peculiar circumstances, a woman was made ruler of the tribe, as Tacitus tells us with much disgust and contempt, but such cases were exceptional. In the beginning women had no right of inheritance, later on they were permitted to become co-heirs.

Every freeborn German had a claim to part of the common land, which, when it was not wood, meadow or water and as such used by all alike, was divided by lot among the members of the community. As soon as the young German married, he received his share of land; if children were born to him he had a further claim to an additional piece. It was also a universal custom to grant a young married couple special privileges for furnishing their household, for instance, a load of beechwood and the timber for their log-hut. The neighbours helped willingly in fetching and building, and in making the implements of agriculture and the utensils for household use. At the birth of a daughter the parents had a right to one load of wood, but if the child were a son, to two loads.* We see that women were estimated at half the value of men.

The marriage ceremony was simple. There was no vestige of a religious act, the mutual declaration sufficed, and as soon as the pair had entered the bridal bed, the marriage was regarded as consummated. The idea that the validity of marriage depended on ecclesiastical sanction was an acquisition of the ninth century, and it was not till the

---

* "Eyn iglich gefurster man, der ein Kindbette hat ist sin kint eyn dochter, so mag er eyn wagen vol bornholzes von urholz verkaufen of den samstag. Ist iz eyn sone, so mag he iz tun of den dinstag und of den samstag von ligendem holz oder von urholz und sal den frauwen davon kaufen win und schon brod dyeweile sie kintes june lit." G. L. v. Maurer: 'Geschichte der Markenverfassung in Deutschland." (History of the constitution of the Marks in Germany).

sixteenth century that the Council of Trent raised marriage to the rank of a sacrament. We possess no historical record that the simplicity of the early marriage ceremony, which had merely the character of a private contract between two persons of different sexes, had any injurious effects on the community or on morality. Morality was endangered, not by the manner in which the matrimonial act was concluded, but by the fact that a freeman might with impunity, in his sexual relations with his wife, abuse a power which placed her in the position of a slave and a bondswoman.

Under the feudal system the lord of the manor possessed unlimited sway over his serfs, and almost unlimited sway over his villeins. He could force any man at the age of eighteen and any girl of fourteen to marry. He could dictate the choice of a husband or wife. He had the same right with regard to widows and widowers. He further possessed the so-called Jus Primæ Noctis (Right of the First Night) which, however, he could relinquish in virtue of a certain payment, the name of which betrayed its nature (Bettmund, Hemdschilling, Jungfernzins, Schürzenzins, Bunzengroschen, &c.).*

It was in the interest of the lord of the manor to promote marriage among his serfs; their children being born into the same bondage as their own, the number of his labourers was thereby increased and his income increased in proportion. For this reason both spiritual and temporal lords favoured matrimony on their estates. The Church pursued a different course in cases which offered her the chance of coming into the possession of property by the prevention of marriage. This however only applied to freemen, and mostly to those of low rank, whose position, owing to circumstances that cannot be discussed here, became in the course of time more and more untenable, and who therefore lent a ready ear to religious suggestions and prejudices, and after making over

---

* It has been latterly asserted that this right never existed, an assertion which appears to me entirely unfounded. It is clear that the right was not a written one, that it was not summed up in paragraphs ; it was a natural consequence of the dependant relationship and required no registration in any book of law. If the female serf pleased the lord, he enjoyed her; if not he let her alone. In Hungary, Transylvania and the Danubian Principalities there is no written Jus Primæ Noctis either, but one learns enough on this subject by enquiring of those who know the country and its inhabitants, as to the manners which prevail between the landowners and the female population, That imposts of this nature existed cannot be denied, and the names speak for themselves.

their belongings to the Church sought peace and protection behind the walls of a cloister. Other landed proprietors, feeling themselves too weak to withstand the encroachments of the greater lords, placed themselves, in return for certain payments and services, under the protection of the Church. But the consequence of this measure was that their descendants were frequently overtaken by the very fate from which their ancestors had endeavoured to escape, they became dependent on or subject to the Church, or their property was swallowed by the cloisters into which they were enticed.

The towns which began to flourish in the Middle Ages, had during the first centuries the keenest inducement to encourage an increase of population, by offering the greatest facilities for settlement and marriage. But this state of things did not last for ever. As soon as the towns had become powerful and possessed a class of well trained and organised artificers all new-comers were regarded with aversion, as unwelcome competitors. While the importance of the bourgeoisie was increasing, the barriers were multiplied against strangers from without. Heavy taxes on settlement, costly master-examinations, limitation of every trade to a certain number of masters and journeymen forced thousands into a position of dependence, into sexual relations outside marriage and to the life of a vagabond.

When the prosperous period of the towns had passed, and their decline had commenced, it followed as a natural consequence of the narrow views of the age, that the checks to settlement and independence were enforced even more strenuously than before. Other circumstances had an equally demoralising effect.

The tyranny of the landed proprietors grew from decade to decade, in such a manner that many of their subjects preferred to exchange their bestial condition for the life of a beggar, highwayman, or robber, a process which was favoured by the existence of large forests and the imperfect means of communication. Or they became mercenaries and sold themselves for the highest price and the promise of the richest booty. A large male and female proletariat of scamps arose and became a scourge to the land. The Church was not behindhand in furthering the universal corruption. The unmarried state of the clergy was in itself one of the chief causes of sexual excess, which an uninterrupted intercourse with Rome and Italy did not fail to promote.

Rome was not only the capital of Christendom and the

head quarters of the Papacy, it was the new Babylon, the European academy of immorality, of which the papal court was the principal seat. The Roman Empire had at its fall bequeathed more vices than virtues to Christian Europe, and Italy was their special nursery, from whence they penetrated into Germany, mostly through the medium of travelling priests. The enormously numerous clergy, chiefly consisting of healthy men, whose sexual desires were excited to the utmost by an idle and luxurious life, but which enforced celibacy compelled them to satisfy outside the pale of marriage or by unnatural means, carried licentiousness into all ranks of society and became a perilous plague for female morality in town and village. Monasteries and nunneries were distinguished from brothels by the greater lasciviousness of the life carried on within their walls, and by the ease with which the numerous crimes committed there, particularly infanticide, were concealed by judges who themselves stood at the head of this system of corruption. The peasants in the country endeavoured to preserve their wives and daughters from clerical seduction, by accepting no pastor who did not bind himself to take a concubine. This practice induced a Bishop of Constance to impose a concubine tax on the clergy of his diocese. All this helps to explain the fact that in the same Middle Ages, the piety and morality of which weak-minded romanticists are fond of describing, not less than 1500 travelling adventuresses appeared at the Council of Constance in 1414.

In addition to all the barriers placed in the way of settlement and marriage, the position of women was made still worse by the fact that during this period their number considerably exceeded that of the men; this disproportion is sufficiently accounted for by constant feuds and struggles, dangerous commercial journeys, greater mortality among the men in consequence of intemperance and gluttony, especially during the frequent visitations of pestilential diseases, which did not cease their ravages throughout the entire Middle Ages. In the period from 1336 to 1400, for instance, 32 years of plague are recorded; between 1400 and 1500, 42 years; and from 1500 to 1600, 30 years.*

Troops of women wandered through the country as mountebanks, singers, musicians, in company with travelling scholars

---

* Dr. Karl Bücher: "Die Frauenfrage im Mittelalter." Tübingen (The Women's Question in the Middle Ages).

and clerks, inundating the fairs and markets, and all other
places in which assemblies or festivities took place. In the
army of mercenaries they formed special divisions with their
own sergeant. In harmony with the corporative spirit of the
times, they were appointed according to beauty and age to
the different ranks among the soldiers, and a heavy punishment was inflicted on any who ventured to prostitute themselves outside their proper circle. In the camps they had to
help the soldier boys in carrying hay, straw, and wood to
fill up ditches, dykes, and pits, and in cleaning the tents. At
sieges they had to fill the moats with branches, fagots, and
brushwood, to facilitate the attack; they assisted in bringing
the artillery into position, and when the cannon wheels stuck
in the mud, in lifting them out again.

In various towns so-called Bettina institutions (Houses of
God) were established and placed under municipal administration, for the purpose of ameliorating the condition of
numbers of destitute women. Here they received shelter and
were obliged to lead a respectable life. But neither these
houses nor the numerous nunneries were able to support all
those who sought admittance.

It was a characteristic feature of the Middle Ages that not
even the most contemptible trade could be carried on without
fixed regulations. Accordingly, prostitution received a guild
organization. In all towns there were brothels, belonging to
the Municipality, to the Sovereign, or even to the Church,
the proceeds of which flowed into the treasury of their proprietor. The women in these brothels elected their own
" head-mistress," whose duty it was to preserve order and
discipline, and who jealously sought to prevent competitors
that did not belong to the guild from spoiling the trade.
Such competitors, if caught, were punished and often savagely
persecuted. The brothels enjoyed special protection. A
doubly severe penalty was inflicted on all who caused disturbances in their neighbourhood. The members of the
guild had moreover the privilege of appearing in processions
and at all festivities in which other corporations took part,
and they were not unfrequently guests at the tables of
councillors and princes.

There was, on the other hand, especially in the early Middle
Ages, no lack of violent persecutions directed against the
public prostitutes, and naturally instigated by the male population whose money and morals were the cause of their
existence. What shall we say when we hear that Charles the

Great condemned a prostitute to be dragged naked to the market place and there beaten with rods while he himself, " the most Christian " King and Emperor, had no fewer than six wives at one time! The same communities which officially organised and protected prostitution and accorded all kinds of privileges to the priestesses of Venus, imposed the severest and most cruel penalties on the unfortunate woman who had been seduced and forsaken. The infanticide who destroyed her own offspring in despair was punished as a rule by the most atrocious forms of death. No one asked any questions about the unscrupulous seducer. Perhaps he sat on the judgment bench and passed sentence on the unhappy victim. Such things are still happening among us to-day.*

In Würzburg the brothelkeeper swore to the Magistrate "to be faithful and friendly to the town, and to enlist women." A similar oath was administered in Nürnberg, Ulm, Leipzig, Köln, Frankfurt and elsewhere. After the brothels had been dissolved in Ulm, in 1537, the guilds petitioned for their re-establishment in 1551 "to prevent greater evils." Prostitutes were provided for guests of rank at the expense of the town. When King Ladislaus entered Vienna in 1452, the municipal government sent a deputation of public women to meet him, the beauty of whose forms was rather enhanced than concealed by their covering of gauze. The Emperor Charles II. was saluted on his entry into Bruges by a deputation of perfectly naked women. Such cases were by no means unusual and no one considered.them indecent.

Phantastic romanticists and calculating persons have endeavoured to represent this period as the age of morality. and of sincere reverence for women. Especially the time of the Minnesingers in Germany from the end of the 12th to the 14th century was made to serve as an exemplification of this imaginary fact. The " Service of Love " practised by French, Italian, and German knights, in imitation of the Moors in Spain and Sicily, was supposed to prove the high respect paid to the women of that day. In reply to this assertion we must remind our readers of several things. In the first place, knights and ladies represented a very small

* Léon Richer, in " La Femme Libre " relates a case in which a Paris servant girl was sentenced for child murder by the father of her child, a pious lawyer of good reputation, who acted the part of juror. Worse still. The lawyer was himself the murderer, and the heroic girl perfectly innocent, as she was afterwards induced to confess.

percentage of the whole population ; secondly, only a small number of knights were devoted to the "Service of Love," and thirdly, the true nature of this service has been grossly exaggerated and misunderstood, or indeed intentionally misrepresented. The period in which it flourished was at the same time that of lynch-law in its worst shape, in which, at any rate in the country, all bands of order were loosened, and knighthood itself had become the profession of highwaymen, robbers and incendiaries. Such a period, characterized as it was by the most brutal acts of violence, was hardly favourable to gentle and poetic feelings. On the contrary, this period succeeded in destroying the little respect for the female sex which existed at its commencement. The knights, both in town and country, were mostly coarse and licentious men, and their chief passions, feuds, drunkenness, and the unbridled gratification of sensual lusts. The chronicles of the time swarm with tales of rape and violence on the part of the nobles, in the country and still more in the towns, where they were exclusive rulers up to the 13th and 14th century; while those subjected to this degrading treatment were powerless to obtain redress. In the towns the nobles sat on the magistrate's bench, and in the country criminal jurisdiction was in the hands of the lord of the manor, squire or bishop. It is quite impossible that a knighthood with such habits and morals should have had any great respect for its own wives and daughters, or have placed them on a pedestal as a kind of superior being.

Still there doubtless remained a small number of sincere admirers of womanly beauty, but these were mostly men with little control over their own senses, in whom, as in Ulrich von Lichtenstein, Christian mysticism and Christian asceticism stood in a peculiar and intimate relationship to a sensuality that was partly innate and partly artificial. Others of a more sober stamp pursued more positive aims. In any case however this service of love was the idolization of the beloved object at the expense—of the legitimate wife, a Hetærism that had been introduced into Christianity, similar to that which we have described in the times of Perikles. As a matter of fact, the mutual seduction of wives was a custom strongly in vogue among the knights of the Middle Ages, much as it is in certain circles of our Bourgeoisie to-day.

So much for the Idealists of the Middle Ages and for their reverence towards women.

Undoubtedly the open allowance made for sexual passion

in mediæval times contained the recognition that every natural impulse, implanted in a healthy and mature being, has a claim to gratification, and this was a victory of unsophisticated nature over the ascetism of Christianity. But on the other hand we must never lose sight of the fact that this recognition and encouragement was only accorded to the one sex, whilst the other was treated as though it neither possessed nor had any right to possess the same impulses, and its [slightest transgression of the moral law imposed by man was punished with uncompromising severity. Long continued oppression and the corresponding education have so accustomed the female sex to the arguments of its master, that it regards this state of things as perfectly right and natural.

Were there not also millions of slaves who thought slavery right and natural, and would never have become free if liberators had not arisen out of the ranks of slaveholders themselves? Did not the Prussian peasants petition, when Stein's legislation abolished serfdom after 1807, that they might be allowed to remain as they were, " for who should care for them when they were sick and old? "

And does not the modern labour-movement prove the same thing? Do not large numbers of workmen still follow their exploiters in leading-strings? The oppressed needs some one to arouse and incite him. He has neither power nor opportunity for seizing the initiative himself. It was thus in the case of slavery, of serfdom, and villeinage, it was thus in the uprising of the Proletarians, and is so still, and it is thus in the struggle for the liberation and emancipation of woman. Even in the contests of the modern bourgeoisie, notwithstanding the comparative advantages of its position, noble and clerical advocates acted the part of pioneer.

In spite of many wants and failings, from which the Middle Ages were naturally not exempt, the fact remains that they possessed a healthy sensuality, which Christianity was unable to suppress, and that they had no share in the hypocritical prudery, shamefacedness, and concealed lasciviousness which characterizes our own day, in which people fear and refuse to call things by their right names and to speak naturally about natural processes. They were also strangers to that piquant ambiguity in which we cloak subjects which a lack of simplicity and the affectation of coyness forbid us to mention openly, and which thereby become doubly injurious, thanks to a language that excites curiosity without satisfying it, that rouses surmise but gives no reply, The conversations carried on in society, our novels and theatres are full of this equivocal piquancy, and the effect is apparent enough. This spiritualism, which is not that of the transcendental philosopher, but of the roué, and which entrenches itself behind religious spiritualism* is a powerful social factor at the present day.

The healthy sensualism of the Middle Ages found its classical interpreter in Luther. I have not here to deal with the religious reformer, whom I judge very differently to the man. Viewed from the human side, Luther's strong, unsophisticated nature stands out in full light; it impelled him to express forcibly and without reserve his need of love and enjoyment. His former position as Roman Catholic priest had opened his eyes, had shown him by practical demonstration, so to speak, in his own body, that the lives of monks and nuns were contrary to nature. Thence the fervour with which he combats the priestly and monastic celibacy. His words apply to all who believe that they may with impunity sin against nature, and with whose ideas of decency and morality it is compatible that state and social institutions should prevent millions from fulfilling their natural vocation. Luther says : " A woman, unless she be peculiarly sanctified from above, can as little dispense with a man, as with eating, sleeping, drinking, or the fulfilment of any other physical need. Neither can a man dispense with a woman. The reason is this : it is as deeply implanted in our nature to beget children as to eat and drink. Therefore has God given the body members, veins, fluids, and everything which is necessary for these purposes. He who seeks to restrain them, and will not let Nature alone, what does he else but seek to restrain Nature from being Nature ; fire from burning ; water from wetting ; and man from eating, drinking or sleeping."

While Luther recognised the satisfaction of the sexual impulse as a law of nature, and by abolishing the celibacy of the priesthood and by dissolving the cloisters, placed the possibility of its fulfilment within the reach of millions, other millions still remained excluded as before. The Reformation was the first protest of the rising class of wealthy citizens against the limitations of feudalism in Church, State, and Society. These citizens strove for liberation from the fetters of guilds, courts and jurisdictions, for centralization of State

---

* Cf., Mallock : "Romance of the Nineteenth Century." Rem. of the Transl.

functions, for reduction in the expenses of an extravagant clergy, for the abolition of sinecures, and for the employment of the idle in production. The bourgeois forms of property and of industrial acquisition were to take the place of the feudal forms, in other words, instead of the corporative protection of small exclusive circles, the free individual struggle of competition was to develop itself.

Luther was the representative of these endeavours on religious ground. When he claimed freedom of marriage he did so merely for the bourgeois marriage, which a few years ago attained its full development in Germany, through civil registration, and its attendants, liberty of migration and free trade. We shall see later on how far the position of woman has been benefited thereby. Meanwhile, at the time of the Reformation things had not got to the pitch which they have reached to-day. Although the above mentioned measures allowed numbers to marry, free sexual intercourse on the other hand was prosecuted with inexorable severity. The Catholic clergy had shown great leniency towards sexual misdemeanours; the Protestant clergy, after it had provided for itself, denounced them with implacable hatred. War was declared against brothels and they were closed on the grounds that they were pits of Satan. Prostitutes were persecuted as " daughters of the Devil," and every woman, guilty of a "fault," was exposed to public disgrace at the pillory as the quintessence of everything that was evil.

The merry citizen of the Middle Ages, who lived and let live, became a bigoted, austere, and gloomy philistine, who scraped the money together, which his wealthy heirs of the nineteenth century were to waste in riotous living. The respectable citizen, with his stiff cravat, his narrow horizon and his severe morality because the prototype of society.

The legitimate wife who had long since become an enemy of the catholic sensuality of the later Middle Ages, gladly welcomed the puritan spirit of Protestantism. Women in general were no better off than before. The changes that took place in production, finance and trade after the discovery of America and of the sea passage to East India were even greater in Germany than elsewhere and their first result was a strong social reaction.

Germany ceased to be the centre of European traffic and commerce. Spain, Portugal, Holland, England took the lead in quick succession, and England has retained it to this day. German trade and commerce consequently declined. The Reformation had moreover destroyed the political unity of the nation. It was the pretence under which the German princes sought to emancipate themselves from the power of the Empire. At the same time the princes endeavoured to subjugate the nobility, and as a means to this end, protected the towns to which they accorded all kinds of rights and privileges. Many towns were induced by the growing uncertainty of the times to place themselves voluntarily under the rule of the princes. The consequence of all this was that the bourgeoisie, alarmed at the decay of its business, erected still more impassable barriers on all sides, with a view to keeping unwelcome competitors aloof. The ossification of society progressed, and poverty along with it. The religious struggles and persecutions which broke out soon after the Reformation in all parts of Germany, and in which Protestants and Catholics took part with equal intolerance and equal fanaticism, the religious wars that followed (Schmalkaldian and Thirty Years' War) sealed the fate of Germany, her dismemberment, her political impotence, her economic weakness and stunted growth, for centuries to come.

During the Middle Ages various towns had admitted women to their membership on a footing of equality with the men. For instance there were female furriers in Frankfurt and in the Silesian towns, female bakers in the towns on the Middle Rhine, embroideresses of coats of arms and female saddlers in Köln and Strassburg, female harness-makers in Bremen, female tailors in Frankfurt, female tanners in Nürnberg, and female goldsmiths in Köln. But they were now expelled from all these trades. And, as is always the case when a phase of society is approaching dissolution, its defenders took refuge in the very measures that tended to increase the evil. An absurd fear of over-population took possession of people's mind, and all concurred in seeking to restrict the number of marriages and of independnet citizens. Although formerly flourishing towns, such as Nürnberg, Augsburg, Köln and others, decreased in population from the 16th century, because commerce and traffic had been directed into other channels, although the Thirty Years' War had decimated Germany, still every town, every corporation, in view of its own decline, dreaded an increase of its numbers. The attempts of absolute rulers to alter this condition of things were as ineffectual as the laws rewarding marriage had been among the Roman citizens of a former time. Louis XIV., as a means of obtaining more inhabitants and more soldiers, established a pension for the parents of ten children ; for families of twelve children the pensions were raised ; his general the Marshal von Sachsen went still further and proposed that no marriage should be allowed to last longer than five years. Frederic the Great wrote fifty years later in the same spirit : " I regard men as a herd of deer in the park of a great lord; the only duty of the herd is to people and fill the park."[*] This was in 1741. Later on his wars went far towards laying the deer park waste.

The position of woman was all this time as bad as can be imagined. She was in numberless case excluded from marriage as a means of subsistence or of the gratification of her natural impulses ; the absence of productive development caused men who had long since learnt to fear competition even among themselves, to shut her out from trade. She had to content herself with menial employments and the lowest forms of labour. But as natural impulses cannot be suppressed, and part of the male population lived under similar conditions, no amount of police persecution availed to prevent illicit relationships and the number of illegitimate children was never greater than under the paternal government of absolute monarchs who ruled in Christian simplicity.

The married woman lived in the strictest retirement ; her duties were so manifold that a conscientious housewife had to be at her post from early in the morning till late at night to fulfil them, and even then it was only possible to do so with the help of her daughters. It was not only a question of the daily household duties that still fall to the lot of the middle-class housekeeper, but of many others from which she has been entirely freed by the modern development or industry and the extension of means of transport. She had to spin, weave and bleach, to make all the linen and clothes, to boil soap, to make candles and brew beer. In addition to these occupations she frequently had to work in the fields and garden, and to attend to the poultry and cattle. In short, she was a veritable Cinderella and her solitary recreation was going to church on Sunday. Marriages only took place within the same social circles; the most rigid and ridiculous spirit of caste ruled everything and brooked no

* Karl Kantsky : "Der Einfluss der Volksvermehrung auf den Fortschritt der Gesellschaft." (The Influence of Increasing Population on the Progress of Society.) Vienna 1880

transgression of its law. The daughters were educated in the same principles ; they were kept in strict home seclusion, their mental development was of the lowest order and did not extend beyond the narrowest limits of household life. And all this was crowned by an empty and meaningless etiquette, whose part it was to replace mind and culture, and which made life altogether, and especially the life of a woman, a perfect treadmill of labour.

Thus was the spirit of the Reformation degraded to a formalism of the worst stamp, while men sought to stifle natural impulses and the joys of life under a mass of dignified but commonplace rules and customs.

Among other things the Reformation robbed women of a privilege which had been granted to them by the Middle Ages, especially in country districts. In West and South Germany, in Alsace and other parts it was the custom to give the country women every year a few days for themselves, in which they could make merry together, and during which no man might molest them on pain of being ill-received. This naive custom of the people was an unconscious recognition of the bondage of women, which they were thus allowed to forget for a short period yearly.

It is well known that the Roman Saturnalia, and the " Fasching " of the Middle Ages, which were an imitation of them, had the same object. During the Roman Saturnalia the master permitted his slaves to imagine themselves free for a couple of days, and to live according to their own tastes, after which the yoke was laid on afresh. The Roman Papacy, which paid great attention to all popular customs and knew how to turn them to account in its own interest, retained the Saturnalia under the name of Fasching (Carnival.) During Fasching all serfs and thralls were their own masters for the three days before Passion Week. The subjected classes were then allowed to drink to the dregs all pleasures within their reach, to ridicule and parody human and divine laws and ceremonies, without the slightest restraint. The clergy even went so far as to join in the wild mirth and to suffer and encourage profanations which at any other time would have entailed the heaviest spiritual and temporal penalties. And why not ? The mass that felt itself master for these few days and exhausted its exuberant energy in them, was grateful for the freedom granted and became all the more docile afterwards, in expectation of a repetition of the same delights next year.

The same thing applied to these festivities among the women, about the origin of which little is known, but at which, according to accounts, the jollity often bordered on frenzy. The sober, ascetic, puritan spirit of the period succeeding the Reformation suppressed them wherever it was in its power to do so. In other places the custom was abolished by degrees.

The old and superannuated social institutions were finally overthrown by the development of industry on a large scale, by the introduction of machinery, and by the technical application of natural science in production, commerce and traffic. We may regard the moment in which Germany attained its political unity, and with it freedom of marriage, of trade, and of migration, as that in which the abolition of the former untenable conditions was consummated.*

Centuries had passed since writers began to appear in one German State and another, urging advance in this direction. A new age has come at last, a new age for woman as well as for man, in which she has received a new position, both as a sexual being and as a social individual. The laws facilitating marriage have permitted a greater number of women to fulfil their natural functions; the laws enacting freedom of trade and of migration widened their possibilities of joining in industrial

---

* Reactionary pedants believed that these measures were the death-knell of all decency and morality, The late Bishop Ketteler of Mainz lamented as early as 1865, before the new legislature had begun to work, "that the demolition of the present barriers to marriage meant neither more nor less than the dissolution of marriage itself, for it was now made possible for all to sever the matrimonial tie at will." A pretty confession, to the effect that the moral bonds of our modern marriage are so weak that only compulsion can hold them together.

The fact that the number of marriages has as a matter of course considerably increased, and that the population has increased correspondingly, while on the other hand the gigantic industrial development under the new era called forth numerous evils unknown before, has rehabilitated the spectral fear of over-population. Conservative and Liberal economists of the bourgeois school meet here on common ground. At the close of this work I shall show what this fear means and explain its origin. Professor A. Wagner is one of the victims of the over-population panic, and consequently demands limitation of the right of marriage, chiefly for the working classes. The workmen, he says, marry too early, earlier than the middle classes. May be, it is mostly the middle classes who make use of prostitution ; if we forbid workmen to marry, we place them before the same alternative. But in that case let us hold our peace, and not shriek over the decline of morality, and not wonder that women, who have the same natural instincts as men, seek to gratify those instincts in "illegitimate relationships."

competition, and gave them a footing of greater pecuniary independence. Their legal status has also undergone essential amelioration. Are they then really free and independent? Have they attained the full development of their being, the normal exercise of all their powers and faculties?

The answer to this question will be given in the following chapters.

WOMAN IN THE PRESENT.

SEXUAL IMPULSE. MARRIAGE. OBSTACLES AND PREVENTIONS
TO MARRIAGE.

At the beginning of this book we expressed the opinion
that woman owed the inferiority of her position to the peculiarities of her sex, which placed her in a situation of
economic dependence on man.

Some who are wise in their own conceit will reply to this
that the natural instinct to which we give the name of sexual
impulse may be overcome; that its gratification is not a
matter of necessity, and that consequently the dependence
resulting from this gratification is easy to avoid. Possibly a
few solitary individuals, favoured by inherited disposition,
may succeed, though at heavy cost to themselves, in over-
coming it, but the race will never do so, seeing that it is the
purpose of sex to propagate the race. But solitary individuals
cannot alter any given social conditions. The reply is therefore invalid and superficial. Luther went to the root of the
matter in his definition of the natural impulse, when he said,
as already quoted: "He who seeks to oppose the natural
impulse and will not let Nature alone, what does he else than
seek to oppose *Nature being Nature, fire burning, water wetting,
and man eating, drinking or sleeping.*" These are words which
deserve to be chiselled in stone over the doors of our
churches, in which the lusts of the flesh are denounced. No
doctor or physiologist can more forciby express the necessity
which every sound person is under of satisfying amatory
desires. It is a law which every individual must fulfil as a
sacred duty towards himself, if his development is to be
healthy and normal, to neglect the exercise of no member of
his body, to refuse gratification to no natural impulse. Each
member must discharge the functions assigned to it by Nature,

on pain of injuring and stunting the entire organism. The laws of our physical development must be as exactly studied and obeyed as those of our mental development. The mental activity of man is the expression of the physical condition of his organs. The soundness of the former stands in most intimate relationship to that of the latter. Disturbance in one part must occasion disturbance in the others. The so-called animal passions occupy no lower rank than the so-called mental passions, both are utterances of the same organic individual, and both are constantly subject to the mutual influence of each other.

It follows as a natural consequence that an acquaintance with the physical properties of the sexual organs is as necessary as an acquaintance with the physical basis of mental activity, and that the same care must be bestowed on the development of the one as on that of the other. Every person must understand that organs and instincts which are common to all, which constitute a very essential part of his being, and even, at certain periods of life, usurp the empire over all other impulses, are not a fit subject for the affectation of mystery, for false shame, and gross ignorance. It follows further that an acquaintance with the physiology and anatomy of the sexual organs ought to be as widely spread among both sexes as any other branch of information. If we possessed knowledge of our physical nature we should regard very many vital questions from quite a different standpoint to our present one. We should find ourselves brought face to face with the question of how to remedy evils which modern society passes by in silence, but which nevertheless force the recognition of their unwelcome reality on well-nigh every family in the land. In all other departments knowledge is regarded as a virtue, as the best and most desirable aim of human endeavour. The only exception is made in those things which stand in the most intimate relation to the character and health of the individual as well as to the foundations of all social development.

Kant says: "Man and woman constitute when united the whole and entire being, one sex completes the other." Schopenhauer asserts: "The sexual impulse is the most complete expression of the will to live, in other words, it is the concentration of all volition." And in another passage: "The affirmation of the will to live concentrates itself in the act of procreation, which is its most positive expression." Mainländer gives utterance to the same opinion when he says : "The sexual impulse is the centre of gravity for human existence. It alone secures to the individual the life which he above all desires . . . man devotes himself more seriously to the business of procreation than to any other; in the achievement of nothing else, does he condense and concentrate the intensity of his will in so remarkable a manner as in the act of generation." And before all these, Buddha wrote : "Sexual desire is sharper than the hook with which wild elephants are tamed ; hotter than flame ; it is like an arrow that is shot into the heart of man.*

When we consider the intensity of the sexual impulse, we cannot be surprised at the effect which abstinence, at a mature age, exercises upon the nervous system and upon the whole constitution ; we cannot wonder at the errors and perturbations, or even at the mental derangement and suicides to which it occasionally gives rise. The degree of perfection which any human being, either man or woman can obtain, depends on the measure in which impulses and vital manifestations accentuate themselves in sex, on the extent to which sexual life finds its expression in organic and spiritual development, in form and character. Only when this expression is complete can the individual reach his own completion. "In civilized society," says Klencke, in his book : "Woman in the Position of Wife," "the impetus towards sexual gratification is, it is true, placed under the guidance of those moral principles which reason dictates ; but not even the most powerful will is able entirely to silence the urgent admonition to propagate the race, which nature has expressed in the normal and organic differentiation of the sexes ; and when healthy individuals of either sex do not fufil this duty at some period of their lives, the reason is not to be sought in their unbiassed resolve to resist nature, even when this is affirmed to be the case, or when free-will is self-deceptively stated as the cause, but in social checks and their consequences, which have encroached on natural rights, stunted the growth of organs, and at the same time stamped the whole organism with the type of retrogression, of sexual imperfection, in appearance and character, while giving birth to morbid nervous tendencies and conditions of body and mind. Man becomes womanish, woman masculine, in form and nature, because sexual differentiation never reached the realization intended in

---

* Mainländer : "Philosophie der Erlösung," 2nd vol., 12 Essays. (Philosophy of Redemption.)

Nature's plan ; the individual remained one-sided, never attaining the completion of himself, the perfection of his own existence." And Dr. Elizabeth Blackwell says in her book : " The Moral Education of Young in Relation to Sex " :—" The sexual impulse exists, as an indispensable condition of life, and as the basis of society. It is the greatest force in human nature. Whatever else disappears, this remains. Often undeveloped, not even an object of thought, but none the less the *central fire of life*, this inevitable instinct is the natural protector against any possibility of extinction."

Thus does modern philosophy agree with the dicta of exact science and with the plain common sense of Luther. The outcome is that every human being has both the right and the duty to satisfy instincts which are not only intimately connected with his innermost being, but form an integral part of it. If social institutions or prejudices prevent the gratification of these instincts, the development of his being is checked, it becomes crippled and stunted. We may learn. the consequences of such a system from our physicians, our hospitals, lunatic asylums, and prisons, to say nothing of the thousand cases in which families are broken up and their happiness destroyed.

A few facts will suffice as illustrations. Dr. Hegerisch, the translator of Malthus' Essay on Population, expresses himself as follows with regard to the forced suppression of the sexual instinct in women :—" Although I agree with Malthus as to the value of virtuous abstinence, the sad conviction is forced upon me as a physician, that the chaste morality of women, which, though it is certainly a high virtue in our modern states, is none the less a crime against nature, not unfrequently revenges itself by the cruellest forms of disease. It is as certain that the virtuous abstinence of women is no rare cause of morbid processes in the breasts, the ovaries and the uterus as it is childish to fear the effects of continence or of natural self-help in men. Inasmuch as these diseases do not attack vital organs, they are a greater source of torment to their unhappy victims than almost any others. The unfortunate women, mostly the best of their sex, who succeed in subduing an ardent temperament in spite of the struggles of nature, present the saddest of all sad spectacles. The deserted girl, the early widow, pines on her solitary couch. . , ..." He then goes on to show that nuns are especially subject to the above-mentioned troubles and diseases.

The evil effects of suppressed passion on both men and

women, and the advantages of even an imperfect marriage over celibacy, are proved by the following figures :—In Bavaria there were, in 1858, 4899 lunatics, of whom 2576 (53 per cent.) were men, and 2323 (47 per cent.) were women. The number of men was therefore greater than that of women. But the percentage of unmarried lunatics of both sexes was 81 per cent., of the married lunatics 17 per cent. ; while the condition of 2 per cent. was unknown. This alarming proportion is somewhat modified by the fact that a number of born idiots are reckoned among the unmarried. In Hannover, the census of 1856 returned one lunatic to 457 unmarried, 564 widowed, and 1,316 married inhabitants. In Saxony there were 1000 unmarried male suicides to 1,000,000 unmarried males and only 500 married male suicides to 1,000,000 married males. Among the women, who on an average commit suicide less frequently than men, the ratio was 260 unmarried women to a million spinsters and widows, and only 125 to a million married women. Similar results have been obtained in many other states. By far the greater number of female suicides falls between the ages of 16 and 21, proof enough that the causes are chiefly ungratified sexual instincts, disappointed love, concealed pregnancy and desertion on the part of men. The same causes occasion madness, in equally unfavourable proportions. For instance, in Prussia, in 1882, there were to every 10,000 inhabitants of the respective categories, 32.2 unmarried male lunatics, 29.3 female lunatics, 9.5 married male lunatics, 9.5 married female lunatics, 32.1 widowed male lunatics, and 25.5 widowed female lunatics.

It is unquestionable that neglected satisfaction of the sexual impulse exerts the most detrimental influence on the mental and bodily condition of men and women, and that no social institutions can be regarded as healthy which prevent the normal gratification of the natural instincts.

The question therefore arises whether society in its present shape meets the demands of a rational mode of life, in the case of human beings in general, and especially in that of women. Can it meet these demands ? And if not, how can they be met ?

" Marriage is the basis of the family, the family is the basis of the State ; if you attack marriage you attack society and the State and undermine both," exclaim the advocates of the present "order" of things. Certainly, marriage is the basis of social development. But we must ascertain which form of marriage is the more moral, or in other words, more likely to conduce to the advantage of humanity in all its phases, a marriage founded on the bourgeois idea of property, and therefore compulsory, with its many attendant evils and mostly imperfect realisation of its object, a social institution beyond the reach of millions, or a marriage founded on the free, untrammeled choice of love, *such as is only possible in a Socialistic society.*

Even John Stuart Mill, whom no one will suspect of being a communist, declares " *Marriage is at the present day the only actual form of serfdom recognised by law.*"

According to the doctrine of Kant, man and woman together represent an entire being. The healthy development of the race depends on the normal union of the sexes. The natural exercise of the sexual functions is a necessity for the healthy development of the individual, whether man or woman. But as man is not only an animal but also a human being, his strongest and most vehement impulse cannot be fully satisfied by mere physical gratification ; he feels the need of mental affinity to the being with whom he unites himself. When this is absent, sexual intercourse becomes purely mechanical and is rightly stigmatized as immoral. Such intercourse cannot fulfil the requirements of a higher humanity, that seeks to enoble a relationship based on purely physical laws by the mutual personal attraction of two sexual beings. The man of finer mould demands that this mutual attraction should outlive the consummation of the sexual act, and extend its elevating influence to the beings called into existence by that act.*

It is therefore consideration for the offspring, duties towards it and pleasure in it, which, under the most various social forms, first causes the amatory relationship of two beings to become permanent. Every couple which desires to unite in sexual intercourse should ask itself whether its reciprocal bodily and mental qualities are capable of advantageous intermingling. The reply can only be an unbiassed one under two conditions. Firstly, the removal of every interest foreign to the proper purpose of union, namely, gratification of the natural instincts and the perpetuation of

---

* " The moods and feelings in and with which husband and wife approach each other exercise without doubt a definite influence on the result of the sexual act and transmit certain characteristics to the fruit." Dr, Elizabeth Blackwell : " The Moral Education of the Young in Relation to Sex." See too Goethe's " Wahlverwandschaften," in which he distinctly depicts the action of such feelings.

the individual in the propagation of the race ; and secondly, a measure of discernment sufficient to bridle the blindness of passion. As both these conditions, in our modern society, are more frequently absent than not, it follows as a matter of course that our modern marriage is very far from fulfilling its true purpose and has therefore no claim to be regarded as either sacred or moral.

It is impossible to prove statistically how large a number of marriages are concluded in the present day on a basis the reverse of that described above. It is in the interest of those concerned to let their union appear to the world other than that which it really is. Nor has the modern State, as the representative of Society, any occasion to instigate researches the result of which might throw a curious light on its own proceedings. The principles which the State lays down with regard to the marriage of numerous categories of its own servants and officials will not bear the application of a standard which the same State declares obligatory in other cases.

We agreed that the matrimonial union should only be entered upon by two persons inspired by mutual love, for the purpose of exercising their natural functions. This motive is rarely pure and unalloyed. On the contrary, marriage is regarded by most women as a kind of almshouse into which they must obtain admittance at all costs, while the man, for his part, generally counts up the pecuniary advantages of marriage with the greatest exactitude. And even into those marriages in which low and egoistic motives have had no place, the stern reality of life introduces so many elements of disturbance and dissolution, that they but rarely fulfil the hopes of youthful enthusiasm and passion.

And very naturally. If married life is to afford satisfaction to both husband and wife, not only mutual love and respect must be present, but also the certainty of possessing that measure of the necessities and agreeables of life which they consider indispensable for themselves and their children. Gnawing anxiety, the hard struggle for existence, are the first nails in the coffin of matrimonial happiness and content. And the more fruitful the union is, in other words, the more the natural purpose of marriage is accomplished, the more pressing does the anxiety become. The peasant, who congratulates himself on the birth of every calf, who counts with complacency his litter of young pigs, and reports the number smiling to his neighbour,—this same peasant listens gloomily when he hears that his wife has brought him an addition to the small number of children that he hopes to be able to rear, and all the more gloomily if the new-born child has the misfortune to be a girl.

The simple fact that the birth of a human being, the image of God, as religious people say, is in so many cases regarded as of very much less importance than that of a domestic animal, proves the degraded condition in which we live. And here again, it is chiefly the female sex that suffers.· In many respects there is little difference between our ideas and those of ancient and modern barbarians. The barbarians put their superflous girls to death, and most girls were superflous, in times when wars of extermination were the order of the day. We are too civilized to kill our daughters, but we mostly treat them as pariahs in society and in the family. Man, as the stronger, drives them back everywhere in the struggle for existence, and when, nevertheless, the instinct of self-preservation forces them to compete, they only too often meet the hate and persecution of the more powerful sex, which fears their competition. In this respect all trades and professions are alike. When short-sighted workmen seek to forbid the employment of women altogether—the demand was made, for instance, in 1877 at the Congress of French Working Men, but rejected by a large majority—their narrow mindedness is excusable, for they support their demand by pointing to the undeniable fact that the increasing employment of female labour is entirely destroying the family life of the workmen, and that a consequent degeneration of the race is inevitable. But prohibition is impossible. Hundreds and thousands of women are compelled to seek work in factories and in many other branches in order to keep soul and body together. Even married women are forced to take part in the competitive struggle, to supplement the earnings of the husband, who is more often than not unable to support the family alone.*

---

* "Mr. E., a manufacturer, tells me that he exclusively employs women at his mechanical looms ; he says that he prefers married women, especially the mothers of families which depend on them for support ; they are much more attentive and tractable than the unmarried women, and are compelled to exert their strength to the uttermost to earn the bare means of subsistence. Thus are the virtues, the peculiar virtues of the female character turned to its abuse ; thus is the morality and tenderness of woman's nature made the instrument of her suffering and slavery." Speech of Lord Ashley on the Ten Hours Bill, 1844. v. Karl Marx, "Kapital," (Capital) 2nd edition.

There can be no doubt that society is to-day more civilized than at any previous period. The position of women is higher, the employments of women are less menial and more manifold, but the relations of the two sexes to each other have remained the same. Professor Lorenz von Stein, in his work, " Woman from the Standpoint of Political Economy," a book which, by the way, corresponds little either to its title or to the expectations which it raises, gives a poetic and ideal picture of modern marriage as it is supposed to exist, but even here the subjected position of women towards the lion, man, is apparent. Herr v. Stein writes, among other things: " Man desires a being that not only loves but understands him, a being whose heart not only beats for him, but whose hand smooths his brow, a being that, wherever it appears, irradiates peace, rest, order, silent control over itself and over the thousand trifles that makes up his daily life ; he desires a being that diffuses over everything that indefinable odour of womanhood which is the vivifying warmth of domestic life."

In this would-be song of praise lies the degradation of woman, the basest egotism of man. The Herr Professor paints woman quite arbitrarily as an airy creature who is nevertheless in possession of the necessary practical knowledge of arithmetic, who knows how to maintain equilibrium between the debtor and creditor columns of her housekeeper's book, and who, for the rest, flits about the master of the house, the all-powerful lion, like a gentle zephyr of spring, reads every wish in his eyes, and with her small soft hand smoothes away the wrinkles which reflections on his own folly have possibly called forth. In short Herr Professor v. Stein depicts woman and marriage such as they neither are nor can be in ninety-nine cases out of a hundred. The learned gentleman neither sees nor knows anything about the thousands of unhappy marriages, of the disproportion between compulsion and choice, of the innumerable solitary women who cannot even dream of marriage, of the millions who toil and slave by the side of their husbands, early and late, to earn a miserable crust of bread for the day as it passes. A rude and pitless reality brushes the poetic bloom from the lives of the poor more easily than the hand dust from a butterfly's wings. A glance in this direction would have brought dire disorder into the lyrical effusions of the Herr Professor, or possibly have spoiled them altogether.

One so often hears the remark : " the best standard for

the civilisation of a nation is the position occupied by its women." We agree to this standard, but it will show us that our own civilisation is far from being what we fondly imagine it to be.

John Stuart Mill remarks in his book on the " Subjection of Women " (a title which sufficiently characterises the author's opinion of the condition of women in general): " The lives of men have become more domestic, growing civilisation lays them under more obligations towards women." The first assertion is not correct, and the second only partially so. In cases in which a sincere marital relationship exists between husband and wife it doubtless applies. Every reasonable man will regard it as an advantage for his wife and himself, if she acquaints herself with the course of public events and the state of public opinion, if she quits the narrow household circle and begins to take part in the affairs of life. But the obligations thus imposed upon him are not pressing. On the other hand we must enquire whether modern life has not introduced factors into matrimony which tend to undermine it more than any which existed before.

Doubtless in all ages, when women were possessed of property, marriages were far oftener determined by pecuniary considerations than by love or affection, but proofs are wanting to shew that marriage was formerly made an object of speculation and exchange in the open market with anything like the same effrontery as to-day. In our times, among the propertied classes—the poor have no need of it— marriage barter is frequently carried on with a shamelessness which makes the phrases about the sacredness of marriage that some people never tire of repeating, sound like the emptiest mockery. This has its reasons, like everything else. In no period has it been so difficult as at present for the great majority to attain to what is generally regarded as prosperity, and in no period has the perfectly justifiable desire for the amenities and enjoyments of life been so universally disseminated as now. And the failure to attain these things is felt the more acutely, because all believe they possess an equal claim to gratification. Theoretically there is no distinction between ranks and classes. The conception of a democratic equality in enjoyment has roused in all the longing to translate this conception into reality. But the majority does not understand that equality in enjoyment is only possible in company with equality in the social conditions of existence. Moreover public opinion and the example of the upper classes prompt the individual to resort to any measures, which, without compromising him, will, as he believes, lead to the end in view. Thus speculation on a wealthy marriage has become one of the chief means of rising in life. On the one side is the thirst for money, for as much money as possible ; on the other, the desire for rank, titles, distinction; these desires, especially in the so-called better classes of society, provide for each other's mutual gratification. In these classes marriage is mostly regarded as a mere business transaction, it is a purely conventional tie, which both parties outwardly respect, while each acts privately as his feelings may direct. We need only allude to political marriage in the highest circles for the sake of completeness. In such cases the privilege of seeking compensation outside marriage, according to desire or caprice, has been accorded as a matter of course and again in far higher degree to the man than to the woman. There was a time when it was etiquette for the monarch to have at least one mistress, who belonged so to speak to his regal attributes. Friedrich Wilhelm I. of Prussia (1713-1740) for instance, kept up a make-believe liaison with the wife of a general, the intimacy of which consisted in an hour's walk daily in the castle yard. It is universally known that the predecessor of the late King of Italy, "König Ehrenmann" as he was called, left no fewer than thirty-two illegitimate children behind him. These examples might be multiplied ad libitum.

The internal history of most of the European courts and noble families is for the initiated an almost uninterrupted chronique scandaleuse, often blackened by crimes of the worst kind. It is therefore very necessary that historical sycophants should cast no doubts on the legitimacy of the successive sovereigns, but on the contrary endeavour to represent them, one and all, as faithful husbands and excellent fathers. The race of Augurs has not yet died out and it lives now, as in Roman times, on the ignorance of the masses.

In all large towns there are certain places and certain days on which members of the upper classes assemble, chiefly for the purpose of arranging betrothals. These meetings have been not unsuitably named the marriage-exchange. Speculation and bargaining play the principal part; deceit and jobbery are not wanting. Officers over head and ears in debt, but in possession of a noble pedigree; roués, whose health has been ruined by debauchery, and who seek repose and a good nurse in the matrimonial haven; manufacturers, with bankruptcy staring them in the face; merchants and bankers in quest of a saviour; officials in money difficulties but with prospects of advancement; finally all who desire the rapid attainment or increase of wealth, appear here as customers and conclude bargains, whether the woman be old or young, pretty or ugly, healthy or diseased, cultivated or ignorant, pious or flippant, Christian or Jewish. According to the opinion of a very celebrated statesman, " Marriage between a Christian stallion and a Jewish mare is much to be recommended." This simile, characteristically taken from the stable, finds, as experience shows, lively approval in the higher circles of society. Money compensates for all dis- advantages and outweighs all defects of character. Numerous and extensively organised marriage-agencies, procurers and procuresses of all kinds hunt up their prey, and secure candi- dates of both sexes for the " sacred state of matrimony." This business is especially profitable when it is carried on in the interests of the upper classes. In 1878 a procuress was tried on a charge of poisoning at the criminal court of Vienna, and sentenced to fifteen years penal servitude. On this occasion it was discovered that the former French ambassador in Vienna, Count Banneville, had paid this woman 22,000 florins (£1,870) for his wife. Other members of the aristo- cracy were also seriously compromised in the trial. It appeared that certain high officials had suffered the procuress to pursue her unclean and criminal trade unmolested. After what we have stated the reason will be plain enough. Similar tales are current in the German capital. Any man or maiden who comes across no suitable object for marriage, confides the needs of his heart to pious Conservative or moral Liberal papers, who for money, but not for love, arrange to bring kindred souls together. This disgraceful business of match- making has reached a pitch at which the authorities occasion- ally consider themselves bound to interfere, and to issue warnings and threats against a traffic that has so little regard to decency. In the year 1876 the local government of Leipzig published a proclamation, calling attention to the illegality of the business, and directing the police to punish all who ex- ceeded the prescribed limits. As a rule, however, the State, which is ready enough to become the saviour of " order and morality" where an inconvenient party is concerned, rarely takes occasion to seriously combat the increase of this scandalous barter.

The part played by Church and State in the sacred ceremony is far from creditable in more respects than one. However certain the State official or the minister of the Church
may be that the bridal pair before him has been brought
together by the dirtiest of tricks, however apparent it may
be that there is not the smallest compatibility between the
two, either in age, or in mental or physical constitution—the
bride may be twenty and the bridegroom seventy, or *vice versa*,
the bride may be young, handsome, full of life and spirits, the
bridegroom old, decrepid, morose,—all this is of no consequence to the representative of Church and State, it does
not concern him ; it is his business to bless the matrimonial
bond, and the blessing on the part of the Church is all the
more solemn the larger the sum paid for the sacred act.

But when, later on, the discovery is made, that such a
marriage, as every one knew beforehand, and the unhappy
victim, who is generally the woman, herself foresaw, is a
disastrous one, and one or other of those concerned desires
separation, both Church and State, who had asked no
questions in the first place as to whether real love, and purely
natural and moral impulses, or base and undisguised egotism
had tied the knot, make the gravest objections. Neither
State nor Church considered itself under the obligation of
calling their attention before marriage to the fact that their
union was obviously contrary to nature and therefore immoral. And after marriage moral disgust is rarely accepted
as a sufficient ground for separation ; as a rule circumstantial
evidence is demanded, proofs which degrade or dishonour
one of the two must be forthcoming before a divorce is
granted. The fact that the Catholic Church only recognizes
divorce in the rare cases in which a dispensation can be
obtained from the Pope, and can generally only with difficulty
be induced even to permit separation from table and bed is a
serious aggravation of the present state of things, under
which the entire Catholic population suffers heavily.

Thus are human beings chained together, the one becomes
the slave of the other, and is forced, in the fulfilment of
matrimonial duty, to submit to the most intimate embraces
and caresses of the other, which he possibly detests more
than blows and abuse.

Now I ask, is not such a marriage—and the number is
great—worse than prostitution. The prostitute is at least to
a certain extent free to withdraw from her shameful trade ;
she has, at least if she is not the inmate of a brothel, the

right of refusing to do business with a man whose personality repels her. But a wife is sold into the hands of her husband, and must endure his embraces though she may have a hundred causes to hate and abominate him.

In other marriages, in which pecuniary advantage was not the principal motive, the state of things is somewhat better. People accommodate themselves, find a *modus vivendi*, accept the inevitable, for fear of scandal or of money loss, or for the sake of the children, although it is precisely the children who suffer most under a cold and loveless parental régime, even without open enmity, altercations and quarrels. The man, who is generally the discordant element in marriage, as the divorce cases shew, thanks to his position as master of the house, can seek compensation elsewhere. It is far more difficult for the wife to diverge from the matrimonial path, firstly because she as the recipient is exposed to dangerous consequences, and secondly because the slightest transgression on her part is regarded as a crime which neither husband nor society forgives. A woman will only make up her mind to divorce in the worst cases of marital unfaithfulness or brutality, for the simple reason that she has as a rule to look to her husband for support. Her position is pecuniarily a dependent one and the social status of a divorced wife is far from enviable. It is a serious proof of the matrimonial sufferings of women that nevertheless a very large proportion of divorce cases is instigated by the wife. In France, for example, the proportion is 88 per cent.* The yearly increasing number of divorces in all countries shews the truth of the statement. The Austrian Judge, who exclaimed in a feuilleton article in the Frankfurter Zeitung, in 1878 : " The actions for adultery are as common as actions for broken window panes," can hardly be accused of exaggeration.

The growing uncertainty of business, and the increasing difficulty of obtaining a moderately secure position in the economic struggle of all against all, afford small probability that under the present social system this marriage traffic will

---

* Petitions for separation from table and bed in France were as follows :—

In the years		from women.		from men.		
1856—1861	on an average	1729	..	184	..	per annum.
1861—1866	,,	2135	..	260	..	,,
1866—1871	,,	2591	..	330	..	,,

Bridel : " Puissance Marital : (Marital Power).

cease or even diminish. On the contrary, the intimate connection between marriage and the existing conditions of society and property cannot fail to aggravate the state of affairs.

While on the one hand the corruption of marriage is increasing, while on the other a large number of women is shut out from marriage altogether, such expressions as "Woman's place is at home, she must fulfil her vocation of wife and mother," are nothing better than mere thoughtless phrases. At the same time the factors already mentioned, the degradation of matrimony, and the action of marriage hindrances which cannot but become more stringent, in spite of the removal of State checks, must foster the spread of illegitimate relationships, of prostitution and of all unnatural vices.*

Among the propertied classes the wife not unfrequently sinks to the level of the Greek woman; she becomes a mere apparatus for procuring legitimate children, a guardian of the house and a sick nurse for the man. The husband finds amusement and gratification of his amatory passions with courtesans and hetæræ, whom we call mistresses, and whose elegant houses form the best quarters in all large towns. At the same time, unnatural matrimonial relations lead to all kinds of crime, to murder and false accusations of insanity. The murder of husband or wife is said to be more frequent than is generally supposed during cholera epidemics, owing to the similarity between the symptoms of cholera and poisoning, and the impossibility of exact examination in consequence of the general panic, the number of corpses, the danger of infection and the necessity of speedy burial.

---

* Dr. Karl Bücher, in his book: "Die Frauenfrage im Mittelalter" (The Woman's Question in the Middle Ages), complains of the dissolution of married and family life; he condemns the increasing employment of women in industrial pursuits, and demands the "return" of woman "to her proper sphere," viz., house and family, in which alone she is "of value" from an economic point of view. The endeavours of modern women, appear to him "dilettantism" and he finally expresses the hope, that "they will soon seek the right path again," though he is obviously incapable of pointing out the way. It cannot be otherwise while he attempts to do so from the middle class democratic standpoint. From this standpoint our entire modern development must appear in the light of an argument on false premises, of a gigantic mistake on the part of civilisation. But civilisation makes no such mistakes, it is governed by immanent laws; and it is the task of the historian to discover these laws and under their guidance to shew how existing evils may be removed, and conditions brought into harmony with nature.

In the classes in which limited means prevent the support of a mistress, recourse is had to public and private places of amusement, to cafés chantants, music halls, balls, and brothels. The increase of prostitution is apparent everywhere.

We have seen that the dissolution of matrimony among the upper and middle classes is brought about by money marriages, by superfluity, idleness, debauchery, with a corresponding nourishment for heart and mind, frivolous theatrical performances, sensuous music, immoral novels, unclean literature, and pictures of a similar nature. Many of the same causes are at work among the lowest classes. It is true that here neither man nor woman is exposed to the temptations of marrying property. As a rule the man's choice is dictated by affection, though not unfrequently also by the calculation that the wife can add to his earnings, or by the prospect that the children will soon be able to work and so cover their own expenses. Sad, but only too true. There is no lack of disturbing elements in the married life of a workman. A large family puts an entire stop to the work of the mother, and increases the expenditure ; gluts in business and trade, the introduction of new machines or improved methods of labour, wars, unfavourable commercial treaties, indirect taxes curtail the wages of the father for a longer or shorter time, or throw him out of work altogether. Such blows as these make a man bitter, and his bitterness finds vent most readily at home, where he is daily and hourly faced by the necessity of providing the requisites of life for wife and children, and has not the wherewithal to do it. More often than not he seeks comfort in despair from bad brandy, the last penny is spent, quarrels and disputes know no end. We see the ruin of marriage and of family life before us.

Let us take another picture. Husband and wife go out to work. The children are left alone or in the care of elder children, who need looking after and educating themselves. In hot haste the parents swallow the meal that is by courtesy called dinner, supposing they have time to come home at all ; tired and exhausted, they return home at night. Instead of a pleasant and comfortable house, they find a small unhealthy dwelling, without light or air, and often without the most necessary arrangements for cleanliness. The wife must set to work at once, in the utmost haste, to get things into something like order. The noisy and crying children are put to bed as soon as possible, the mother sits sewing and mending till late in the night. The necessary mental recreation and refreshment are altogether wanting. The man is ignorant, the woman still more so ; they soon come to the end of the little which they have to say to each other. The man goes to the public-house in search of the entertainment which his home cannot provide; he drinks, and however little he may spend, it is too much for his means. Sometimes he falls a prey to the vice of gaming, which claims so many victims among the upper classes ; and loses three and ten times as much by cards as by drink. Meanwhile the wife remains at home in dudgeon : she must work like a beast of burden ; there is no rest or recreation for her ; the man makes use of the freedom which the chance of birth has given him. The discord is complete. Or, if the wife be less conscientious, if she too seeks a well-earned recreation when she comes home, weary, at night, the household is neglected and its wretchedness doubled. Truly, we live in the best of worlds.

All these things tend more and more to destroy the married life of the proletarian. Even good times have a destructive influence, for they force him to work over hours on Sundays and weekdays, and thus rob him of the time which he might devote to his family. In thousands of cases he has at least an hour's walk to his work ; it is frequently a simple impossibility for him to come home during the dinner hour, he starts early in the morning, while the children are still asleep, and returns late at night, after they have been put to bed. Many workmen, especially masons in large towns, remain away the whole week, on account of the distance, only coming home on Sunday; and family life is supposed to flourish under circumstances such as these. Moreover the employment of women and children is continually on the increase, especially in the textile industries, whose thousand steam-looms and spindle frames are worked by the cheapest hands in the market. There relations of sex and age have been pretty well reversed. The wife and children are in the factory ; the man, who has no work to do, remains at home and attends to the house. In Kolmar, at the end of November 1873, 8109 hands were employed in the cotton and kindred branches. 3509 of these were women, 3416 men, and 1184 children, so that the number of women and children together was 4693, that of the men 3416. In the English cotton industry, in 1875, among 479,515 hands, 258,667, or 54 per cent were women, 38,558, or 8 per cent children of both sexes between the ages of 13 and 18, 66,900, or 14 per cent, children under 13, and only 115,391 or 24 per cent men. What can the family life of these people be like ?

Our "Christian" State, whose Christianity one seeks in vain, where it ought to be practically applied, and finds where it is superfluous or harmful, this Christian State acts in precisely the same way as the Christian bourgeois, a fact which does not surprise those who know that the Christian State is nothing more than the clerk of the Christian bourgeois. Not only does it refrain from introducing laws to restrict the employment of women within permissible limits and forbid the employment of children altogether; it does not even secure the Sunday's rest, or a normal working day to a large number of its own officials, upon whose family life it thus encroaches. Civil servants in the Post Office, on the railway and in prisons are frequently obliged to work long after hours and their wages stand in inverse ratio to their service. But this is everywhere the case to-day, and most people imagine it must be so.

Further, house rent is out of all proportion to the income of the lower officials and of the poor, who are consequently forced to limit themselves to the utmost extent in dwelling room. Young men or women are taken as lodgers, often both. Old and young are crowded together in the smallest space, with no separation of the sexes, even for the most private acts. Terrible experiences shew the influence of this state of things on decency and morality. And what must be the result of factory work on the children? Undoubtedly both physically and morally the worst that can be imagined.

The increasing employment of married women, especially in cases of pregnancy and birth, and in the period after birth, when the children depend on the mother for nourishment, cannot fail to have the most pernicious effects. A woman is thereby exposed to many accidents during pregnancy, which are alike injurious to her offspring and to herself, abortion, premature and still-birth. After her confinement, the mother is forced to return to the factory as soon as possible, or her place will be filled by another competitor. The inevitable consequences for the children are neglect, unsuitable food, slow starvation; they are fed with opiates to keep them quiet, and the results are innumerable deaths, chronic ailments, stunted development, in a word, the degeneration of the race. The children grow up in countless cases without having ever felt a father's or a mother's tenderness, while the parents, on the other hand have never known what it was to love their children. So is the Proletariat born, so does it live and die. And a Christian State and a Christian Society are surprised at the increase of brutality, immorality and crime.

During the North American Slave War, at a time when thousands of women were thrown out of work in the English cotton districts, doctors made the remarkable discovery that in spite of the terrible distress of the population, the mortality among infants decreased. The reason was plain. The children were better looked after and better fed than they had been in times of the greatest prosperity. The same observation was made some years later during the North American glut, in New York and Massachussetts. Want of work forced the women to remain at home and gave them time to attend to their children.

The condition of family life and of morality is not one jot better in domestic industry, which romantic theorizers are fond of representing as so idyllic. Here both husband and wife are tied to their work from morning to night, and the children are trained to the same thing from the tenderest years. Parents and children, young men and girls are crammed together in the smallest possible space, in the midst of dust and leavings, in a pestilential atmosphere, with no means of providing for the most elementary cleanliness or ventilation. The sleeping rooms are no better than the combined workshop and sitting-room ; they can only be described as dens, without light or air, but which nevertheless contain a number of persons that would suffice to make rooms four times the size in the highest degree unhealthy. In short, the state of things which exists is enough to make anyone who is accustomed to a less bestial existence shudder.

The struggle for existence, which is becoming fiercer year by year, not unfrequently compels men and women to commit actions and suffer indignities which would otherwise fill them with disgust. For instance it was ascertained in München, in 1877, that among the registered prostitutes under the surveillance of the police no fewer than 203 were the wives of day-labourers and artisans. And how many married women are driven by hunger to carry on this disgraceful trade, without subjecting themselves to a police control which so shamelessly violates every feeling of decency and of personal dignity ?

We know by experience that the high price of corn during a single year diminishes the number of marriages and births ; still more detrimental is the influence of periods of distress, which extend over many years and are inseparably connected

with our present economic system. This is strikingly shown
by the marriage statistics of the German Empire. In the
year 1872, a year of increasing prosperity, 423,900 marriages
were concluded; in 1879, when the panic had reached its
climax, only 335,133. The numbers had decreased 25 per
cent., indeed, if we take the increase of the population into
account, 33 per cent. During the years of depression, 1876—
1879, the numbers fell off in Prussia year by year.

> In 1876 there were 224,773 marriages.
> In 1877   ,,   ,,   210,357   ,,
> In 1878   ,,   ,,   207,754   ,,
> In 1879   ,,   ,,   206,752   ,,

The number of children was also considerably lessened. Insufficient means, the fear of not being able to give the children
an education befitting their station impel women in all
classes of society to commit actions that are contrary to
nature and conflict with criminal law. We refer to the
various measures for preventing conception, or, when conception has already taken place, to the expulsion of the
immature fœtus by abortion. It would be a mistake to suppose that this measure is only resorted to by frivolous,
unscrupulous women. On the contrary, extremely conscientious women will often expose themselves to the dangers
of artificial abortion, rather than refuse to gratify the desires
of their husbands, and forcibly suppress their own sexual
impulses, or from fear of seeing their husbands seek compensation elsewhere, which the latter are generally ready
enough to do. On the other hand there are women, especially
among the upper classes, who do not recoil from criminal
actions, in which they easily procure the well-paid assistance
of doctors and midwives, in order to conceal a "fault," or
from dislike to the trouble of pregnancy, childbirth and child-
rearing, or from fear of losing their charms and forfeiting the
admiration of their husbands or of other men. An instance
of this was afforded in the spring of 1878 by the suicide of a
woman in New York, who possessed a sumptuous residence
and carried on her shameless trade for more than a generation
under the eyes of the New York police and justices, but was at
last overtaken by her Nemesis in the shape of an action which
threatened to ruin her. In spite of her luxurious life this
woman left behind her property to the amount of a million-
and-a-half of dollars. Her clientèle was exclusively confined
to the richest circles in New York.

To judge from the growing number of advertisements in the daily press there is also a considerable increase of establishments in which opportunity is offered to married and unmarried women of awaiting the consequences of " faults " in seclusion.

The dread of having more children than one has means of bringing up and providing for has caused the systematic use of preventive checks to spread among whole classes and nations to a degree that must be regarded as a public calamity. It is a well-known fact that the Two-children System is carried out through all strata of French society. In no civilized country in the world are marriages relatively so numerous as in France, and in no country is the average number of children so small, or the increase of population so slow. In the last respect, indeed, France is even behind Russia. The French bourgeois of the upper and middle classes and the peasant proprietors adopt this plan, and the French workmen follow in their wake.

The same thing applies to the Saxon colony in Transylvania. The endeavour to keep their large possessions together, as a means of retaining their political power and the consequent desire to avoid all unnecessary partition among their heirs, causes the Germans in Transylvania to restrict the number of their *legitimate* offspring as much as possible. On the other hand the men are accustomed to gratify their sexual impulses outside marriage, a fact which explains the curious ethnological phenomenon of light-haired gypsies and teutonic Rumanians, as well as their occasional possession of such qualities as industry and thrift, which are by no means usual characteristics of the latter people. Thanks to these principles, the Transylvanian Saxon population has hardly yet reached 200,000, although the territory was colonized by large numbers towards the end of the 12th century. In France on the other hand, where there are no foreign races for sexual exploitation, cases of infanticide and exposure are considerably increasing, favoured it is true, by the prohibition of the French civil code to instigate the research of paternity.*

The French bourgeoisie, conscious of the cruelty of preventing deserted women by law from turning to the father of the

---

* Paragraph 340 of the Civil Code runs as follows: " La recherche de la paternité est interdite," and Paragraph 341, " La recherche de la maternité est admise." It is illegal to enquire after the father: It is legal to enquire after the mother. All attempts to abolish paragraph 340 have been hitherto unsuccessful.

child for support, endeavoured to ameliorate their condition
by establishing Houses for Foundlings. As we know, our
impartial morality does not permit the existence of paternal
feelings towards illegitimate children but only towards
legitimate "heirs." In the Foundling-Homes the new-
born babes were robbed of the mother as well. They
came into the world as orphans. The bourgeoisie rears
its illegitimate children at the expense of the State, as
children of the Fatherland. An admirable institution!
Nevertheless, in spite of these asylums, in which the care
is insufficient and where the little one die en masse, infanticide and abortion are increasing in France out of all
proportion to the population.

From the year 1830 to 1880, 8563 cases of child murder
were tried before the French Assizes. The number was 471
in 1831 and 980 in 1880. During the same period 1032
women were sentenced for abortion; in the year 1831, over 41;
in the year 1880, over 100. Naturally only a very small
percentage of abortion cases come before the courts, generally
only when they have resulted in serious illness or death.
75 per cent of infanticides were committed by the country
population, and 67 per cent of abortions by the town population. In the towns, women have more means to prevent
birth, hence the relatively large number of abortions, and the
relatively small number of infanticides. In the country these
conditions are reversed.

This is the picture offered us by marriage at the present
day, in the overwhelming majority of cases. It differs
materially from that painted by poets and poetic phantasts,
but it has the advantage of being true to nature.

But the picture would be incomplete if I omitted to add a
few important touches.

However the dispute with regard to the mental capacities
of the two sexes may be decided—a subject to which we
shall return later on—there can be no difference of opinion
as to the fact that the average woman is at present inferior
to the average man. Balzac, it is true, who was by no
means a friend of women, asserted: "A woman that has
received a masculine education possesses the most brilliant
and fertile qualities, with which to secure the happiness of
her husband and herself;" and Goethe, who was certainly a
connoisseur in the men and women of his day, remarks with
cutting sarcasm in "Wilhelm Meisters Lehrjahre" (Confes-
sions of a Beautiful Soul,) "People ridicule learned women

and dislike even women who are well informed, probably because it is considered impolite to put so many ignorant men to shame." But neither of those assertions prove anything with regard to women in general as they at present are. There is an undeniable difference between the sexes, and there must be, because women are what men, their masters, have made them. The education of woman has been as a rule even more neglected than that of the proletarian, and the improvements that are being made in this direction are in every respect inadequate. We live in a time in which all circles recognize the necessary of interchanging ideas, in the family as well as elsewhere, and the neglected cultivation of woman makes itself felt as a defect under which the husband has to suffer heavily.

The distinguishing features in a man's education are the strengthening of the understanding, the sharpening of the powers of thought, the extension of knowledge, the acquisition of scientific facts and methods, in short, the development of the functions of the mind. The education of a woman on the other hand, when it deserves the name at all, concerns itself with the purely external cultivation of the feelings and of "esprit." The results are overstrung sensitiveness, nervous irritability, and a heightened imagination, the product of music, light literature, art and poetry. This is the most unhealthy and insane course which could possibly be pursued; it clearly shows that those persons on whose decision both the quantity and the quality of woman's education has depended have been guided in this decision only by their inherent prejudices with regard to the nature of woman's character and her circumscribed sphere of life. What our women want is not stimulation of the feelings and the imagination, an increased nervosity or a superficial acquaintance with literature; in all these respects the female character has been amply formed and deformed; a woman's education has only tended to aggravate her failings. But if our women had a good dose of sharpened wits and logic instead of superfluous feeling, which is often the reverse of what it aspires to be; if they possessed physical courage and strong nerves, instead of timidity and nervous debility; a knowledge of the world, and of men and of natural forces, instead of ignorance, or at best a slight, belletristic culture, it would be better for themselves, and undoubtedly better for the men as well.

As a general rule the development of the heart and fancy has hitherto been cultivated in woman to an altogether disproportionate extent; the development of her reasoning faculties on the other hand has been checked or grossly neglected. She consequently suffers literally from an hypertrophy of feeling and is therefore generally accessible to every kind of superstition and fraud; she is a fruitful soil for all forms of religious and other charlatanism, and a willing tool in the hands of every reactionary party. This is frequently regretted by short-sighted and narrow-minded men, who suffer from the results but do nothing to mend matters, because they are mostly over head and ears in prejudices themselves.

The great majority of women answers to the description given; as a natural consequence they regard the world from quite a different standpoint to that of the men, and the end of the chapter is a state of perpetual disagreement between the two sexes.

It is one of the most important duties of every man at the present day to take part in public life; this fact is not altered by the failure of many men to comprehend it. The number of these who recognise that public institutions have the most intimate connection with the so-called private concerns of each individual is continually increasing. People are beginning to understand that the prosperity and adversity of persons and families depend far more upon the condition of public and general organization than upon the personal qualities and actions of the individual, inasmuch as the utmost exertions of the individual are absolutely powerless to overcome evils which are caused by circumstances and by which his own position is determined. On the other hand the struggle for existence demands far greater efforts than formerly, and if a man is to fulfil all the claims made upon him by public and private life, he must perforce encroach upon the time devoted to his wife. But the wife, owing to her deficient education, is from her point of view incapable of understanding that the interest which her husband takes in public affairs can have any other object than the society of his men friends, in which he spends money, ruins his health, and gets into trouble, while she has to suffer from the consequences. Thus the family quarrel begins. The husband is not unfrequently placed before the alternative of giving up his public activity and accommodating himself to his wife, which does not increase his happiness, or of sacrificing his matrimonial peace and domestic comfort, if he decide in favour of the public duties which, as he knows, are so closely connected with the welfare of himself and his family. If he is able to convince his wife and to come to an understanding with her, he has passed a dangerous rock in safety, but this rarely occurs. A man is generally of the opinion that his wife cannot comprehend his affairs, and need not concern herself with them. He gives himself no trouble to enlighten her. " You can't understand that " is the stereotyped reply when the wife complains, and wonders that he, as she imagines, should neglect her so unaccountably. This want of comprehension on the part of women is only aggravated by the folly of most men. And should the wife discover that her husband has only made use of subterfuges in order to get away from her, fresh fuel is added to the family disputes. The husband's need of enjoyment is not always particularly ideal, but even such as it is, it cannot be gratified at home.

These differences of education and opinion, which are easily overlooked in the beginning of marriage, while passion still holds its sway, become accentuated in maturer years, and make themselves all the more painfully felt at a period in which sexual feeling has cooled down, and must necessarily be replaced by mental conformity.

But whether or not the man recognises and fulfils his civil duties, his vocation and the constant intercourse with the outer world which it involves give him a hundred opportunities of coming in contact with a variety of people and a corresponding variety of views, and this mental atmosphere enlarges his horizon, without any trouble on his part. His condition might be described as a perpetual state of moulting, whilst the wife, tied to her household work, which occupies her from morning to night, leaving her little or no time for the cultivation of her mind, becomes crabbed or ossifies.

There is a good description of the life led by most wives of the present day, in a little book entitled " Randglossen zum Buche des Lebens " (Marginal Notes to the Book of Life), by Gerhard von Amyntor (Samuel Lucas, Elberfeld.) The author remarks, among other things, in the chapter on " Fatal Gnat-bites " :—

" It is not the great misfortunes which spare none, such as the loss of her husband, the moral ruin of a beloved child, severe illness, the failure of a cherished plan, that undermine the strength and freshness of the housewife, but the little daily cares that eat out bone and marrow. . . . . . How many millions of good house-mothers have cooked and scrubbed away their vital energy, their rosy cheeks and roguish dimples in the service of household cares, till they became wrinkled, broken-down, dried-up mummies. The everlasting question, "What shall we have for dinner to-day?" the perpetual necessity of sweeping and beating and brushing and dusting is a constantly falling drop, that slowly but surely wears out body and mind. The kitchen fire is the place where the saddest debtor and creditor accounts are drawn up, where the most depressing reflections are made on the rising price of food and the growing difficulty of obtaining the necessary means of purchase. At the flaming altar on which the soup pot boils, youth and candour, beauty and good humour, are offered up in sacrifice, and who recognizes in the aged, decrepit, hollow-eyed cook the once blooming, high-spirited, chastely coquet-tish bride in her myrtle crown.

"The ancients regarded the hearth as sacred, and placed their Lares and guardian deities beside it ; let our hearth too be sacred to us, on which the duteous German housewife slowly dies a sacrificial death to make the house comfortable, to spread the table and keep the family well."

That is all the comfort which the bourgeois world has to offer the unhappy victims of the present order of things.

In the case of women whose pecuniary and social position affords them more liberty, a false, one-sided, and superficial education, acting on the hereditary peculiarities of the female character, has the most injurious results. These women only care for mere externals, only trouble about dress and ornament and seek occupation and satisfaction only in the cultivation of degenerate tastes and in the gratification of wanton passions. They take but little personal interest in the education of their children, whom they leave as much as possible to the care of the nurse and the servants, and later on the boarding school.

We see that many and various causes combine to trouble and destroy marriage, and in an enormous majority of cases render it incomplete or nullify it altogether. It is impossible to ascertain the extent to which this takes place, because every married couple is anxious to draw a veil over its mutual rela-tions, and as a rule, especially in the upper classes, succeeds admirably in doing so.

Further Obstacles and Preventions to Marriage.—The Numeric Proportion of the Sexes; Its Causes and Results.

The conditions described before have combined to develop in women's character not only good but also very many bad qualities, which have been inherited from generation to generation, becoming more and more accentuated in the process. Men are fond of laying particular stress on the bad qualities, forgetting that they have been called forth and nurtured by themselves. As examples, we may mention the much abused garrulity and love of gossip, the tendency to carry on endless conversations on the most unimportant and frivolous subjects, the habit of occupying their minds with mere external things, such as dress and the morbid desire to please, their proneness to every folly of fashion, their easily roused envy and jealousy of other women.

These qualities are the almost universal characteristics of women, differing in degree, but making their appearance in quite young children; we must therefore regard them as to a great extent inherited, and developed by education. A mother who has been badly trained herself cannot train her own children well.

In order to understand the origin and evolution of the good and bad qualities of sexes or nations, the same methods must be applied and the same laws examined as those by whose help modern science explains the origin and evolution of species and genera with their respective characteristics in the animal world. We refer to the laws named Darwinian, from their main discoverer, and based on the material conditions of existence, Inheritance, and Adaptation, *i.e.*, breed and training.

Man can form no exception to laws which apply to all organisms in Nature; he does not stand outside Nature, but is from a physiological point of view nothing more than the most highly developed animal. Unfortunately this is very far from being generally recognised. The ancients, thousands of years ago, when nothing was known of our modern science, had, in many things relating to humanity, more rational ideas than we, and, what is still more to the point, they turned the results of their experience to practical account. One often hears people speak with enthusiastic admiration of the surpassing beauty and strength of the free Greek men and women, but overlook the fact that the race did not owe its character and physique to its favourable climate or to the advantages of a country embraced by a thousand arms of the sea, but to the system of bodily exercise and training which was consistently carried out by the State in the case of all freeborn citizens, with a view to developing their physical beauty, power, and agility, combined with elasticity and acuteness of mind. And although the mental culture of women was neglected in comparison with that of men, it was not so with their bodily training.* In Sparta, for example, where the greatest attention was paid to the physical development of both sexes, boys and girls went about naked till they had reached the age of puberty, and were trained together in bodily exercises, games and wrestling.

The spectacle of the naked human body and the natural treatment of natural things were the best safeguard against the sensual excitement artificially produced by the modern plan of separating the sexes from the earliest childhood. The forms of the one sex and the functions of its specific organs were no secret to the other. There was no possibility of trifling with ambiguities. Nature remained nature. One sex delighted in the beauty of the other. And our only salvation lies in a return to nature and to natural intercourse between the sexes, in casting off the unhealthy, spiritualistic ideas of humanity which cling to us to-day.

Certainly our views on female education are as far removed from those of the old Greeks as light from darkness. The notion that women require strength, courage, and resolution, is regarded as very heterodox and very "unwomanly," although no one can deny that these qualities would protect a woman from many a small and great injustice and an-

---

* For instance, Plato demands in his " Republic " that women be brought up in the same manner as men, and orders that the rulers of the ideal State be chosen by careful selection, in the Darwinian sense ; from which it appears that he was aware of the importance of selection in the development of human beings. Aristotle lays down the educational maxim ; " First the body must be trained and then the understanding."

noyance. Accordingly, women are checked as much in their bodily as in their mental development. This repressive system is favoured by strict separation of the sexes in social intercourse and at school, an educational régime that owes its origin to that spiritualistic mode of thought which Christianity has so deeply implanted within us, with regard to everything concerning human nature.

It is impossible for a woman with meagre physical development and crippled mental faculties, imprisoned in the narrowest circle of opinions and condemned to exclusive intercourse with her nearest female friends, to rise above the banalities of every-day life. Her mental horizon is bounded by the most trivial household concerns, the affairs of relations, and similar topics of interest. Long-winded conversations about nothing, the love of gossip and scandal, are the natural and inevitable results. Her mind demands activity and exercise, and her husband, whom she often compromises or drives to the brink of despair, abuses and execrates defects, for which he, as " Lord of Creation," is principally responsible.

Whilst marriage is so exclusively the one resource of woman, to which she is bound to cling with every fibre of her nature, it is only natural that love and matchmaking form the main subject of her thoughts and talk. Moreover the tongue is the only weapon which she can make use of in her position of physical inferiority and subjection to man by law and custom, and it is not surprising that she employs the only means of self-defence within her reach. The same thing applies to her love of dress and thirst for admiration, for which she is overwhelmed with such violent invectives, which assume such alarming dimensions in the follies of fashion and drive husbands and fathers, who know no remedy, to despair.

The explanation is not far to seek.

Woman is at the present day chiefly an object of enjoyment for man ; her pecuniary circumstances oblige her to look to marriage for support ; she thus becomes dependent on man, in other words, she becomes his property. Her position is rendered still more unfavourable by the fact that the number of women is as a rule larger than that of men. To this subject we must return later on. This disproportion, which is further augmented by those men who for one reason or another remain unmarried, heightens the competitive struggle among women, and forces them to pay the greatest attention to the attractions of their personal appearance, if they are to have any chance of successful emulation with their fellow-women in the favour of men.

When we remember that these evils have been in existence and in action for hundreds of generations, we shall not be surprised that the results, under the influence of the natural laws of inheritance and adaptation, have at length reached the extreme development in which they present themselves to-day. We must further take into account that in no former age was the competition of women for husbands so violent as at present, owing to the disproportionately large number of women, a fact some of whose causes have been already mentioned, and some of which still remain to be pointed out. Finally, the difficulty of securing an existence, added to the demands of society, make marriage as a means of support more indispensable than ever before.

Men are well contented with this state of affairs, and turn it to their own account. It gratifies their vanity, feeds their pride, and suits their interest to play the part of master and lord, and in this rôle, they are, like all rulers, well nigh inaccessible to reason. This makes it all the more imperative on women to exert themselves in bringing about new conditions, which will enable them to free themselves from this degrading position. Women have as little to hope from men as the workmen from the middle-classes.

If we further recall to our minds the characteristics which mark competition in other branches, for instance in the industrial line, where one manufacturer competes with another, with what base and often rascally weapons the struggle is carried on, how hate, envy and calumny are called into play, we must acknowledge that it is only natural, if the competition for husbands generates the same qualities among women. For this reason women generally agree among themselves less than men, and a quarrel easily arises among the best friends, about questions such as the regard of a man, or the more pleasing personal appearance of a rival. And the same cause explains the fact that when two women meet, though they be perfect strangers, each regards the other in the light of an enemy, and discovers at a single glance if an unsuitable colour has been chosen, a bow put on in the wrong place, or any other cardinal crime of a similar nature been committed. In the eyes of each, one may read the involuntary sentence pronounced on the other; it is as though one heard the words: " I am much better dressed, and know how to attract attention better than you."

The education and surroundings of women, mainly tending, as they do, to develop the feelings at the expense of the other faculties, furnish moreover an explanation for the greater passionateness of the sex, which finds on the one hand distorted expression in rage and fury, on the other in extreme self-sacrifice: for instance, in the heroism with which a mother immolates herself for her child, or in which un-assisted widows provide for their families.

But we have not yet exhausted the list of checks and hindrances to marriage. In addition to the influence of a pernicious mental education, we have to deal with the results of a no less pernicious or deficient physical training with reference to the natural functions. All doctors agree that the preparation of a woman for her vocation of mother and educator is very far from being what it should be. " The soldier is exercised in the use of his weapons, the artisan in the use of his tools. Every profession demands a special education, even the monk has his novitiate. Women alone are not prepared for their important maternal duties."* Nine-tenths of the girls who ever have an opportunity of marrying enter matrimony almost completely ignorant concerning motherhood and all that it entails. We have already called attention to the unpardonable aversion on the part of even the mother to speak to her grown-up daughter about such eminently important functions as those of the sexual organs, and to the consequent total unenlightenment of young women on the subject of their duties towards themselves and their future husbands. In entering marriage a girl enters a strange country, of which she has formed a picture in her imagination generally from novels and not the best novels, which is as far removed from reality as light from darkness.† We need only

---

* " Die Mission unseres Jahrhunderts. Eine Studie zur Frauenfrage " von Irma von Troll-Borostyani. Pressburg and Leipzig. (" The Mission of our Century. A Study on the Women's Question,") A fluent and energetic book, demanding fairly comprehensive reforms.

† In " Les Femmes qui votent et les Femmes qui tuent." (Women who vote and Women who kill). Alexandre Dumas *fils* records a remark made to him by a Roman Catholic priest of high rank, to the effect that at least eighty per cént. of his former girl pupils came to him a month after marriage, saying that they were disappointed and regretted the step. That sounds very probable. The Voltairean French bourgeoisie finds it consistent with its principles to have its daughters educated in nunneries, on the theory that the more ignorant a woman is, the more easily can she be led. Disagreement and disappoint-ment are the natural consequences. Laboulaye distinctly advises his readers to keep women in a state of moderate ignorance, for " notre empire est détruit, si l'homme est reconnu. (Our empire is at an end, when man is found out.)

allude in passing to their want of training in household matters, which cannot at present be dispensed with, although, for reasons mentioned above, women have been relieved of much of this kind of work which formerly fell to their share. It is an undeniable fact that large numbers of women often from no fault of their own, but in consequence of general social conditions, are entirely unprepared to fill the post of wife, mother and housewife, and thus naturally enough give occasion to disputes after marriage.

Another cause which nullifies marriage for many men is the deficient bodily development of women. Injudicious training, miserable social conditions (food, dwelling, occupation) produce weak, bloodless, nervous beings, incapable of fulfilling the duties of matrimony. The consequences are menstrual troubles and disturbances in the various organs connected with the sexual functions, rendering maternity dangerous or impossible. Instead of a healthy, cheerful companion, a capable mother, a helpmate equal to all the the calls made upon her activity, the husband has a nervous, excitable wife, permanently under the doctor's hands, too fragile to bear the slightest draught or noise. I will not enlarge on this subject; every reader—(and whenever I say reader, I mean as a matter of course the reader of both sexes)—can complete the picture for himself; he will find examples enough in his own circle of acquaintances.

Experienced doctors assure us, that the greater number of married women, especially in towns, are in a more or less abnormal condition. According to the degree of the complaint, and the character of husband and wife, such unions will be more or less unhappy ones, and public opinion gives the man in such a case the right of seeking compensation outside marriage, a fact which is not calculated to improve the temper or increase the happiness of the wife. Sometimes a difference of sexual temperament is the cause of fatal discord, but a hundred considerations prevent the divorce which under such circumstances would be so desirable.

Thus we see that in an overwhelming number of cases, the most various factors combine to hinder marriage from becoming what it ought to be, a covenant of two persons of opposite sexes to belong to each other in mutual love and respect, and, according to the striking words of Kant, to represent in their unity an entire human being.

It is therefore a recipe of doubtful worth, when even scholars imagine that they have settled the question of women's emancipation by pointing them to family and married life, which, as we shall show further on, thanks to our social conditions, is becoming more and more distorted, is failing more and more signally to fulfil its true purpose.

But such a recommendation, which the majority of men never tire of thoughtlessly applauding, sounds like the bitterest contempt, when these counsellors and their admiring public do nothing to provide every woman with a husband. Schopenhauer, the celebrated philosopher, is one of these scholars, and has if possible even less comprehension than his brother-philosophers for women and their position. His remarks on the subject are not only impolite, but vulgar. For instance: " Woman is not called to great things. Her characteristics are not active but passive. She pays her debt to life by the throes of birth, care of the children, subjection to her husband. The most intense utterances of volition and sense are denied her. Her life is destined to be less eventful and more trivial than that of man. It is her vocation to nurse and educate children, because she is herself childish, and remains an overgrown child all her life, a kind of intermediate thing between the child and the man, who is the only proper human being. . . . Girls should be brought up to habits of domesticity and servility. . . . Women are the most complete and hopeless Philistines."

It seems to me that Schopenhauer in his judgment on women was no philosopher, but one of the most complete and hopeless Philistines himself. This is the kind of reasoning which one expects from a Philistine, but not from a philosopher, who is supposed to be a wise man. Moreover, Schopenhauer was never married, and thus never did what lay in his power to enable at least one woman to fulfil the lot which he assigns her. This brings us to the other, but not the fairer side of the medal.

Many women do not marry, because they never have the chance. Everyone knows this. Custom forbids a woman to choose and woo; she must wait till a suitor seeks that which she may not bestow unasked. And if no suitor comes, she joins the great army of those unfortunates who have missed their vocation in life, who have no assured income, and who are therefore exposed to want and misery, and often enough to ridicule. Very few know the reason of this disproportion between the sexes, or recognise its full extent. Most people have an answer ready to hand ; " Too many girls are born," and many draw the conclusion, that if marriage be a woman's only purpose in life, polygamy ought to be introduced.   But those who assert that more girls are born than boys are mis-informed.   And those who, because they must acknowledge that celibacy is unnatural, and are at a loss to provide for the numbers of unmarried women, imagine that nothing remains but the adoption of polygamy, whether we like it or not, fail to understand the true nature of the case.   Leaving our present morality, which will never consent to reckon with polygamy, out of the question, such a condition must under all circumstances be a degrading one for women.   It is true, this did not prevent Schopenhauer, in his scorn and con-tempt of women, from declaring roundly : " Polygamy is a benefit for the whole female sex."   Notwithstanding, poly-gamy will be checked by barriers erected by Nature.

Many men do not marry, because they cannot support a wife.   For the same reason by far the greater number of married men could not support a second wife.   The few who could, cannot be taken into account ; as a rule they have already two and more wives.   One is legitimate and the others illegitimate.   Those who enjoy the privilege of riches allow neither law nor morality to interfere between them and the gratification of their caprices.   Even in the East, where polygamy has been recognised by law and custom for thousands of years, few men have more than one wife.   We so often hear people speak of the demoralising influence of Turkish harems, and of the consequent degeneration of the race, and people are quite right.   But they forget that the institution of the harem is only possible among a small fraction of the male population, and that this fraction belongs exclusively to the ruling class, while the mass of the people are monogamous like Europeans.   In the town of Algiers shortly before 1879, 18,282 married men were registered.   Of these men, no fewer than 17,319 had but one wife, 888 had two wives, and only 75 had more than two wives.

We shall not go far wrong in supposing that the propor-tions are much the same in Constantinople, the capital of the Turkish Empire.   Among the Turkish country population the number of monogamous marriages is relatively even larger.   The same pecuniary circumstances which compel most men to limit themselves to one wife come into force in Turkey as well as among ourselves.   But even supposing that all men were in a position to support a plurality of wives, polygamy would still be impracticable, for want of the sufficient number of women. *The almost equal numbers of men and women under normal conditions of life point us everywhere to monogamy.* This assertion must be proved at more length.

The table on page 78 and the remarks to which it gives rise will show that, as a matter of fact, there is no appreciable numeric disproportion between the sexes, and still less an excess of women. The relations of the populations, according to the numbers and sexes of the inhabitants, give the results shown on the next page.

We see therefore that while the sum total of inhabitants in the States quoted amounts to 248,484,524, the excess of women is in round numbers 2,000,000, making a percentage of 101·22 women to 100 men. The difference is small, but it becomes still smaller when we take into account that the above numbers in most cases do not include the seafaring population, that was out of the country when the census was taken. It is included only in England and Italy, but it is an important figure in all the other countries, especially in the United States and Germany. Moreover, the troops absent in the different colonies of their respective countries are not mentioned in the lists. These troops and the omitted sailor population must amount together to something like several hundred thousand heads. And lastly we must not forget that the European emigration to all parts of the earth is recruited chiefly from among the men, a fact which is clearly pointed out by the excess of men in the United States.

A few more figures may serve to establish the assertion. In 1878, in the colony of Victoria, the total number of inhabitants was 863,370, while the men outnumbered the women by 100,000 ; in other words, there were 20 per cent fewer women than men. The population of Queensland amounted at the end of 1877 to 203,084 ; 126,900 of the inhabitants were men, 76,100 were women ; again a disproportionately large number of men. The colony of New Zealand possessed a population of 414,171 inhabitants, without counting the natives or the 4,300 Chinese ; 230,898 of the number were men, and and 183,373 women. The population of India shews over 6,000,000 more men than women. These figures suffice to prove that if the inhabitants of the whole earth were distributed according to their sex, the men would rather predominate over the women than *vice versâ*. And in addition to this, there are several other circumstances to be considered, which, under favourable conditions, might easily cause a relative increase in the number of men, as we shall see farther on.

	Country.	Total.	Male.	Female.	Excess of Males.	Excess of Females.
1875	German Empire	42,752,554	21,005,461	21,747,093	—	741,632
1872	France	36,102,021	17,982,511	18,120,410	—	137,899
1871	Italy	26,801,154	13,472,262	13,328,892	143,370	—
1869	Austria and Hungary	35,904,435	17,737,175	18,167,270	—	430,095
1871	Great Britain and Ireland	31,845,379	15,584,132	16,261,247	—	677,115
1870	United States	38,558,371	19,493,565	19,064,806	428,759	—
1870	Switzerland	2,670,345	1,305,670	1,364,675	—	59,005
1869	Netherlands	3,309,128	1,629,035	1,680,093	—	51,058
1866	Belgium	4,827,833	2,419,639	2,408,194	11,445	—
1860	Spain	15,673,481	7,765,508	7,907,973	—	142,465
1864	Portugal	4,188,410	2,005,540	2,182,870	—	197,330
	Sweden and Norway	5,850,513	2,880,339	2,980,164	—	99,825
		248,484,524	123,270,837	125,213,687	583,574	2,536,424

It is interesting to compare the numeric proportions in the different States. We find the men numerically inferior wherever wars have been carried on, or an extensive emigration has taken place ; indeed, the latter seems to exercise a greater influence than the former. The Teutonic States, Germany, Switzerland, Austria, England, shew the greatest differences. The States, with a mixed or Celtic population, such as Belgium and Italy, have an excess of males. In France, whose contingent of emigrants is too small to be taken into account, the proportions have become irregular since the war of 1870-71. In 1866 France had only 26,000 more women than men ; but in 1872, the excess amounted to 137,899. The greater excess of women in Spain and Portugal is explained by the large colonies of both countries, to which the male population emigrates, and by the frequent internal disorders and the precarious state of society.

The United States, on the other hand, present a very different aspect. The consequence of the extensive and for the most part male immigration, is an excess of men, which almost entirely covers the deficiency in Europe. Indeed, if the numbers of the European population in the Cape, Australia, South America, and all the other European settlements in different parts of the earth were known, we should probably find that the total number of men of European extraction exceeded that of the women, so that if every man married, no woman would remain single. The question might then possibly arise as to whether polyandry must not be introduced instead of polygamy.

The birth statistics support this assertion. It has been ascertained that in all countries in which an enquiry into the sex of infants has been made, to every 100 girls, 105 to 107 boys are born. It has been further ascertained that more boys die, on an average, in the first year than girls, and that among stillborn children the proportion of boys to girls is 138 to 100.

The statistics of the sex of infants in the year 1877 in Paris throw an interesting light on the subject. According to these statistics 27,720 male and 27,138 female children were brought into the world, while the total number of deaths among the former (without reference to age) amounted to 24,508 and among the latter to 22,855. The excess of male births was therefore 528, and the excess of female deaths 1,788. There was also a remarkable difference between the sexes in the number of deaths from consumption. 4,788 male and 3,815 female individuals died of this disease in Paris in 1877. The cause of this greater mortality among men, which is more apparent in the towns than in the country, lies principally in a more unhealthy and dissipated manner of life. According to Quetelet more men die between the ages of 18 and 21 than women between the ages of 18 and 25. A further cause is that men are exposed to greater dangers than women in many of their callings (in factories, on board ship, on the railway).

The cause for the greater number of stillborn boys is sought in the greater average size of their heads, which increases the difficulty of birth, and in the supposition that they partake more than girls of the weakly constitution of the mother* and are therefore less easy to rear.

People have tried to explain the remarkable fact that more boys are born than girls, by assuming that the sex of the child is influenced by the age, strength, and energy of the father, which are as a rule superior to the age, strength, and energy of the mother. The greater the difference of age between man and wife, the greater will be the number of boys, with the exception that old men are at a disadvantage towards young women. According to this theory the law would seem to prevail that the stronger nature asserts itself in the sex of the offspring.

We may at least conclude one thing from the data given, namely, that if women attain a better physical and mental development through training and manner of life in harmony with natural laws, the number of stillborn children and the mortality among boys will decrease, and possibly that by this development of the bodily and mental powers, and a suitable selection with regard to the age of the husband, it may, and under healthy social conditions probably will, become possible to regulate the sex of children.

In Prussia, in 1864, there were 3,722,776 boys under 14, but only 3,688,985 girls of the same age. There were therefore 33,791 more boys than girls. Nevertheless the census of the entire population showed that there were 313,383 more women than men. The disproportion had therefore arisen in

---

* It is worthy of remark that the women of savage or half-savage tribes bear children with great ease, and generally return to their ordinary occupations soon after birth. The same thing applies to the hardworking women of our own lower classes, especially in the country, whose deliveries are much easier than those of women in the upper classes.

maturer years, and had been caused, as we have already remarked, principally by war and emigration. Immediately
after the wars of 1864, 1866, and 1870 the emigration from
Germany increased to a very considerable extent, and was
mostly recruited from among those young men who had not
yet entered on their term of military service, as well as from
among the older members* of the reserve forces who had
returned from the field alive and did not care to expose themselves a second time to the dangers and sacrifices of a levy.
It is therefore the healthiest and strongest men in the nation
who form the largest contingent of emigrants, and thus
prevent many thousands of German women from fulfilling
their natural vocation in marriage.

According to the official reports on the levy of recruits in
the year 1876 the number of the men bound to serve in the
German army was 1,149,042; of these 35,265 could not be
found, 109,956 remained away without excuse, 15,293 had
been sentenced for illegal emigration, and 14,934 were on
trial for the same cause. These figures need no commentary.
But the women who read them will understand the degree to
which they are concerned in the regulation of our military
and political affairs. Whether the time of military service is
to be lengthened or shortened, the army increased or decreased,
whether we pursue a peaceful or warlike policy, whether the
treatment of soldiers is humane or inhumane, and the number
of deserters and suicides rises or falls in consequence—these
are questions which affect women quite as much as they
affect men. Men have to suffer very much less from the
results of a military régime than women. They comfort
themselves moreover by the belief that when their numbers
decrease from any of the causes mentioned, wages will rise.†

---

* That is, men under 42, and generally under 32.

† The absurdity of this idea is best shown by following it out to it
ultimate consequences. Let us suppose, for the sake of argument, that
wages increase in proportion to the size of standing armies and the fre-
quency of wars. The enormous sacrifices that must be made year by year
to support some hundred thousands of unproductive men, the disturbances
caused by war, and the economic losses resulting therefrom are generally
quite left out of sight by the defenders of this remarkable theory. According to them wages would lowest in countries which have a smaller or
no standing army, e.g., in Switzerland, England and America; but as we
know the reverse is the case. If large standing armies were favourable
to wages, by lessening competition, it would follow that the community
would be benefited if the State considerably increased the number of its
officials. But it is clear that the cost of supporting unproductive soldiers
and officials must be borne by productive workers.

But women are more than ever exposed to the danger of not being able to fulfil their natural vocation, and have to bear more than their share of the evils arising from overgrown armies, wars and the panics of war.

On the whole men have not shown any particular degree oi wisdom or insight so far, in the legislation which is their work ; if they had things would not be in the miserable condition that they are. Hitherto the majority has placed itself at the discretion of a small minority that abused its power at pleasure. This is one reply in passing to the objection that politics are no concern of women's.

The number of accidents in factories, which increase in proportion to the more extensive use of machinery, without the simultaneous introduction of protective measures, is not one of the least important factors in the numeric inferiority of women. It is true that they too are beginning to be more and more employed in every branch of industry and consequently to supply their contingent to the sum total of these accidents.

The official reports of accidents in factories and agriculture in Prussia for the year 1869 state that of 4,769 fatal cases 4,245 were men and 524 women, the latter hardly amounting to 12½ per cent. of the former. In the year 1876 the total number of deaths from accident was 6,141, and that of injuries 7,059. Of the dead 5,748 were men and 663 women ; the latter were therefore a little over 12 per cent. of the men. Among 6,693 male and 366 female injured the latter hardly represented 5½ per cent. It has also been statistically proved that many more women than men die between the ages of 24 and 36, owing to puerperal fever, difficult births, and the various specific diseases of the sex ; after 40, on the other hand, the excess of deaths is on the side of the men.

Male mortality among inhabitants of the sea-coast is even greater than that in manufacturing districts. Though I am not in a position to show this by figures, the fact is proved by the unusually large number of widows left behind by those whose dangerous vocation obliges them to seek their living on the sea. But all these unfavourable conditions put together, if we except emigration, would not suffice to cause any appreciable disproportion between the sexes ; moreover, they are one and all capable of considerable amelioration.

As soon as any essential improvement has been made in the social conditions of men, when their discernment has increased, and respect for human life has become greater, the large mortality among children will be lessened, the dangers of machinery, of mines, &c., will be reduced to a minimum by extensive protective measures, and the same thing will apply to the occupation of sailors. This is a field in which at present the most unwarrantable carelessness reigns supreme. Mr. Plimsoll in England has proved by exact evidence that a large number of shipowners, in criminal thirst for gain, sacrifice highly-insured, unseaworthy ships together with their crew to the chance of any slight accident, with a view to obtaining the very considerable insurance premium, and certain German proprietors are said not to be models of conscientiousness either. Moreover the arrangements for rescuing the shipwrecked on the sea-coast are still very deficient and incomplete, because they almost entirely depend on private beneficence. The State seems utterly indifferent to the question as to whether hundreds and thousands of its members shall annually be rescued from death or not. On foreign coasts the chance of escaping from shipwreck is small indeed. A community whose highest and only function it would be to promote the equal well-being of all, would improve shipping and navigation and introduce safety measures to a degree sufficient to make an accident the rarest occurrence. But the present economic system of depredation, that reckons with men only as figures, with which to achieve as large a gain as possible, annihilates the life of a human being for a profit of half-a-crown.

Radically reformed social conditions would also abolish standing armies, and put an end to disturbances to production, and consequently to all that part of emigration of which they are the cause.

There are still other reasons which limit the number of marriages. The State itself compels a large category of men to remain single. People indignantly condemn the immorality involved by the enforced celibacy of Roman Catholic priests, but do not open their lips to complain of the far greater number of soldiers who are condemned to similar abstinence. Officers are not only obliged to obtain the consent of their superiors, but their free choice is restricted to a considerable extent by the regulations requiring that their wives must possess a certain amount of property. This is a striking illustration of the stand-point occupied by the State with regard to marriage. The subaltern officers are subjected to the same binding conditions ; they too are not allowed to marry without permission. which is accorded reluctantly and only in a certain number of cases. For the great majority of common soldiers there is no question of marriage at all; it is simply not allowed.

Public opinion is tolerably unanimous in regarding marriage as unreasonable for young men before the age of 24 or 25. 25 is the age at which the imperial civil marriage law declares a man to be his own master for the purposes of matrimony. The reason is that few men are in a position to support a wife and family sooner. Public opinion makes an exception in the case of those fortunate persons, for instance members of the royal family, who are not forced to work their way through difficulties to independence. Public opinion allows such persons to marry earlier—the young man at 18 or 19 and the young girl at 15 or 16 years of age. Indeed the heir apparent is declared of age at 18, and is then considered capable of governing the most extensive empire and the most populous nation. Ordinary mortals do not attain the capability of managing any property which they may possess till the age of 21.

This difference of opinion as to the age at which marriage is desirable proves that the public judges the right of individuals to marry according to their social positions, and that this judgment has nothing to do with man as an organic being or with his natural instincts. But natural instincts are not limited by any given social position, or by the ideas and prejudices inherent to it. As soon as man has attained maturity his natural instincts claim their right, with all the vehemence which characterises the strongest and most intense impulse of nature. They are the incarnation of the whole being and demand gratification on pain of serious mental and bodily suffering.

The development of the sexual faculties varies with the individual, with the climate and with the manner of life. In hot climates it takes place among girls as early as ten and eleven, and one meets women of this age with their first child in their arms, but who are faded at 25 or 30. In northern climates the rule is between the 14th and 16th year, in some cases even later; there is moreover a difference in this respect between town and country women. Healthy, robust peasant girls, who work hard all day in the open air, develope, on an average, a year later than our delicate nervous, etherial young ladies in the town. Among the former, development takes place normally with no accompanying disturbances; among the latter a normal development is the exception, various troubles occur and bring the physician to despair, because custom and prejudice prevent proposing and carrying out the only remedies which would be of any avail. How often are doctors obliged to declare that marriage and a totally different manner of life are the only radical measures by which they can hope to cure our anemic, narrow-chested, excitable ladies of fashion. But how can these measures be put into practice? Insuperable difficulties lie in the way, and one cannot blame a man for considering twice, before marrying a creature who resembles a walking corpse and threatens to succumb to her first delivery or to the diseases arising from it.

All these things point the same way, and show us that we can only hope for improvement in an absolutely different mode of education, which takes the body as well as the mind into account, and provides for a complete reform in work and manner of life, such as is only possible under a corresponding *reform of social conditions.*

This contradiction between man as a natural and sexual being and man as a member of society—a contradiction which at no former period made itself so much felt as to-day—is the parent of numerous and perilous evils. It is the cause of various diseases upon which I need not dwell here, and which chiefly befall the female sex. One reason for this is the more intimate connection of woman's organism than that of man with the sexual functions, and another the greater difficulties which oppose the gratification of their intensest natural impulses in a natural way. This contradiction between organic needs and social compulsion leads to perverted instincts, to secret vices and excesses, in a word, to unnatural means of gratification, which undermine all but strong constitutions. These unnatural means of gratification, especially among women, have been carried on with the greatest effrontery for years under the eyes of the law. We refer principally to the covert recommendation of certain articles of trade, which one finds announced for sale in the largest newspapers, and especially in the advertisement sheet of the periodicals that are mostly read in families. These recommendations are as a rule addressed to the middle and upper classes, as the price of the articles in question generally places them beyond the reach of the poor. Alongside of these shameless advertisements, another branch of trade flourishes even more openly, and is supported by both sexes; we mean the announcements of obscene pictures, particularly of entire series of photographs, and of poetry and prose of a similar kind, the titles of which are calculated to rouse sexual excitement, and the existence of which calls for the interference of the police and public prosecutor. But police and public prosecutor are too much taken up with the dangers that threaten civilization, morality, marriage and family life from the machinations of of social democracy. A considerable part of our novel literature has the same tendency. Under such circumstances it would be strange indeed, if sexual irritation and excesses did not make themselves felt in a most unhealthy and injurious manner, and in fact assume the character of a widespread social disease. The idle and luxuriant life of so many women in the upper classes, the nervous stimulant afforded by exquisite perfumes, the overdosing with poetry, music, the stage, in a word with every form of so-called artistic enjoyment, which is regarded as the chief means of education and is the chief occupation of a sex suffering already from hypertrophy of nerves and sensibility, and certain branches of which are cultivated like hothouse plants, all these things rouse sexual feeling to the highest pitch of excitement and excesses are the inevitable result.

In the case of the poor, various kinds of fatiguing but mostly sedentary employment occasion a determination of blood to the pelvic organs, while sexual impulses are stimulated by the pressure of constant sitting. One of the most injurious and most widely spread of these employments is working at the sewing-machine. Its effects on the nervous and sexual system are at the same time so exciting and wearing that a working day of ten to twelve hours is sufficient to ruin the best constitutions in a few years. Undue sexual irritation is also caused by long hours of work in a high temperature, for instance, in factories for refining sugar, for bleaching and calico printing; by nightwork in overcrowded, gas-lighted rooms in which both sexes often work together.

Thus we see again a number of circumstances which throw a glaring light on the folly and unsoundness of our times. But these evils are deeply rooted in our social system, and cannot be reformed either by the sermons or palliative measures which social and religious charlatans of both sexes are so ready to prescribe.

The axe must be laid to the root of the tree. A healthy manner of life, healthy employments and a healthy education in the broadest sense of the word, combined with the natural gratification of natural and healthy instincts must be brought within the reach of all. There is no solution short of this.

A man is free from a number of restrictions which a woman is bound to observe. He alone, thanks to his position as ruler, has the right of exercising choice in love. a right which is limited only by social considerations. The nature of marriage as a means of subsistence, the numeric excess of women, and custom conjoin in forbidding a woman to express her desires; it is her lot to wait till she is sought, and to accept her fate whatever it may be. As a rule she seizes the first opportunity that presents itself for securing a maintainer, who rescues her from the social proscription and contempt which is the portion of the unfortunate old maid. And having done this, she shrugs her shoulders at those among her fellow-women who have preserved enough sense of their human dignity not to sell themselves into matrimonial prostitution to the first comer, but prefer to tread the thorny paths of life alone.

But a man who desires to satisfy his amatory needs in marriage is limited by social considerations, He must first ask himself the question, " Can I support a wife and possibly a family, without incurring the danger of seeing my happiness destroyed by pressing cares." The purer his intentions in marriage, the higher his ideal, the more determined he is to marry for love and only to choose a wife of congenial mind, all the more seriously must he ask himself this question. It is simply an impossibility for many to answer in the affirmative, under the present conditions of earning and possessing; they prefer to remain unmarried. Many, less conscientious, are met by other difficulties. Thousands of young men in the middle-classes do not fill an independent position, which satisfies their notions, until comparatively late ; they are unabled to support a wife " as becomes their station," unless she have property of her own. In the first place, the notions of many of these young men as to what is becoming to their station, are out of harmony with their income ; in the second place, in consequence of the utterly perverse education which the generality of women receives, a man must expect his wife to make claims on his purse which he is entirely unable to satisfy. Well trained, unpretending women do not often come in his way; they are reserved and are not to be found where people have gradually accustomed themselves to look for women. Those whom he does meet generally endeavour to catch a husband by external attractions, and make a purposely false impression by concealing their pecuniary position and personal defects behind an artificial brilliancy. The nearer these ladies get to an age in which a speedy marriage becomes desirable, the more anxiously do they seek to decoy their prey. And by the the time such a woman succeeds in getting a husband she is so accustomed to outward show, ornaments, finery and expensive amusements, that she is by no means prepared to give these things up after marriage. Thus men walk on the brink of a precipice, and many prefer to leave a flower un-plucked which is only to be reached at the risk of their neck. They go on their way alone, and seek recreation and enjoy-ment without the sacrifice of their liberty.

In the lower and poorer classes checks and hindrances to marriage are often caused by the necessity which obliges many girls to take up some employment in shops or factories, to support themselves and often to support the family, and which leaves them neither time nor opportunity to train themselves in domestic matters. In many cases the mother is unable to give her daughter the needed instruction in those things, because all her time is taken up in earning, frequently away from home.

The number of men who are withheld from marrying for one or other of those reasons is increasing to an alarming extent. According to the census of 1875 there were 1,054 women to every 1,000 men between the ages of 20 and 80. We must allow for at least 10 per cent. of these men re-maining single. Only 84 out of a 100 women would therefore have the prospect of marrying. But this proportion is even far more unfavourable in certain ranks and places. The greatest number of batchelors is generally found in the upper classes, firstly because the expenses incurred by marriage are too great ; and secondly, because the men in these circles can find compensation elsewhere. Towns in which many pen-sioned officers and officials live with their families are particularly overdone with girls in comparison to the young men. In such towns the number of women who get no husband can easily rise to 30 or 40 per cent. The deficiency in marriage candidates chiefly affects those classes of women, who, owing to their education or the social position of the father, are accustomed to a certain degree of refinement, but have only their persons to offer a man on the look out for property, while they would neither be suited to nor deign to accept a man of humbler station. This applies especially to the large category of female members in families which live on a fixed income who are socially eligible but pecuniarily penniless. The life of these women is relatively the saddest among all their companions in distress. Social prejudices force them to avoid various occupations by which they might possibly have ameliorated their lot. It is mostly for them that the so-called Women's Societies for Promotion of Needlework under the patronage of noble and royal ladies are endeavouring to make their way. It is a Sisyphus labour, similar to that of the associations instituted by Schulze to improve the position of working men. Small results are obtained, results on a large scale are impossible. At the same time, the aristocratic patronage is injurious, inasmuch as it exercises a moral pressure, which stifles and brands as treason every effort to effect a radical change, every suspicion that the foundations of our state and social organism are not based on immutable laws. It cost the workmen trouble to cast off the tutelage of these aristocratic friends, and it is harder still for the women to do so. For this reason, those societies have hitherto remained free from so-called revolutionary tendencies, and for the same reason they have had no significance for the real emancipation of women.

It is difficult to estimate how large a number of women are compelled by the causes quoted to give up all thought of matrimony. Still we have some means of judging. In Scotland, about 1870, the number of unmarried women over 20 amounted to 43 per cent. of all the women above this age, while the proportion of women to men was 110 per cent. In England (without Wales) there lived 1,407,228 more women than men between the ages of 20 and 80; 359,969 unmarried women over 40; 42 per cent. of the women were unmarried. How does this strike those superficial critics who reply to women's demand for an independent and equal position in life by pointing them to marriage and the family circle? It is not for want of good will on the part of the woman that so many remain single, and as for married happiness, we have already seen what it only too often amounts to.

And what is the fate of these victims of our social conditions? The revenge of neglected and outraged nature imprints itself on the faces and characters of both men and women, and stamps so-called old maids and ascetic old bachelors in all countries and climates as different beings to the ordinary race. They bear witness to the powerful and fatal influence of suppressed instincts. It is asserted that men of high intelligence, for instance Pascal, Newton, Rousseau, suffered for this reason towards the end of their lives from serious mental derangement. The so-called nymphomania of women, as well as the various forms of hysteria, spring from the same source. Hysteria is also caused by want of satisfaction in marriage with an unloved man, and consequent sterility.

This is the picture of our modern marriage and its results. We see, it is an institution most intimately related to the present condition of society, with which it stands or falls; it is impossible to regenerate it within the framework of existing society, and all attempts to do so are doomed to hopeless failure. The bourgeois world is incapable of satisfactorily re-modelling marriage, or of satisfactorily providing for the unmarried.

Prostitution, a Necessary Social Institution of the Bourgeois World.

Marriage represents one half of the sexual life of the bourgeois world, and prostitution represents the other. Marriage is the front, and prostitution the back, of the medal. When a man finds no satisfaction in marriage, he generally resorts to prostitution, and when a man for one reason or another remains unmarried, it is again prostitution to which he has resource. Provision is thus made for men who are celibates by choice or by force, as well as for those whom marriage has disappointed, to gratify their sexual instincts in a manner forbidden to women.

Man has in all times and climes regarded the use of prostitutes as his natural and exclusive right. All the more strictly and severely does he watch over and judge every woman outside the pale of prostitution. He does not trouble himself with the consideration that a woman has precisely the same impulses as a man, indeed, that these impulses at certain periods (during menstruation) are far more vehement than his. In virtue of his position as master, he demands the forcible suppression of her intensest instincts, and makes her chastity the condition of marriage and social eligibility. Nothing can afford a more drastic and at the same time more revolting illustration of the subjection of woman to man, than the diametrically different manner in which the gratification of the same natural impulse is regarded and judged according to the sex of the person in question.

The unmarried man is particularly favoured by circumstances. Nature has burdened woman alone with the consequences of the act of generation, the man has the enjoyment without trouble or responsibility. This privileged position has led in the course of history to that unbridled license in sexual matters which characterizes a considerable portion of the masculine world. And legitimate gratification being, as we have already shewn, prevented or checked by a hundred causes, the consequence is illegitimate gratification in the broadest sense of the word.

Prostitution becomes a necessary social institution, just as much as the police, the standing army, the church, the capitalist, etc., etc. This is no exaggeration but an assertion that can be proved.

We have described in what light the ancient world regarded prostitution, that it considered it inevitable and organised it by state regulations, in Greece as well as in Rome. We have also quoted the opinions which prevailed on the subject during the Christian Middle Ages. Even St. Augustine, next to Paul the chief pillar of Christianity, although an ardent advocate of asceticism, could not refrain from exclaiming: " If you put down public prostitutes, the State will be over-turned by the violence of passion." The provincial spiritual council in Milan, in the year 1665, expressed itself to the same effect.

Let us hear what the modern world has to say. Dr. F. S. Hügel declares in his " History, Statistics and Regulation of Prostitution in Vienna : " " Advancing civilization will gradually clothe Prostitution in more pleasing forms, but not till the end of the world will it be banished from the earth." That is saying a good deal, but it is certain that no one who is incapable of looking beyond the horizon of bourgeois society, and of recognising the changes which must take place within the community before the latter can attain to natural and healthy conditions, can fail to agree with Dr. Hügel's assertion.

For this reason Dr. Wichern, the well-known orthodox director of the Rauhe Haus, near Hamburg, Dr. Palton in Lyons, Dr. William Tait in Edinburgh, and Dr. Parent-Duchâtelet in Paris (celebrated for his investigations on the subject of prostitution and venereal disease) declare unani-mously: " It is impossible to eradicate Prostitution, because it is an integral part of our social institutions," and one and all demand its regulation by the State. It has not occurred to any one of these men, that we must alter the social institu-tions that necessitated prostitution. Their want of economic training, and their inherent prejudices make such a solution appear an impossibility to them. The *Wiener Medicinische Wochenschrift* (Viennese medical weekly paper) for 1863, No. 35, asks :

" How can the large number of voluntary and involuntary

celibates satisfy their natural needs otherwise than by pluck-
ing the forbidden fruit of Venus Pandemos?" and the writer
comes to the conclusion that if prostitution is therefore a
necessity, it has a right to existence, to exemption from
punishment, and to protection by the State. Dr. Hügel expresses precisely the same opinion in the work quoted above.

The Leipzig Police-Surgeon, Dr. J. Kühn says in his book,
"Prostitution in the Nineteenth Century from the standpoint
of the Sanitary Police" : "Prostitution is not only an evil
that must be endured, it is an inevitable evil, for it shields
women from unfaithfulness" (of which only men have a right
to be guilty) "and virtue" (of course, female virtue, men
have no need of any) "from being attacked (sic) and therefore from falling." These few words of Dr. Kühn's suffice to
characterise the crass egotism of men in all its nakedness.
That is the proper standpoint of a police-surgeon, who
sacrifices himself in watching over prostitutes, in order to
preserve men from unwelcome diseases.

Was I wrong, when I said prostitution is at present a
necessary social institution, just as much as the police, the
standing army, the church, the capitalist, &c., &c. ?

In the German Empire prostitution is not, as in France,
sanctioned, organized and controlled by the State, but merely
suffered to exist. The official brothels have been abolished
by decree of the Federal Council. The consequence of this
abolition was that in the second half of the last decade,
numerous petitions were addressed to the Reichstag, requesting that these houses might be rehabilitated, on the ground
that vice was spreading without let or hindrance, and that
an alarming increase of syphilitic disease was the result. A
commission appointed by the Reichstag to examine the subject,
and numbering a fair contingent of doctors, concluded to
recommend the petition to the Imperial Chancellor, inasmuch as the prohibition of public brothels involved the most
dangerous consequences for the morality and health of
society and especially of family life.

These testimonies may suffice. They prove that for
modern society, the prostitution question is a sphynx, whose
riddle it cannot read ; it sees no way out of the difficulty but
that of state sanction and control, if greater evils are to be
avoided.

Thus society which is so proud of its morality, its religion,
its civilization, and culture, must suffer licentiousness to
permeate its body like a slow poison. But our testimonies

prove something more. *The Christian State makes the official declaration, that the present form of marriage is insufficient and that men have a right to seek the illegitimate gratification of their sexual impulses.* This same State only recognizes the unmarried woman as a sexual being, inasmuch as she surrenders herself to illegitimate male desires, in other words, becomes a prostitute. And the surveillance and control exercised by the officers of the State do not touch the men, as they ought to do as a matter of course, if the sanitary superintendence were to have any *raison d'être* and any chance of success, even if we leave the equality of the sexes before the law in the interest of ordinary justice out of the question, but they touch the women alone.

This protection of man against woman by the State turns the true nature of the relationship upside down. It would appear as though men were the weaker sex, and women the stronger, as though women were the seducers, and poor, helpless men the seduced. The myth of Adam being beguiled by Eve in Paradise still holds its own in our ideas and laws, and justifies the dictum of Christianity ; " Woman is the great seductress, a vessel of iniquity." Strange that men are not ashamed to play the part of such miserable weaklings.

The popular notion that it is the duty of the State to superintend prostitution, in order to preserve men from disease, naturally causes those protected to believe that they are really safe from infection, and this belief promotes prostitution to an enormous extent. This is proved by the fact that wherever the police has proceeded with particular severity against non-registered prostitutes, the man have felt secure, and the number of syphilitic cases has considerably increased.

No doubt exists in the mind of any experienced judge as to the delusion of supposing that either brothels under the control of the police, or the police superintendence and medical examination of prostitutes, afford any security against infection. In the first place the nature of these diseases prevents their being easily recognizud, and in the second place nothing short of several examinations a day would guarantee safety. The number of women and the expense involved render such a method quite impossible. While 50 or 60 prostitutes have to be " got through " in an hour, the examination is a mere farce, and its repetition once or twice a week in every respect inadequate. Finally the fact that the men carry infection from one woman to another would of itself be sufficient to frustrate the success of the system. A prostitute who has been examined and declared sound, receives the contagion from a diseased man an hour later, and transmits it between then and the next controlling day, or until she becomes aware of it herself, to a number of other visitors. The control is therefore not only illusory; it is worse than this. A compulsory examination, made by men instead of women doctors, outrages a woman's sense of decency, when it does not annihilate it altogether. Prostitutes endeavour to avoid the control by every means in their power. A further consequence of these police measures is to make the return of a prostitute to an honest manner of life well-nigh if not quite impossible. A woman who has fallen into the hands of the sanitary police is lost to the community; she generally perishes miserably within the next few years.

England affords a striking proof of the uselessness of this medical police control. A law was passed there in 1866, enacting the examination of prostitutes in all places in which army or navy troops were stationed. From 1860 to 1866, before this law came in force, the milder cases of syphilis had sunk from 32.68 per cent to 24.73 per cent. After it had been in force six years, in 1872 the number of cases was still 24.26, i. e., not ½ per cent lower than in 1866, while the average number of these six years was one-sixteenth per cent higher than in 1866.

Owing to this experience, a commission appointed in 1873 to investigate the working of the Acts came to the unanimous conclusion that the periodical examination of women who associated with soldiers and sailors had at the best not occasioned the slightest diminution in the number of cases; the commission consequently advocated the suspension of these periodical examinations.

But the effects of the Acts on the women subjected to them were very different to those on the troops. In 1866 among a thousand prostitutes there were 121 cases of disease; in 1868, after the law had been in force two years, 202; they then gradually decreased but in 1874 they were still more numerous than in 1866 by 16. The deaths among prostitutes increased under the Acts to an alarming degree. In 1865 the proportion was 9.8: 1000, in 1874 it had risen to 23. When the English Government made the attempt shortly before 1870 to extend the Acts to all English towns, a storm of indignation arose among the women of England. They

regarded the law as an insult flung in the face of the whole
sex. They exclaimed that the Habeas Corpus Act, the
fundamental law which protects the English citizen from
the encroachments of the police, was to be suspended for
women, that any brutal policeman, instigated by a desire for
revenge, or by any other base motive, was to be allowed to
assault any honest woman, whom he suspected of illicit
intercourse, while the licentiousness of men was not only
unchecked but protected and fostered by the law.

Although this intervention for the outcasts of their sex
exposed the English women to misrepresentation and con-
temptuous treatment at the hands of narrow-minded men
and women, they did not let such things hinder their energetic
protest against the introduction of this degrading law. The
subject was discussed under all its aspects in articles and
pamphlets, by men and women, it was brought before Parliament and at last the extension of the Acts was prevented.
The German police is everywhere in possession of similar
powers, and cases that have leaked into publicity from
Leipzig, Berlin, and other places, prove that abuses, or let us
say mistakes, easily occur in their application, but we hear
nothing of an energetic opposition against these regulations.
Frau Guillaume-Schack very rightly remarks with regard
to the protective measures taken by the State in the interests
of men; " why do we teach our sons to respect virtue and
morality, if the State declares that immorality is a necessary
evil, and presents the young man, long before he has reached
mental maturity, with woman, stamped by the authorities
as an article of trade for his passion to trifle with ? "

A man affected with venereal disease may, in his licentiousness, transmit the contagion to any number of the miserable
creatures, who, to the honour of women be it said, are generally
driven by bitter necessity or by seduction into their igno-
minious profession ; the foul man remains unmolested, but
woe to the diseased woman who has delayed to submit
to medical examination and treatment. Garrison towns,
universities, etc., with their large population of strong and
healthy men, are the hot-beds of prostitution and of its
dangerous consequences, which are carried from thence into
the remotest corners of the land, and everywhere spread
destruction. The same thing is to be said of seaport towns.
" Thy sins shall be visited upon the children, unto the third
and fourth generation." This Bible sentence applies to the
dissipated and venereal man in the fullest sense of the words.

Syphilitic poison is the most tenacious and the most difficult to extirpate of all poisons. Years after the primary infection, when the patient believes that every trace has been destroyed, the contagion can wake to fresh life in the wife or new-born child. * A certain number of the children born blind owes this misfortune to paternal sins; the poison has been transmitted to the wife, and through her to the infant. Weak-minded children and idiots have frequently the same cause to thank for their deficiencies, and recent years have furnished us with some terrible examples of the consequences that can arise from the presence of the smallest drop of syphilitic blood in vaccine lymph.

In proportion to the voluntary or involuntary celibacy on the part of men and their consequent recourse to the illicit gratification of natural impulses, seductive allurements to illegitimate intercourse increase also. The large profits to be made in all undertakings based on immorality induce numbers of unscrupulous men of business to employ all the artifices in their power to entice and retain customers. Every demand of these customers, whatever their rank and station, is met by the supply; in all cases the pecuniary position and readiness to pay are taken into account. If certain of these public brothels in our large towns could betray their secrets, we should find that their inmates, mostly of low birth, with neither breeding nor education, often scarcely able to write their own names, but possessed of personal charms, stand in a relationship of the greatest intimacy to the leaders of society, men of high intelligence and scholarship. We should there see cabinet ministers, officers of rank, privy counsellors, members of parliament, judges, etc., entering side by side with representatives of the aristocracies of birth, finance, trade, and industry. These men appear by day and in society with the grave and dignified air of guardians of morality, order, marriage and the family; they are at the head of Christian charities and of societies for the suppression of prostitution. Our social organization resembles a great carnival festival, in which everyone seeks to dupe and deceive everyone else, in which everyone wears his official disguise with decorum, and indulges his inclinations and passions all the more unrestrainedly in private. And meanwhile public life is running

---

* Fourteen per cent. of the patients treated in the English hospitals in 1875 were suffering from hereditary syphilis. Out of 190 fatal cases, one died of the same disease in London; the proportion in all England was 1:159, and in the French almshouses, 1:160.5.

over with propriety, religion and morality.   The number of
the Augurs increases daily.

The supply of women for the purposes of lust grows even
faster than the demand.   The augmenting precariousness of
our social conditions, necessity, seduction, love of a seemingly
free and dazzling life, furnish candidates from all ranks of
life.   A novel of Hans Wachenhusen* contains an excellent
description of the state of things in the capital of the
German Empire.   The author makes the following remarks
on the purpose of his work.   " My book treats principally of
the victims among women, and of the increasing depreciation
of the sex through the unnatural condition of society and
of the middle classes, through its own faults, through neglected
education, craving for luxury, and through the growing, ill-
judged supply in the market of life.   It treats of the increasing superfluity of the sex, which is daily making the future of
the new-born more hopeless, more desperate.   I write much
in the same way as the public prosecutor recapitulates
the life of a criminal, in order to sum up his guilt.   If
therefore a novel is generally supposed to be a work
of the imagination, the reverse of reality, and therefore free to be represented with impunity, the following book is no novel in this sense of the word, but
a true and unadorned picture of life."   Now things are
neither better nor worse in Berlin than in any other large
town.   It would be difficult to decide which most resembles
ancient Babylon, orthodox Greek St. Petersburg, Catholic
Rome, Christian Germanic Berlin, heathen Paris, puritan
London, or lively Vienna.   The same social conditions beget
the same results.   " Prostitution possesses its written and its
unwritten laws, its resources, its various resorts, from the
poorest cottage to the most splendid palace, its numberless
grades from the lowest to the most refined and cultivated ; it
has its special amusements and public places of meeting, its
police, its hospitals, its prisons, and its literature."†

Under such circumstances the trade in Women's Flesh
has assumed enormous dimensions.   It is carried on with an
admirable organization, on a most extensive scale, without
attracting the attention of the police, in the midst of all our

---

* Was die Strasse verschlingt.   (What the Street Swallows).   Social
novel in 3 vols.   A. Hoffmann and Co., Berlin.

† Dr. Elizabeth Blackwell.   " The moral education of the young in
elation to sex."

culture and civilization. A host of brokers, agents, carriers of both sexes is engaged in the business with the same cold-bloodedness as though it were a question of any other article of sale. Birth certificates are forged and invoices are made out, which contain an exact description of the qualifications of the separate " packages," and which are handed over to the carrier as a statement for the purchaser. The price depends, as in the case of other wares, on the quality, and the different categories are sorted and sent to different places and countries according to the tastes and demand of the customers. These agents make use of the most elaborate manipulations to avoid rousing the suspicion and incurring the pursuit of the police, and not unfrequently large sums are spent in closing the eyes of the officers of the law. Some such cases have become public, especially in Paris.

Germany enjoys the reputation of stocking the woman-market for half the world. The innate German love or wandering seems to have taken possession of some of the German women, who provide a larger contingent than the women of any other nation for the supply of international prostitution. German women fill the harems of the Turks and the public brothels from the interior of Siberia to Bombay, Singapore and New York, One writer, W. Joest, speaks as follows of the German. trade in girls, in his book of travels " From Japan to Germany through Siberia " :—" People excite themselves in our moral Germany often enough about the slave trade that is carried on by some West African negro prince, or about the condition of things in Cuba or Brazil ; they would do better to take the beam out of their own eye, for *in no country of the world is such a trade with white slaves carried on as in Germany and Austria ; aud from no country of the world are such numbers of these human wares exported.* The road which these girls take can be followed exactly. They are sent from Hamburg to South America ; Bahia and Rio de Janiero receive their quota, but the greater number is intended for Montevideo and Buenos Ayres, while the small remainder passes through the Straits of Magellan to Valparaiso. Another batch is sent direct or *viâ* England to North America, but here it finds difficulty in competing with the native product and is therefore dispersed along the Mississippi to New Orleans and Texas, or westward to California ; from thence the coast is provided as far as Panama, while Cuba, the West Indies, and Mexico receive their supply from New Orleans. Under the title of ' Bohemians ' other troops

of German girls are exported over the Alps into Italy, and
from thence further south to Alexandria, Suez, Bombay,
Calcutta and Singapore, and even to Hong-Kong, and
Shanghai.   Dutch India, the East Indies and Japan are bad
markets, as Holland suffers no white girls of this sort in its
colonies, and in Japan the daughters of the country are too
good-looking and too cheap.   Moreover competition from San
Francisco prevents much profitable business being done.
Russia is supplied from East Prussia, Pomerania and Poland.
The first station is generally Riga.   Here the dealers from
St. Petersburg and Moscow pick out what suits them, and
send their wares in large numbers to Nischnij-Nowgorod and
over the Oural to Irbit and Krestofsky, as far as the interior
of Siberia ; I met, for instance, a German girl in Tschita
who had been negotiated in this way.   This enormous business
is thoroughly organized, it is transacted by agents and commercial travellers, and if the Ministers of Foreign Affairs
were to demand reports from all the German consuls very interesting statistical tables might be made out."

Similar complaints have come from another quarter, which
occasioned the German Reichstag in its session of 1882-83 to
pass a resolution requesting the Imperial Chancellor to unite
with Holland in its endeavours to restrict and suppress this
odious trade.   A hundred reasons make the success of such
measures doubtful.

It is exceedingly difficult to even approximately estimate
the number of prostitutes and impossible to ascertain it
with exactitude.   The police is in a position to state with
tolerable accuracy the number of those whose principal profession is prostitution, but it cannot do this with regard to the
far greater number of those who resort to prostitution as a
partial means of subsistence.   In any case the numbers
which are known are alarmingly great.   According to von
Dettingen, the number of prostitutes in London about 1870
was estimated at 80,000.   In Paris there are only 4,000 registered prostitutes, but the actual number is said to be 60,000,
by some even 100,000.   In Berlin about 2,800 women are at
present under the direct control of the police, but von
Detingen tells us that as early as 1871 15,065 women were
known or suspected to be prostitutes, and as, in the year 1876
alone, 16,198 were arrested for disregard of the regulations
issued by the Police of Morals, we shall not go far wrong in
assuming the total number to be 25—30,000.   In Hamburg,
in 1860, every ninth woman above the age of 15 was a prosti-

tute; at the same time in Leipzig there were 564 registered women, but the number of those depending principally or exclusively on prostitution was estimated at 2,000. Since then it has considerably increased. As we see, we have here to do with whole armies of women who regard prostitution as a means of livelihood, and a corresponding number of victims is claimed by death and disease.

Another cause which swells the ranks of prostitution from one decade to another, in all large towns and centres of industry, are the sudden economic panics. Hand in hand with the concentration of manufacturing, *i.e.*, with the development and improvement of machinery, goes the tendency of capitalistic production to fill its workshops with women and children instead of grown men, a tendency which is becoming more and more marked. In 1861, for example, there were in England, in the branches subject to the Factory Act, 308,278 women and 467,261 men. But in the year 1868, when the total number of hands had risen to 857,964, the women numbered 525,154 and the men only 332,810. The female hands had therefore increased by the enormous number of 216,881 within seven years, while the male hands had suffered a decrease of 134,551. When panics occur, as they must occur under the bourgeois *régime*, the women who are thrown out of employment take refuge in prostitution to a great extent, and once within its clutches their fate is sealed. According to a letter of the chief constable of Bolton on the 31st October, 1865, to a factory inspector, the number of young prostitutes had increased more during the English cotton famine, occasioned by the North American Slave War than in the preceding five-and-twenty years.[*]

With regard to the decimating effects of venereal disease, we will only mention that in England between 1857 and 1865 the authenticated cases which ended fatally amounted to over 12,000, among which no fewer than 69 per cent. were children under twelve months, the victims of parental infection. At the same time, S. Holland estimated the number of persons annually infected in the United Kingdom of Great Britain and Ireland at 1,652,600.

The Parisian doctor, Parent-Duchatelet, has made out an interesting statistical table, containing an account of 5,000 prostitutes, with a view to ascertaining the principal causes which drive women to prostitution. Of these 5,000, 1,440

---

[*] Karl Marx: "Das Kapital" (Capital). Second edition, p. 480.

had been induced to enter the trade by want and misery, 1,250 had neither parents nor means of livelihood, and therefore belong to the first category, 80 prostituted themselves to support poor and aged parents, 1,400 were concubines deserted by their lovers, 400 girls seduced by officers and soldiers and dragged to Paris, 280 had been deserted by their lovers during pregnancy. These figures and rubrics speak for themselves.

We only need to consider the miserable wages earned by the greater number of workwomen, wages from which it is impossible to exist, and which the recipients are forced to eke out by prostitution, to understand why things are as they are. Some employers are infamous enough to excuse the lowness of the salary by pointing to this means of indemnification. Such is the position of sempstresses, dressmakers, milliners, workwomen in all kinds of factories, counting by hundreds of thousands. Employers and their officials, merchants, manufacturers, landed proprietors, etc., who engage workwomen and female servants do not unfrequently regard it as their peculiar privilege to use the former for the gratification of their lusts. The Jus Primæ Noctis of feudal lords in the Middle Ages exists to-day in another shape. The sons of our well-to-do and cultured classes consider it for the most part their right to seduce and then desert the daughters of the people. These confiding and inexperienced girls, whose lives are generally friendless and joyless, become only too easily the victims of a fascinating and brilliant seduction. Disappointment and misery, and finally crime, are the consequences. Suicide and infanticide among women are generally traceable to those causes. The numerous trials for child murder present a dark but instructive picture. A woman is seduced and heartlessly abandoned, helpless, in desperation and shame she is driven to the last resource ; she kills the fruit of her womb, is tried, condemned and sentenced to penal servitude or death. The unscrupulous man, the moral author of the crime, in reality the true murderer, is unpunished ; he probably soon after marries the daughter of a " nice, respectable family," and becomes a pious, honest, and much respected man. There are many, occupying positions of honour and dignity, who have thus defiled their name and their conscience. If women had a word to say in the legislature, a good many things would be altered in these matters.

The cruellest procedure, as we have already remarked, is

that prescribed by French law, which forbids enquiry after the father, and builds Foundling Houses instead. The decree of the Convention, dated June 28th, 1793, runs as follows:—
"La nation se charge de l'education physique et morale des enfants abandonnés. Désormais ils seront designés sous le seul nom d'orphelins. Aucune autre qualification ne sera permise." (The nation undertakes the physical and moral education of abandoned children. They will henceforth be only designated as orphans. No other name will be allowed.) That was a convenient arrangement for the men, who could thus throw their individual responsibility on to the shoulders of the community, without compromising themselves publicly or before their wives. Accordingly Foundling Houses were erected in all parts of the country. The number of orphans and foundlings amounted in 1833 to 130,945, and it was estimated that every tenth child was legitimate. But as these children are by no means well-cared for, the mortality among them is very great. Over 50 per cent. died at that time in their first year, 78 per cent. died in the first twelve years, so that only 22 per cent. lived beyond the age of twelve.

Similar arrangements exist in Austria and Italy, where a "humane" society has also founded these institutions for murdering infants.* "Ici on fait mourir les enfants." (Children killed here) is said to be the inscription recommended by a monarch as a suitable one for Foundling Asylums. History does not tell us that men have endeavoured to restrict this slaughter of the innocents by providing better nursing and more efficient protection. In Prussia where there are no such orphanages for foundlings, about 1860, 18·23 per cent. legitimate and 34·11 per cent. illegitimate children died in the first year. The mortality among the latter was nearly twice as large as among the former, but still very considerably less than in the French Foundling Houses. In Paris 193 illegitimate children died to 100 legitimate, and in the country as many as 215. Want of nourishment during pregnancy, weakly children, and insufficient care after birth are the natural causes. Bad treatment, the notorious "angel-making," helps to increase the number of victims. Twice as

---

* The large Foundling Asylum in Vienna is an honourable exception. Its arrangements are based on hygienic principles, and dictated by humanity But the fact that this and doubtless some other similar institutions are conducted with as much regard for the health and welfare of the inmates as circumstances allow cannot redeem a system that is intrinsically bad. [Translator's Note.]

many illegitimate as legitimate children are stillborn, probably owing to attempts made by the mothers to destroy the
children before birth. The surviving illegitimate children
revenge themselves on society for the ill-treatment received,
by forming a disproportionately large percentage of criminals
of all grades.

Another evil, which is being developed more and more by
the present state of things must be cursorily alluded to. Too
much sexual indulgence is even more injurious than too little.
A misused organism can be ruined even without the aid of
venereal disease; impotency, sterility, spinal complaints,
idiocy or imbecility, and various other derangements are the
consequences. Moderation is therefore quite as necessary in
sexual enjoyment as in eating or drinking or the gratification
of any other human requirements. But moderation is a hard
thing, especially for young men. Thence the crowd of aged
youths, particularly in the higher ranks of society. The
number of old and young roués is immense, and all, surfeited,
palled by superfluity, feel the need of keener irritants. Some
resort to the unnatural practices of Greek times, others seek
stimulation in the abuse of children. The so-called liberal
professions furnish 5 per cent. of ordinary criminals; but
12 per cent. of the criminals sentenced for violation of
children, and the percentage would be much higher if the
members of these circles did not possess such ample means
of concealing their offences that the majority of cases remains
undiscovered.

Thus we see that vice, depravity, error, and crime of all
kinds, are bred by our social conditions. The community is
kept in a state of permanent unrest. But it is women who
suffer most from these things.

Many women are conscious of this, and seek redress. They
demand in the first place the greatest possible economic
independence; they demand that women be placed on the
same footing as men with regard to all those occupations for
which their bodily and mental powers and faculties appear to
qualify them; they demand especially admittance to those
forms of activity characterized as the liberal professions.
Are these demands justified? Can they be realized? Will
they mend matters if realized? These are the questions that
now call for our attention. Let us enquire into them.

The Commercial Position of Woman. Her Mental Faculties. Darwinism and the Social Condition of the Community.

The women's struggle for independent vocations and personal freedom has to a certain extent been recognized as legitimate by bourgeois society, in the same manner as the struggle of the working classes for independence has been recognized. The reason for this acknowledgement lay in the class interest of the bourgeoisie. The bourgeoisie needed the liberation of male and female working power, in order that production on a large scale might attain its utmost development. And the number of women employed in industrial pursuits will increase in proportion to the extension of machinery, the division of labour into more and more single acts, and to the consequent competition of manufacturers against each other, of one branch of industry against another, of country against country and continent against continent.

The cause of this increasing employment of women in a growing number of branches must be looked for in their individuality and in their social position. Woman, always regarded as an inferior being by man, has acquired the character of humility, docility, and servility to a much greater extent than the male proletarian. She has therefore no chance of being employed side by side with man, or in his stead except when her claims on remuneration are less than his. Another circumstance, founded on her character as a sexual being, which forces her to work at a much lower rate of pay, is the fact that she is as a rule subject to more physical disturbances than man which necessitate an interruption of work, and, under the present combination and organization of labour in capitalistic industry, are felt as a serious disadvantage. Such pauses are prolonged by pregnancy and birth. The manufacturer turns this fact to account, by claiming double compensation for the threatened inconvenience in the shape of considerably lower wages.

On the other hand female labour and especially the labour of married women, has, as we saw in the note to page 50, a certain attraction for the manufacturer. A woman is more tractable and patient, she lets herself be more easily exploited than a man, and bears bad treatment better. If she is married, she is, in the words of the note referred to, " much more attentive and teachable than a single woman, and is forced to exert her strength to the uttermost to provide the necessary means of livelihood." The value of a workwoman as an object of exploitation is considerably enhanced in the eyes of her employer by the fact that she rarely dares to combine with her fellow-workwomen for the purpose of obtaining more favourable conditions of labour ; the manufacturer regards her in the light of a useful trump to be played out against the refractory workmen. And lastly there is no doubt that owing to her greater patience, dexterity and taste a woman is far better qualified than a man for various branches of work, and especially for those requiring delicate manipulation.

The capitalist is not at a loss to appreciate all these female " virtues," and the field opened to women by the development of industry is growing larger year by year, but—and this is the decisive point—without any accompanying improvement in their social condition. Wherever women's labour is employed the labour of men is as a rule set at liberty. The men thus elbowed out of place must live ; they offer them-selves at the lowest possible wages. This supply depresses women's wages still more. The lowering of pay almost becomes a screw without end, which tends all the more to keep the ever revolving machinery of working forces in motion, as each revolution sets female labour free, and furnishes the market with a fresh supply of hands. Newly developed employments and branches of industry have some effect is neutralizing this constant production of relatively superfluous labour, but they are not sufficient to secure a higher rate of remuneration. For every rise in wages above a certain level is an occasion for the employer to seek to improve his machinery, and replace human heads and hands by inanimate, automatic apparatus. At the commence-ment of the capitalistic era of production workman was pitted against workman, now sex is pitted against sex, and later on age against age. Men must make way to women and women to children. This is the moral " order " of modern industry.

The efforts of the employers to lengthen the working day, in order to extract " surplus-value " from their workmen, are particularly facilitated by the inferior power of resistance possessed by women. This explains the fact that in the German textile industry, in which the women often outnumber the men, working hours are longer than in any other branch. The women have learnt at home that there is no limit to their time of work, and they submit without opposition to the greater requirements made on their strength. In other branches, millinery, flower-making, etc., in which the work is principally done by hand, the women spoil their own chances of obtaining good wages and a reasonable working day, by taking home extra work, which keeps them busy till midnight and later. They forget that at the end of the month they have not earned more by sixteen hours a day than they would have earned in ten or twelve.

We have already more than once shewn by figures what enormous dimensions the employment of women has assumed. In the year 1861 the number of women working in factories in England and Wales, exclusive of various less important branches, amounted to 1,024,277, and is now probably double as great. In London, according to the last census, there were 226,000 female servants, 16,000 female teachers and governesses, 5,100 female bookbinders, 4,500 flower-makers, 58,500 milliners, 14,800 dressmakers, 26,800 sempstresses, 4,800 female shoemakers, 10,800 women working at sewing machines, and 44,000 washerwomen. And a considerable number of occupations, in which women are more or less numerously employed, is not included in this list at all.

Owing to the want of similar statistics we have no trustworthy report with regard to the extent in which women are engaged in industrial and commercial pursuits in Germany. The statistics which we do possess only refer to limited branches, and afford no standard of comparison.

At present the trades and manufactures from which women are still excluded are few in number, while there are on the other hand a considerable number of occupations, especially those connected with the making of articles for women's use, in which women are exclusively or almost exclusively employed. In other branches, for instance as already mentioned in the textile industry, the women have equalled or outnumbered the men, and are taking their place more and more. Women have moreover also found employment as assistants in a large variety of trades, and special forms of business, and are still pressing forward and gaining ground. The final result is that the number of women engaged in occupations outside their homes, as well as the occupation open to them in manufacturing, commerce and traffic is rapidly increasing. And this increase does not confine itself to those branches which are best adapted to the weaker physical frame of women, but comprises, regardless of this inferiority, all the forms of activity in which modern exploitation sees the chance of making higher profits by their employment. These occupations are frequently not only those involving the greatest bodily exertion, but also the most disagreeable and detrimental to health: a fact which reduces to its true value the fantastic conception of woman, as the delicate, finestrung creature that poets and novelists have depicted for the gratification of man.

Facts are obstinate things, and it is with facts alone that we are concerned, for they only preserve us from false conclusions and sentimental twaddling. Now these facts show us that women are at the present day employed in the following occupations among others: in the cotton, linen and woollen branches, in cloth and spinning factories, in printed calico and dyeing works, in steel pen and pin factories, in sugar and paper mills, in bronze works, in glass and china works, in glass painting, in silk spinning and weaving, in ribbon making, in soap, candle and indiarubber works, in wadding and mat factories, in the carpet, portfolio and cardboard branches, in the making of lace and trimmings, in embroidery, in the shoe and leather trade, in jewellery, in galvanoplastic institutions, in the refining of oil and fat, and in chemical factories of all kinds, in the treatment of rags and refuse, in bast manufactures, in woodcutting, wood engraving and earthenware painting, in the making and cleaning of straw hats, in potteries, in the tobacco industry, in glue and gelatine factories, as glovers, curriers and hatters, in the making of toys, in flax and shoddy mills, in the hair branch, in watchmaking and room painting, in the cleaning of feather beds, in brush and wafer factories, in making looking-glasses, explosive materials, gunpowder, and phosphorous matches, in arsenic factories, in the tinning of iron, in the dressing of stuffs, as printers and compositors, in polishing precious stones, in lithography, photography, chromolithography, and metachromotype, in brickmaking and ironfounding, in metal works, in the construction of houses and railways,, in mines, in the transport of barges on rivers and canals. Further, in the wide field of horticulture, agriculture and cattle-breeding, and the industries connected with these pursuits, and lastly, in the various occupations that have long been regarded as their special monopoly, in the making of women's linen and clothing, in the branches of fashionable dressmaking, as saleswomen, and of late years more and more as clerks, teachers, Kindergarten teachers, authoresses, artists, etc. Moreover, thousands of women in the lower middle-classes are slaves in shops, or are engaged in markets, and are thus entirely prevented from undertaking any household occupation, particularly the training of children. Nor must we forget to mention one branch in which young and good looking women are being more and more employed, greatly to the detriment of their physical, mental and moral development; we refer to their engagement as barmaids and attendants in public-houses, restaurants, and other places of general resort, as a means of attracting men in quest of amusement.

Many of these various occupations are highly dangerous. For instance, the exposure to sulphuric acid and alkaline gases in the making and cleaning of straw hats, and the inhalation of chlorine gas in bleaching vegetable materials, is exceedingly injurious. In the manufacture of coloured wall-papers, coloured wafers and artificial flowers, in metachromo-type, in the preparation of poisons and chemicals, in the painting of leaden soldiers, and in making leaden toys, the dangers of poisoning are great. The results of working with quicksilver in making looking-glasses are generally fatal to the unborn children of pregnant women, the making of phosphorous matches, and the employment in silk and shoddy mills are also highly injurious. Machine work in the textile industry, the manufacture of explosive materials, and the use of agricultural machines involve danger to life and limb. Moreover, a glance at the list will suffice to show every reader that many of the occupations quoted demand excessive physical exertion, and tax even the strength of men. People may say as often as they like, this or that kind of work is unfit for a woman; their protest will remain ineffectual as long as they are unable to provide her with another and more suitable occupation.

It is truly anything but an agreeable sight to see women, and often pregnant women, wheeling heavy wheelbarrows, and otherwise competing with navvies on the railway, or to watch them in the capacity of hod-carriers on buildings, mixing cement and mortar, and carrying heavy stones, or to observe them in coal-pits and iron works. Such employments rob a woman of her proper attributes, and tread her womanhood under foot ; while on the other hand men pursue a hundred different occupations which strip them of every manly characteristic. These are the consequences of social exploitation and social war. Our corrupt conditions turn Nature upside down.

Considering therefore the extent to which female labour has been and still threatens to be introduced into all branches of industrial enterprise, it is easy to understand and only natural that men should regard the process with looks far from friendly, and demand its entire suppression and legal prohibition. There can be no doubt that the extension of women's occupations is tending more and more to destroy the family life of the workman, that the dissolution of marriage and the family are its natural consequences, and that depravity, demoralization, degeneration, all forms of disease and mortality among children are increasing to an alarming degree. But nevertheless, and in spite of all this, development in this direction means progress, precisely as the introduction of freedom in trading, liberty of migration and of marriage, and the abolition of all barriers to the investment of capital on a large scale meant progress, although these innovations were a death-blow to small and middle-class trade, which is being irretrievably ruined by them.

The workmen have no inclination to assist handicrafts whose members endeavour to keep miniature trade artificially alive for a time—to do more is beyond their power—by all kinds of reactionary efforts, such as the limitation of free-trade, and of the liberty of migration, and the reintroduction of guild and corporative restrictions. And it is equally impossible to return to the old condition of things with regard to female labour. This of course does not exclude the prevention of the exploitation of women's and children's work, by rigorous factory acts, and the entire prohibition of children's labour during their school years. This is a point at which the interests of the workmen meet those of the State, of humanity, and of civilization.* But our final aim must be to eliminate the evils occasioned by the advance of civilization, by machinery, improved tools, and the entire modern method of labour, and, *while retaining their advantages, to make the latter accessible to all members of the State.*

* The degeneration of the race caused by the modern factory *régime* has compelled the State to reduce the minimum height of recruits several times during the last few decades.

It is an absurdity and a crying abuse that the improvements of advancing civilization, the products of human development in its entirety, should only benefit those who, thanks to their pecuniary position, are able to make them their own, while on the other hand thousands of industrious workmen and mechanics learn with anxiety and alarm that human intelligence has made a fresh discovery, by which twenty and forty times as much as can be accomplished as by hand, and that they consequently have the prospect of being turned out of doors as useless and superfluous.*

Thus an event that ought to be a source of satisfaction to all rouses the keenest enmity, and was not unfrequently, in former decades, the cause of factories being stormed and machinery demolished. The same enmity exists to-day between men and women as competitive workers. This is equally unnatural. Consequently we must endeavour to found a society in which all the means of production are the property of the community, a society which recognizes the full equality of all *without distinction of sex*, which provides for the application of every kind of technical and scientific improvement or discovery, which enrolls as workers all those who are at present unproductive or whose activity assumes an injurious shape, the idlers and the drones, and which, while it minimizes the period of labour necessary for its support, raises the mental and physical condition of all its members to the highest attainable pitch. Only thus can woman become as productively useful as man, only thus can she become possessed of the same rights, only thus can she fully develop her bodily and mental capacities, fulfil her sexual duties and enjoy her sexual rights. Such a position of freedom and equality as this will place her for the first time beyond the reach of every degrading demand.

We shall show further on that our entire modern develop-

---

* In a lecture given at Bradford, in December, 1871, by the factory inspector, A. Redgrave, the speaker expressed himself as follows : " I have been struck for some time past by the altered appearance of the wool factories. Formerly they were filled with women and children, now machinery seems to do all the work. On enquiry, a manufacturer gave me the following information : " Under the old system I employed 63 persons, after the introduction of improved machinery I reduced my hands to 33, and latterly, in consequence of new and extensive alterations, I was able to reduce them from 33 to 13." Thus we see a diminution of labour, amounting to nearly 80 per cent., taking place within a few years in one factory, in spite of an equal quantity of manufactured articles, under our present system of production on a large scale. Much interesting information on this subject is contained in Karl Marx's " Capital."

ment is tending in this direction, and that precisely the great
and overwhelming evils of this development must at no very
distant period bring about the conditions described. How
this will come to pass will be the subject of a later chapter.

Although this change in the condition of women in our
social life must be evident to all who have eyes to see, one
daily hears the same idle talk about the natural vocation of
women being comprised by the home and the family. And
this phrase is heard loudest when women make an attempt to
force their way into the so-called liberal callings, *i.e.*, into
the fields of higher instruction, of natural science, of the
administration, of the medical and legal professions. The
most untenable and ridiculous objections are brought forward
and defended under the cloak of " scholarship." The same
thing frequently applies to this appeal to scholarship and
science as to the appeal to " order and morality." Probably
no one ever represented disorder and immorality as a desirable condition, with the exception, perhaps of those individuals who made use of them to get power in their own
hands, and even in this case they always endeavoured to
make their actions appear necessary for the maintenance of
order, morality, and religion. Nevertheless these injurious
catchwords are invariably employed against those who seek
to establish true morality and order, by the introduction of
conditions more consistent with human dignity than the
present ones. Similarly the reference to scholarship and
science is made to do service in defending what is most
absurd and reactionary. Its advocates argue, for instance,
that nature and the physical peculiarities of women point her
to the home and family life, within which she has to fulfil her
purpose in creation. We have already seen how far this is
possible now-a-days. And the highest trump is the assertion
that woman is inferior to man in mental capacity, and that it
is therefore ridiculous to suppose that she can achieve anything worth mentioning on intellectual ground.

These objections raised by scholars harmonise so completely with the general prejudice of men with regard to the
proper sphere and faculties of women, that he who expresses
them can reckon on the approval of his own sex, and for
the present at least, on that of the majority of women. But
the fact that the decision in such matters rests with the
majority, and that nothing can be carried through against its
will and pleasure, does not prove that its decision is always
a reasonable one. New ideas must inevitably meet with

stubborn opposition as long as education and intelligence are at their present low level, and as long as social institutions involve the necessity of encroaching on vested interests in the realization of ideas. It is easy for the representatives of these vested interests to turn popular prejudices to their own account, and therefore new ideas when first broached will never convince more than a small minority; they are ridiculed and defamed and persecuted. But if these ideas are good and reasonable, and the necessary product of circumstances, they will spread; the minority will in time become a majority. This has been the fate of all new ideas in the course of the world's history, and the Socialistic idea, which is so intimately connected with the true and complete emancipation of woman, presents the same spectacle.

Was not Christianity once the creed of a small minority? Was not the idea of the reformation of modern citizenship combated by all-powerful opponents? And have these ideas not outlived all opposition, nevertheless? And does anyone suppose that Socialism is crushed because it is gagged by party legislation in the German Empire, and can not move hand or foot? Its victory was never more certain than now when its enemies believe it exterminated.

There are Socialists who are not less opposed to the emancipation of women than the capitalist to Socialism. Every Socialist recognizes the dependance of the workman on the capitalist, and cannot understand that others, and especially the capitalists themselves, should fail to recognize it also; but the same Socialist often does not recognize the dependance of women on men because the question touches his own dear self more or less nearly. The effort to defend real or imaginary interests, which of course are always indubitable and unassailable, makes people so blind.

The argument that it is a woman's natural vocation to be housekeeper and nurse has quite as little foundation as the parallel argument, that we must always have kings because there have always been kings in one country or another since the commencement of history. Although we do not know where the first king arose any more than we know where the first capitalist discovered his "natural vocation," we do know that the kingly office has undergone very material changes in the course of centuries, and that the tendency is to divest it more and more of its authority, and we may reasonably conclude from this that a time will come in which the monarchy will be regarded as superfluous altogether. In the same way

I

every other institution of state or society is subject to constant alterations, transformations, and finally to decay. Precisely the same process is taking place with regard to marriage and the position of women. The position of married women at the time of the ancient patriarchal family was very different to their position in Greece, where, as we learnt from the words of Demosthenes, their only object was " to bear legitimate children and to be faithful warders of the house." Who would venture now-a-days to declare that such a condition was a woman's natural vocation without incurring the reproach of contempt of the sex. Doubtless there are still persons who privately have the opinion of the Athenians, but no one dares to proclaim publicly that which in Greece, 2,200 years ago, one of the most eminent men could frankly and openly acknowledge as a matter of course. This is precisely a measure of the progress that has been made. And although our whole modern civilization, and especially our industrial development, has undermined millions of marriages, it has at the same time not failed to exert a beneficial influence on marriage, especially in cases in which the social position of husband and wife kept the destructive elements at a distance. For instance, not many decades ago, it was a matter of course in every farmer's or middle-class house, that the wife not only sewed, knitted and washed—and even this has already gone out of fashion to a great extent—she baked the bread, spun, wove, bleached, brewed beer, and made soap and candles. To have a garment made out of the house was regarded as a piece of unparalleled extravagance in the whole town ; it was an event that was criticized and condemned alike by men and women. Although such a state of affairs may still exist here and there, it is certainly an exception. More than 90 per cent. of women have given up these occupations, and they are quite right in doing so. On the one hand, many things can be done better, more practically, and more cheaply elsewhere, and on the other, at any rate in towns, the necessary domestic arrangements are entirely wanting. Thus a great revolution has taken place in our family life within a few decades, and yet it appears so natural that we hardly notice it at all. Man readily accommodates himself to new facts, which do not force themselves on his attention too abruptly, but new ideas, which threaten to quicken his ordinary jog-trot, rouse his opposition and stimulate his obstinacy.

This revolution which has taken place and is still progressing in domestic life, has materially altered the position of women in the family in more directions than one. She has become freer and more independent. Our grandmothers never dreamt, and would not have been allowed to dream, of having workmen and apprentices who did not live and board in the house, of going to theatres, concerts, places of amusement, still less—awful thought—of doing so frequently on a week-day. And which of these good old women would have thought, or have dared to think of troubling herself about public affairs, to say nothing of politics, as many women are already beginning to do. They form societies with all sorts of objects, they read newspapers and call congresses together. Working women join Trades Unions, frequent public meetings, and men's societies, and possess in some parts of Germany the right of voting for arbiters in workmen's disputes.

What pedant would seek to annul these changes, although it cannot be denied that they have not only a bright but also a dark side, the natural consequence of the fermentation and dissolution going on in our society, and that the brightness does not predominate. A plebiscite among women, conservative as they still generally are, would probably show that they have very little desire to return to the old and narrow patriarchal conditions of the beginning of the century.

In the United States, where, although Society still rests on a bourgeois foundation, people have not had to combat decrepid European prejudices or obsolete institutions, and are much more open than here to new ideas which promise to be beneficent, the position of women has for a considerable time throughout large classes of the population been different to what it is with us. In many cases, for instance, the Americans have made the common-sense discovery, that it is not only troublesome and unpractical and trying to the purse for the wife to bake her own bread and brew her own beer, they already regard it as an unnecessary tax on the family treasury for her to cook in her own kitchen. The private kitchen is replaced by the cooperative cooking establishment, with steam-engines and machinery; the women do the work by turns, and the result is that the food is one-third cheaper, more palatable, more varied, and takes considerably less trouble to prepare. Our officers in the army, who are not generally decried as Socialists and Communists, have adopted the same plan. They form a household association in their messes, and appoint a steward, who purchases the articles of food at a wholesale rate; the bill of fare is arranged in common, and the food prepared in the steam kitchen of the barracks. The officers live much cheaper than they would at a table d'hôte, and the meals are by no means inferior to those at an hotel.

When in addition to the steam kitchen we introduce the steam washhouse, with the steam drying rooms, such as already exist; when we replace our unpleasant and wasteful coal fires by the convenient central heating that has been adopted in so many hotels, first-class private houses, hospitals, schools, barracks, etc., though frequently in a defective and incomplete form, women will be relieved of many occupations which are extremely disagreeable and waste a considerable amount of time. At present people shrug their shoulders at these and similar plans. If we had proposed to our wives fifty and sixty years ago to save their daughters and servants the trouble of fetching water by laying water-pipes, they would have declared that it was absurd and unnecessary and only taught daughters and servants idleness. Did not Napoleon I. declare that the plan of propelling a ship by steam was ridiculous. And how our railways were condemned out of consideration for the poor carriers!

Thus does modern middle-class society everywhere contain the germs which a future society only needs to generalize and develop on a large scale to accomplish a vast and radical reform.

All this makes it clear that the whole tendency of our social life is not to restrict women again to house and hearth, as the fanatics of domesticity prescribe and for which they sigh, as the Jews in the desert for the flesh-pots of Egypt. On the contary, the tendency is for them to advance out of the narrow household circle, to take their full share in the public life of the people—which will then no longer comprehend the men alone—and to fulfil their part in all the tasks of human civilization. This is completely recognized by Laveleye, when he writes : * " In proportion to the development of that which we are accustomed to call civilization, the feelings of filial devotion and family ties become weaker, and exercise less influence on the actions of men. This fact is so universal that we may regard it as a law of social development." Precisely so. Not only has the position of the

---

* " Primitive Property." Chapter XX. Household Community.

wife undergone a change, the same thing applies to the position of the son and daughter in the family; they have gradually attained an independence that was formerly unknown, especially in the United States, where the training to manly self-reliance is carried to a far greater extent than here in all ranks of Society. The disadvantages which still cling to this form of development are not inherent to it; they can and certainly will be avoided under higher social conditions.

In company with Laveleye, Dr. Schaeffle also recognizes the entirely altered character of the family in our time as the result of social causes.* He says: "It is true that the tendency mentioned in Paragraph II. to reduce and limit the family to its specific functions constantly reappears in history. The family relinquishes one provisional and temporary function after the other; its only purpose being to fill up gaps in social offices, it made way to independent institutions for law, order, authority, divine service, education, technology, etc., as soon as these institutions arose."

The women themselves are pressing forward, though so far only in small numbers, and without being perfectly clear as to the object in view. They not only claim to measure their strength with that of men in trade and commerce; they not only demand a freer and more independent position in the family; their special aim is the exercise of their mental capacities in the higher walks of life, Here they are met by the objection that they are unqualified because not destined to these callings by nature. Although the question of the admission of women to the liberal professions in the present condition of society only concerns a small number, it is important as a matter of principle. For if we were forced to answer this question in the negative, the asserted possibility of higher development and equality for women would be negatived at the same time. Moreover considering that the majority of men seriously believe that women are and must always remain mentally inferior, it is urgently necessary to disprove the fallacy.

It is amusing to see how the self-same men who have not the slightest objection to make when women are employed in occupations which demand the utmost exertion of physical strength, which are injurious to their health and highly

* "Bau und Leben des Socialen Körpers." Vol I. (Structure and Life of the Social Body.)

dangerous to their morals and which notoriously compel them to neglect the duties of wife and mother—it is, I repeat, amusing to see how these self-same men declared that women must be excluded from professions in which all these drawbacks and dangers exist in a much slighter degree, and which are in every way better suited to the delicate frames, whose strength would nevertheless bear comparison with that of many a male scholar.

Among the German scholars who advocate the entire, or almost entire exclusion of women from advanced studies, we may name Prof. L. Bischof in München, Dr. Ludwig Hirt in Breslau, Prof. A. Sybel, L. von Bärenbach, Dr. E. Reich, and very many others. Bärenbach founds his refusal to admit women to scientific pursuits and his disclaimer of their capacity for such pursuits, on the assertion that the sex has never yet produced a genius, and that women are obviously unfit to study philosophy. It seems to me that the world has had quite enough male philosophers and can afford to dispense with their feminine counter-parts. And the objection that women have brought forth no genius appears to be equally inadequate and inconclusive. Geniuses do not fall from heaven, they must have opportunities to form and mature, and not only have such opportunities been hitherto almost entirely denied to women, as the foregoing historical sketch of their mental development has abundantly shewn, but men have kept them for thousands of years in a state of the deepest subjection. It is just as mistaken to say that a woman can never become a genius, because people can discover no spark of genius among the tolerably large number of intellectual women that exist, as to affirm that no more geniuses have been possible among men than the few who have been recognized as such, thanks to the opportunities that were offered them of development. The simplest village schoolmaster knows how much faculty among his scholars remains uncultivated, because there is no possibility of bringing it to maturity. The amount of talent and genius in male humanity is certainly a thousand times greater than that which has hitherto been able to reveal itself: social conditions have crushed it, just as they have crushed the capacities of the female sex, which has for centuries been oppressed, fettered and crippled to a much higher degree. We have at present absolutely no scale by which to measure the amount of mental power and capacity which will develop itself in men and women, when they are enabled to mature under natural conditions of existence.

To-day the same thing applies in the human as in the vegetable world, in which millions of valuable seeds perish because the soil on which they fall is already occupied by other plants that deprive the young germs of nutriment, light and air. The same laws hold good in nature as among men. If a gardener or agriculturist were to assert that a given plant could not be improved or perfected, although he had never given it a fair trial, or, may be, had even hindered its growth by wrong treatment, he would be regarded by his enlightened neighbours as a simpleton. And they would be quite right. The same judgment would be passed on him if he refused to cross one of his female domestic animals with the male of a superior race, with a view to obtaining an improved breed. But there is hardly a peasant in Germany to-day still so ignorant as not to recognize the advantages of rational treatment in the case of his cattle and vegetables. It is another question whether his means allow him to act accordingly. Among men alone even scholars refuse to recognize that which they accept as an infallible law for the rest of the universe. And yet everyone, without being a scientific man, has ample opportunity of learning by observation in every-day life. Why are peasant children different to town children? Why are the children of the upper classes as a rule different to the children of the poor in face and frame, and in various mental qualities? On account of the difference of life and training.

The monotony which lies in the education for one special calling stamps a man with the peculiar character of that calling. A clergyman and a schoolmaster are generally easily recognised by their carriage and expression, and so is an officer even in plain clothes. It is easy to distinguish a shoemaker from a tailor, or a carpenter from a blacksmith. Two twin brothers who resembled each other strongly in youth, often become extremely unlike at a later age, if their occupations have been dissimilar; if one has done hard work, for instance as a smith, while the other studied philosophy. We see that heredity and accommodation play an important part in the development of man, as well as in that of the lower animals; indeed man appears to be the most pliant and adaptable of all organic beings. A few years of altered occupation and manner of life suffice to make quite a different man of him. This speedy change, at any rate in externals, never shows itself more strikingly than when a man is suddenly transferred from poor and limited to considerably improved circumstances. Such a man betrays his past most by his want of culture, not because it would have been impossible for him to educate himself further, but because people who have reached a certain age rarely feel the desire of self-improvement or regard it as in any way necessary. The chief reason of this is that want of information is a defect from which a parvenu has little to suffer. Our money-loving age bows before the man with a heavy purse far more readily than before the man of genius and culture, if the latter have the misfortune to be poor and untitled. It is certain that the children of a parvenu hardly ever retain any trace of their origin in their manners and deportment, nor is there mentally any difference between them and other people.

But we see in our manufacturing districts the most striking example of the results of a diametrically opposite manner of life and education. There the contrast presented by the working and middle-classes is such that they might belong to two entirely distinct races. Although this contrast is nothing new to me, it struck me afresh with something almost like terror, at an election meeting which I held in the winter of 1877 in an industrial town of the Erzgebirge. The meeting, at which I had a debate with a Liberal professor, was so arranged that both parties appeared in large numbers and filled the hall in two divisions. The front was occupied by the opponents, almost without exception, strong, powerful, and often tall forms, with the appearance of perfect health ; at the back and in the galleries stood workmen and trades-men, nine-tenths weavers, mostly small, thin, narrow-chested, pale-cheeked men, on whose faces trouble and want were written. The former represented well-fed virtue and solvent morality, the latter were the working bees, the beasts of burden, from the fruits of whose toil the others had gained their good looks, while the labourers starved. *Put both under equally favourable circumstances for one generation, and the contrast will disappear ; it will have entirely vanished in their offspring.*

Again, it is worthy of remark, that it is as a rule more difficult to estimate the social position of women than of men because they accommodate themselves with greater ease and adaptability to new surroundings, and adopt the manners of a higher class with more readiness than men. Their capacity in this direction is greater than that of the opposite sex, which is generally more awkward. What reason have we then to doubt that they are also capable of a high degree of mental development ?

All these things show us the great importance of natural laws for the growth and condition of society.

It is real or wilful blindness to deny that improved social, *i.e.*, improved physical and mental, conditions of training could raise our women to a degree of perfection of which we have no idea to-day. The achievements of solitary women make this appear unquestionable, for these women are at least as superior to the mass of their sex, as male geniuses to the mass of their fellow men. In the government of States women have on an average given proof of even more talent than men, considering their number and measuring their actions by the standard usually applied to princes. We may allude, for example, to Isabella and Blanche of Castille, to Elizabeth of Hungary, Elizabeth of England, Catherine of Russia, Maria Theresa, &c. For the rest, many a great man in history would shrivel up till but little remained, if people always knew what he owed to himself and what to others For instance a German author, Herr von Sybel, describes Count Mirabeau as the most brilliant orator, and one of the greatest geniuses of the French Revolution. And, now research has shown that this mighty genius was indebted for the manuscript of almost all his speeches, and of the most important without exception, to the ready help and support of some few scholars who worked in retirement and whom he was clever enough to turn to his own account. On the other hand, unusual pheno-mena among women, such as Madame Roland, Madame de Stael, and George Sand, beside whom many a masculine star grows pale, are worthy of the greatest attention. The influence exercised by women as the mothers of remarkable men is also well known. Taking all into consideration, the intellect of women has achieved everything that it was pos-sible to achieve, and this justifies the best hopes for further mental development.

But supposing the case that women were on the whole less capable than men, and had no chance of becoming geniuses or great philosophers, was this the criterion by which the majority of men was judged, when the latter, at any rate according to the wording of the law, were placed on an equal footing with the geniuses and philosophers? The same scholars who deny the higher capacity of women are only too inclined to do the same in the case of artisans and workmen. When the aristocracy appeals to its blue blood and its genealogical tree, they laugh contemptuously and shrug their shoulders, but in comparison with the lower classes they regard themselves as aristocrats, who have become what they are, not thanks to any favourable conditions of life,—oh, dear no! that would be a degradation of their persons,—but purely and simply through their own peculiar talent and sense. The same men who on the one hand are free from every prejudice, and look down on those who are less free-thinking than themselves, become on the other hand, as soon as the interests of their rank or class, their vanity or self-love is concerned, the narrowest of the narrow, whose opposition assumes the character of fanaticism. Thus does the man of the upper classes regard and judge his lower class neighbour, and the same position is occupied by nearly the entire male sex towards women. Men rarely see anything in women but the instruments of their own advantage and pleasure; it is repugnant to their prejudices to acknowledge them as equals. A woman must be humble and meek, confine herself exclusively to the affairs of the house, and leave everything else to the lords of creation as their peculiar domain. A woman must bridle her own thoughts and desires to the utmost extent, and accept in silence the decisions of her earthly providence, *i.e.*, her father or husband. The better she fulfils these injunctions, the more reasonable, modest and virtuous is she declared to be, although her moral and physical health is being ruined meanwhile by sufferings caused by the constraint of her position. But if people talk of the equality of all mankind, it is an absurdity to exclude one half the race from this equality.

A woman inherits from Nature the same rights as a man; the chance of birth cannot alter this fact. It is as senseless and unjust to cut a woman off from the enjoyment of the common rights of humanity because she happens to have been born as a woman instead of as a man,—an accident of which both are equally innocent,—as it would be to make the exercise of these rights depend on religion or politics, or for men to regard each other as enemies, because they happened to belong to different races or nationalities. These notions and restrictions are unworthy of a free being, and the progress of humanity demands their removal at the earliest possible date. *The only dissimilarity which has a right to permanence is that established by Nature for the fulfilment of a natural purpose, which is externally unlike but in substance the same.* Neither sex can overstep natural boundaries, as it would destroy its proper purpose in doing so; upon this we may confidently rely. Neither sex is justified in erecting barriers for the other, any more than one class for another.

With these remarks we might close the chapter on the injustice of shutting women out from mental activity, or indeed denying her capacity for it, but one principal objection still remains to be examined. The highest trump of the opposition is that woman has a smaller brain than man, and that her eternal inferiority is proved by this fact. The first assertion is correct, the deduction must be enquired into.

The size of the brain and the corresponding weight of the cerebral mass is on an average smaller in the female than in the male sex. According to Huschke * the mean capacity of the European skull is 1,445 c.ctm. for men and 1,226 for women. The difference is therefore 220 c.ctm. Prof. Bischof estimates the male brain as on an average 126 grammes heavier than the female brain. Prof. Meinert states the difference to be 90 to 100 grammes. But the weight of the brain is exceedingly variable among different individuals of the same sex. According to Prof. Reclam the brain of the zoologist Cuvier, weighed 1,861, Byron's, 1,807; Direchlet, the mathematician's, 1,520; Gaus, the celebrated mathematician's, only 1,492; Hermann, the philologist's 1,358; and Hausmann, the scholar's, 1,226 grammes. We see here a very considerable difference in the brain weight of intellectual men. Hausmann's brain was about the same weight as the average female brain. These differences prove at any rate that it would be rash to measure mental capacity exclusively by the weight of the brain. Altogether the investigations on the subject are too recent and too few in number to allow of any definite conclusions. Moreover, in addition to the average weight of the brain in both sexes, the rest of the physical organism must be taken into account, and it then becomes apparent that, in proportion to the average size and weight of the bodily frame, the brain of women is larger than that of men. Possibly the mere cerebral mass is no more a measure of mental strength than bodily size is a measure of bodily strength. We have very small animals (ants, bees) who exceed much larger animals (e.g., sheep, cows) in intelligence, just as we often see that tall and powerful people are far inferior in intellectual capacity to people of small and insignificant appearance. It is therefore extremely probable that the weight of the brain mass is by no means the most important factor in brain power, but that the organization of

* Dr. L. Büchner, " Die Frau, ihre natürliche Stellung und gesellschaft. liche Bestimmung." (Woman, Her Natural Position and Social Destiny') Neue Gesellschaft, 1879--80.

the brain is of more consequence, and practice and use of the brain no less so.

The brain must be regularly used and correspondingly nourished, like any other organ, if its faculties are to be fully developed; if this is neglected, or if the brain is cultivated in a wrong direction, if instead of stimulating and training the organs of the understanding, the organs of feeling and imagination are favoured, the former not only remain stunted, but the whole brain is crippled. One part is nourished at the expense of the other.

Now nobody who is even superficially acquainted with the history of woman's development can deny that in this respect she has been and is still being grievously sinned against, and this has been going on for thousands of years. When Prof. Bischof nevertheless maintains that woman might have cultivated her brain and intelligence just as much as man, this assertion shews unpardonable and incredible ignorance on the part of a scholar with regard to the subject which he is discussing. How then can the striking fact be explained that among tribes in a low state of civilization, *e.g.*, among the negroes and almost all savage races, there is much less difference in the weight and size of the brain of men and women ¡than among civilized nations? Surely only by the training which the brain functions of men in civilized nations have received, whilst the brain functions of women have been cramped. In the first section of this book it was shewn that at the begining the mental and physical faculties of the sexes can hardly have differed from one another, but that in consequence of the dominant position of man over woman, the differentiation became more and more marked during a long period of development.

If our scholars make any claim to the title of scientists, they must understand that the laws of their narrower science are applicable to human life and human development. They must learn that the laws of growth, of heredity, of adaptation, have exactly the same reference to man as to any other organic being, that man is no exception in nature, and that, with better knowledge of his various phases of development, the theory of development, applied to the latter, will appear clear, instead of remaining dark and obscure, the object of scientific mysticism or of mystic science.

Some writers, for instance, Dr. L. Büchner, assert that the relations of the brain in the sexes differ in different civilized nations. The distance is greatest among the Germans and

Dutch, then come the English, Italians, Swedes, and French. In the last nation the sexes approach most nearly to each other with regard to their brain. Büchner does not enter into the question as to whether this signifies that the French women are more highly developed, and that therefore more like men, or the men less developed, and that therefore the similarity between them and women is greater. Either of these suppositions might be correct. Judging by the condition of civilization in France, the former is probably nearer the truth.

And as a matter of fact, the growth of the brain has corresponded to the training it received, if the word training be permissible at all for long periods of the past and some such expression as "bringing up" be not better chosen. All physiologists agree that the functions of the understanding depend on the foremost parts of the brain, *i. e.*, the parts lying over the eyes, directly behind the front wall of the skull. The parts of the brain in which the "feelings," as we call them, principally have their seat, are said to be in the middle brain. The difference in the shape of the heads of men and women corresponds to this disposition of functional organs ; the front head is more developed in men and the middle head in women.

And the ideal of male and female beauty has developed in conformity to this formation of the head, which has arisen from a relationship of supremacy and subjection. According to the Greek ideal of beauty, which is regarded as law up to the present time, a woman should have a narrow and rather low forehead, and a man, a high, broad forehead. And this ideal, so degrading to women, is impressed upon their minds to such an extent, that they regard the possession of a forehead higher than the ordinary average, as a deformity, and endeavour to improve nature by art in combing their hair over their forehead to make it appear lower than it is.

After all this we need not wonder that women are what they are. Darwin is perfectly right in saying that a list of the most distinguished women in poetry, painting, sculpture, music, science, and philosophy, will bear no comparison with a similar list of the most distinguished men. But surely this need not surprise us. It would be surprising if it were not so. Dr. Dodel-Port* answers to the point, when he maintains that the relative achievements would be very different,

---

* "Die neuere Schöpfungsgeschichte." (The Modern History of Creation).

after men and women had received the same education and the same training in art and science during a certain number of generations. Women are also on an average physically weaker than men, which is not the case in many savage tribes, indeed we may sometimes observe the reverse. The results of practice and training from childhood on the bodily development can be seen in female acrobats and circus riders, who could compete with any man, in courage, daring, dexterity, and strength, and whose performances are frequently astonishing.

As all these things depend on education and on the conditions of life, or, in the plain language of natural science, are a question of "breeding," and as natural laws have already been applied in the case of domestic animals with startling results, there can be no doubt, that by the application of these same laws to the physical and mental development of mankind, even more unforseen results will be attained, in as much as man, the object of training, being conscious of the aim in view, takes an active part in the endeavour.

We see from all this, how close and intimate is the connection between modern natural science and our entire social life and growth, and that scientific laws, applied to human society, can explain conditions, which without them would remain obscure. In the light thrown by these laws on the development of the human organism, we discover the motor forces and perceive that relationships of supremacy, character and bodily pecularities of individuals as well as of whole classes and nations depend primarily on the *physical conditions of existence, in other words, on the social and economic distribution of power.** This again is influenced by the nature of the land, the fertility of the soil, and by the climate. Marx, Darwin, Buckle have all three, each in his own way, been of the greatest significance for modern development, and the future form and growth of human society will to an extreme degree be shaped and guided by their teaching and discoveries.

If then we recognize that bad and unfitting conditions of existence, *i. e.*, deficiencies in social arrangements, are the cause of perverse and incomplete individual development, it

---

* A discovery which Karl Marx was the first to make and to establish by a classical demonstration in his works, especially in "Capital." The Communist Manifesto of February 1848, draw up by K. Marx and F. Engels rests on this fundamental theory, and may still be regarded as the pattern of an admirable agitation pamphlet.

necessarily follows that an improvement in these conditions of existence would effect a corresponding improvement in the individual. From this we conclude further, that the systematic application of the natural laws known as Darwinism to the individual will produce a different individual, but demand at the same time correspondingly different social arrangements, and therefore, according to the doctrine of Marx, lead to Socialism. It is useless to kick against the pricks, " und bist du nicht willig, so brauch' ich gewalt " (and art thou not willing, I must use force)—that is, the force of reason.

The Darwinian Law of the struggle for existence, which finds its expression in nature in the elimination and destruction of lower by stronger and more highly developed organisms, arrives at a different consummation in the human world. Men, as thoughtful and reflecting beings are constantly altering, improving, and perfecting their conditions of life, *i. e.*, their social arrangements, and everything connected with them, until finally all mankind will exist under equally favourable circumstances. Humanity will gradually create conditions, laws, institutions, which permit each individual to develop his talents and faculties, to the advantage of himself and of the community, but which deprive him of the power to injure any third person or the community, because, in so doing he would injure himself. This state of things will by degrees become so impressed on his intelligence and discernment that there will be no more room in his brain for thoughts of supremacy and the damage of others.

Darwinism, like every other real science, is eminently democratic* and if its proper advocates refuse to recognize this, or even assert the contrary, that only proves that they are unable to grasp the range of their own science, which is no uncommon occurrence. The opponents and especially the reverend clergymen, who always have a scent for everything that concerns their own advantage or disadvantage, have understood the matter better, and accordingly denounce Darwinism as Socialistic and Atheistic. It is by no means to the credit of Prof. Virchow that he agreed with this class of person, and, in the year 1877 at the meeting of Scientific men in München, played out the following assertion as a

---

* "The Hall of Science is the Temple of Democracy." Buckle: " History of Civilization in England," 2nd vol., 2nd part, 4th edition, translated into German by A. Runge.

trump against Prof. Häckel: "The Darwinian theory leads to Socialism," with the intention of thereby denouncing and discrediting the doctrine, as an answer to Häckel's proposal to introduce the History of Evolution into schools.

If the Darwinian theory leads to Socialism, as Virchow asserts, this is no argument against the theory, but rather in favour of Socialism. But it is not for science to enquire whether the conclusions drawn from it lead to one State form or another, to one set of social conditions or another. It is her part to examine whether her theories are correct, and if they are, they must be accepted with all their consequences. He who acts differently from motives of personal advantage, of favour from above, in the interests of a party or class, acts contemptibly and dishonours science. It is true, the science of the guilds, that flourishes in our universities, can rarely lay claim to independance and character. The fear of losing their salaries, of forfeiting the good will of the authorities, of renouncing titles, orders and advancement, causes most of the representatives of science to crouch, to conceal their convictions or even publicly to assert the contrary of that which they inwardly believe or know. When a Dubois Reymond, 1870, on the occasion of a declaration of allegiance at the Berlin University exclaimed: " The Universities are the training schools for the spiritual body guard of the Hohenzollern ! " one may judge what the majority of those who stand far below Herr Dubois-Reymond, in scholarship and prestige, think about the purpose of Science.* Science is degraded to the position of a servant-maid of power.

It is therefore quite natural that Prof. Häckel and his followers, such as Prof. Schmidt, Herr von Hellwald and others should protest energetically against the fearful accusation that Darwinism plays into the hands of Socialism, and for their part maintain : "on ths contrary, Darwinism is aristocratic, for it teaches that everywhere in nature the lower organism is annihilated by the stronger and more highly developed. As therefore the cultured and moneyed classes represent these stronger and more highly developed organisms among men, their supremacy is a law of nature and as such justified."

The false deduction may be easily detected after what we have already said on the subject. Supposing these gentle-

---

* Herr Dubois-Reymond repeated this sentence, with reference to the attacks made upon him at that time, in February 1883, at the celebration of the anniversary of Frederick the Great's birth.

men to be convinced of the truth of the doctrine, this is at best a rude, mechanical application of it to humanity. They assume that because the struggle for existence in nature is carried on unconsciously by animals and organisms without knowledge of laws, that the same things must take place among men. Fortunately, however, with or without the consent of these scholars, humanity learns to recognize the laws upon which its development depends, and only requires to apply this recognition to its political, social, and religious institutions, in order to effect their complete transformation. The difference between man and a lower animal lies in the fact, that though man is a reflecting animal, the animal is not a reflecting man. This has been overlooked by the Darwinian professors, in their erudition and hence the false conclusions at which they arrive.

Of course Professor Häckel and his adherents deny further that Darwinism leads to Atheism, and after they have dethroned the Creator by all their scientific proofs and arguments, they make the most violent efforts to smuggle him in again by the backdoor. According to this plan people arrange their own peculiar kind of "religion," which they call "higher morality," "moral principles," and so forth, for themselves. Professor Häckel even endeavoured, in 1882 at the Assembly of Scientific Men at Eisenach, in the presence of the Grand Ducal family of Weimar, not only to rescue religion but to represent his master Darwin as a religious man. The endeavour proved a miserable failure as every sane person knows, who has read the lecture and the letter of Darwin's that was quoted in it. Darwin's letter expressed precisely the contrary of that which Professor Häckel was anxious to make it express, very cautiously it is true, because Darwin, out of consideration for the piety of his English countrymen, never ventured publicly to state his real religious opinions. Privately he did so, as was made known shortly after the meeting in Eisenach, to Professor Büchner, to whom he confessed that he had believed nothing since his fortieth year, *i.e.*, since 1849, because he had been unable to find any proof for his belief. Moreover, during the latter years of his life, Darwin anonymously supported an atheistic paper that appeared in New York.

So much on modern natural science, its influence on the advance of humanity, and the attitude of its most distinguished German representatives, who either consciously deny or fail to recognise its scope.

K

Dr. Dühring also joins Professor Virchow in his attacks on Darwin and Darwinism, in a tone of angry abuse. For this purpose he draws a picture of Darwinism as it is not, and combats it with weapons borrowed in part from its own armoury. This is a perversity of mind which excludes argument.

To return to our proper subject, one fact still remains to be emphasized. Natural science and the artificial breeding which is based upon it is able purposely to produce quite new forms and species among animals and plants. This breeding has been carried so far in the case of domestic animals that the head of a certain kind of ox is bred shorter to increase the relative weight of meat on the other parts of the body, the legs of pigs are shortened for the same reason, and other almost incredible changes are brought about through applying the recognized laws of growth. Therefore, if these laws were applied to the training of men and women, the final result would be the formation of certain given qualities of mind and body and the possibility of an harmonious development for the individual.

*   *   *   *   *   *

Women are already determined, thanks to their innate instinct towards perfection, to enter on the competitive struggle with man on intellectual ground, without waiting until it shall have pleased the latter to educate their brain functions. The spirit of the times, this secret but elementary force of nature, the origin of all the material and spiritual currents in humanity, comes to their assistance. Here and there they have already, in co-operation with men, removed all hindrances and forced their way into the intellectual arena. Their success has been greater in some countries than others, greatest of all in North America and Russia, two countries which are the political, and to a great extent the social, extremes of each other. There is already in America and Russia a considerable number of women doctors, many of whom have an excellent reputation and a large practice.*

---

* There were women doctors and operators of high renown, as early as the 9th and 10th century among the Arabians, especially under Arabian dominion in Spain, during which period they studied at the University of Cordova. Women were far freer then under the empire of the Mohammedan Arabians than at the present day in the East. It was Mohammed himself who materially improved their social position. But Asiatic

There can be no doubt that women, whose qualifications as sick-nurses are gladly acknowledged, are peculiarly fitted for the medical profession. Moreover, women doctors would be the greatest blessing to their own sex. The fact that women must place themselves in the hands of men in cases of illness or of the various physical disturbances connected with their sexual functions, frequently prevents their seeking medical help in time. This gives rise to numerous evils, not only for women, but also for men. Every doctor complains of this reserve on the part of women, which sometimes becomes almost criminal, and of their dislike to speak freely of their ailments, even after they have made up their minds to consult a doctor. This is perfectly natural; the only irrational thing about it is the refusal of men and especially of doctors to recognize how legitimate the study of medicine for women is.

Medical women would further be of use, especially in the country, where the number of doctors is insufficient; our bourgeois youths, who avoid serious exertion as much as possible, do not press in to fill up the gap. The zeal and industry of the youths in question leave much to be desired in more respects than one:—cf. the annual examinations of one year recruits—and female competitors would have a very healthy effect.

Here again we find a good example in the United States, where to the horror of learned and unlearned pedants of both sexes, numerous colleges exist in which large numbers of young men and women are educated together. And with what results? President White, of the University of Michigan, expresses himself thus: "For some years past a young woman has been the best scholar of the Greek language among 1,300 students; the best student in mathematics in one of the largest classes of our institution is a young woman, and many of the best scholars in natural and general science are also young women. Dr. Fairshild, President of Oberlin College in Ohio, in which over 1,000 students of both sexes study in mixed classes, says: "During an experience of eight years as professor of the ancient languages, Latin, Greek, and Hebrew, and in the branches of ethics and philosophy, and during an experience of eleven years in theoretical

---

Persian and Turkish influence degraded them later on to their original state. Interesting information on this subject is to be found in von Kremer's "Kulturgeschichte des Orients" (History of Civilization in the East). In the 12th century women also studied medicine in Bologna and Palermo.

and applied mathematics, the only difference which I have observed between the sexes was in the manner of their delivery." Edward H. Machill, president of Swarthmore College, in Delaware County, Pa., author of the work from which the foregoing data are taken, tells us* that an experience of four years has forced him to the con- clusion tha the education of both sexes in common leads to the best moral results. This may be mentioned, in passing, as a reply to those who imagine that such an education must endanger " morality." There still remain many pigtails† to be cut off in Germany, before reason will come to her own.

Another objection is that it is unseemly to admit women to medical lectures, to operations and deliveries, side by side with male students. If men see nothing indecent in studying and examining female patients in the presence of nurses and other female patients, it is difficult to understand why it should become so through the presence of female students. A great deal depends on the manner of teaching, and on the influence exercised by the teacher on the attitude of his male and female pupils. It is moreover probable that women who devote themselves to such studies under present circum- stances, will be inspired by a degree of seriousness and determination generally exceeding that of their male col- leagues. Professors who have taught mixed classes confirm this statement. The zeal of the female students is on an average greater than that of the male. Finally, experienced medical women might undertake to educate the students of their own sex, if people will insist in regarding it necessary to maintain an unnatural separation of the sexes in dealing with natural things.

In reality, the motives which induce most medical pro- fessors and indeed the professors of every faculty to oppose women students have quite another origin. They regard the admission of women as synonymous with the degradation of science, which could not but lose its prestige in the eyes of the enlightened multitude if it appeared that the female brain was capable of grasping problems, which had hitherto only been revealed to the elect of the opposite sex.

The fact is that our universities, and indeed our whole system of education, in spite of all phrases to the contrary, is thoroughly out of repair. In the National School the child is

---

* An Address upon the Co-education of the Sexes. Philadelphia.

† " Pigtail "—Zopf. Antiquated prejudice. (Translator.)

robbed of valuable time, in order to have his mind filled with things that have nothing to do with common sense or scientific information, he is burdened with a mass of ballast which he can turn to no account in life, but which on the contrary is a hindrance to his development and to his success. The same thing applies to our higher schools. During his preparation for the University, the scholar is crammed with a quantity of dry and useless material, which he learns by rote, and which occupies most of his time and demands his best intelligence. The same process is continued at the University. A mass of old-fashioned, worn-out, superfluous information is given him with little else that he can make use of. Manuscript lectures, including the jokes scattered about in them, are read and reread by the majority of professors one half-year after another. The high office of instructor becomes in many cases a mere handicraft, and the students need not be very acute to discover this. Moreover the traditional notions of life at the University prevents the years of study being treated too seriously, and many who have come with the best intentions are repelled by the pedantic and unpalatable method of most teachers. When the time comes for the examination, the student crams mechanically and hastily for a few months, till he knows what is barely necessary to scramble through. This happy consummation being attained and an official post or a profession entered on, these " University men " generally become purely mechanical workmen, but take it very much amiss if a non-academic person fails to shew them the greatest respect, to regard them as beings of another and a better order, and to treat them accordingly. Only the really earnest worker discovers later that what he has learnt is to a large extent useless, and that he has not learnt what he most needs, and begins to learn aright for the first time. During the best part of his life he has been plagued with unnecessary or injurious things, he needs the second part of his life to divest himself of them, and adapt himself of the character of his age, and not till this is accomplished can he become a really useful member of society. Many never get beyond the first stage, others remain at the second, a few only have energy to work up to the third.

But, nevertheless, it is considered decorous to retain the cumbrous and useless heritage of the Middle Ages, and as girls, in virtue of their sex, are as a matter of course excluded from the schools and preparatory colleges of boys, this circumstance supplies a convenient pretext for closing the university doors upon them. One of the most celebrated professors of medicine in Leipzig did not hesitate to remark to a lady: " A public-school education is not a necessary introduction to the study of medicine, but we must make it a condition of admittance to preserve the prestige of science."

Prof. Bischof in München gave as one reason among others why he could not recommend the study of medicine to women, " The brutality of the students," — truly a very characteristic remark. The same Professor goes on to say in another passage of his pamphlet on the subject in question —a passage which deserves attention,—" Why should not he (*i.e.*, the professor) occasionally allow a woman, who is at the same time interesting, intelligent, and pretty, to attend a lecture on some innocent subject." This opinion is apparently shared by Herr v. Lybel, who expresses himself as follows : " Some men are rarely equal to the task of refusing a studious and charming pupil their sympathy and assistance."

It would be a pity to waste a word in refuting such argu· ments and notions. The time will come in which people will not trouble themselves about the brutality of academic youths or about the pedantry and sensual lusts of scientific men, but will be guided only by the dictates of reason and justice.

As we have already seen, the traditional prejudices which infest Europe, and specially Germany, are very much less marked in North America. There women have attained good positions as doctors, lawyers, teachers, in the highest as well as in the lowest grades,—in fact American women form the majority in the last named profession,—and, further, as civil servants in the different state and communal offices. In Russia too public opinion is far more liberal and higher in tone than in Germany * Many Russian women have devoted themselves successfully to various branches of science. In the spring of 1878, a Russian student in Bern, Frau Litwinow from Tula, passed such a brilliant examination, especially in mathematics, that the Philosophical Faculty unanimously bestowed on her the title of Doctor, with the highest marks that could be given. The same thing applied to Frau Suslowa-Erismann, who studied medicine in Zurich, and has now been practising for years as a doctor in St.

---

* In Berlin too the ice has been broken at last. In the spring of 1883 five women doctors were practising there with success. The scholarly German pigtail shakes with serious misgivings when its owner hears such things.

Petersburg. Prof. Rokitansky in Vienna, a well-known specialist for women's diseases, whom no one suspects of any unusual partiality for women's emancipation, remarked with respect to this lady, evidently in sincere admiration, "It was a pleasure to see her operate." Such an admission will have especial value for those who know from experience how critically men are accustomed to regard women's work, and more particularly that of female competitors in their own department.

In the few exceptional cases in which the German State has appointed women to posts in the Civil Service, it has, like a genuine exploiter, regarded them merely as cheap labour, and paid them considerably less than it pays men for the same work. But as, under present circumstances, men are the competitors and therefore the enemies of women to start with, and become doubly so when the latter threaten to undersell them, the position of the women in these appointments is anything but an agreeable one, and frequent disputes are the result. In addition to this, our military system provides us annually with so many subaltern officers, who have served their time, and with so many pensioned officers, as aspirants for official posts, that there is no room for other candidates. Hence the speedy removal of the women who had been appointed. Moreover, it cannot be denied that the exorbitant amount of work demanded of women by private employers as well as by the State, involves serious disadvantages, especially in cases in which the women in question have household duties to attend to. Our present manner of house-keeping is just as great a contradiction to the claims made by life on millions of women, as our whole system of economics to the human dignity of the individual.

Women have proved, and are still more and more proving, that they have plenty of sense in spite of its neglected development, and that they are already capable of entering into competition with men in a great many branches. They have produced first-class authoresses and artists of various kinds, and representatives of other professions as well. This is a sufficient reply to the reactionary shriekers, and proves that the recognition of women's equality is only a question of time. But it is just as certain that under existing social circumstances neither they nor men will attain the end in view. When a greater number of men press into the higher callings —although only a minority can do so—the final result must be the same as in the industrial branches. Here, too, women will not only be worse paid in proportion as the supply is increased by their competition, but beaten down to a very much lower price, owing to the same causes as those quoted for working women in factories. A case has come to my personal knowledge, in which a woman was to take the place of a man, in one of the highest posts in a public school, *but with half the salary which her predecessor received*. It was a shameless proposition, but quite in keeping with current middle-class principles ; it was made, and, under the pressure of circumstances, accepted. There cannot be the slightest doubt that admission to the liberal professions does not signify liberation from social wretchedness, either for women or for men. We must advance further.

The Legal Position of Woman. Her Relation to Politics.

Whenever a rank or class is in a condition of dependence or subjection, this condition will find its expression in the laws of the country in question. The laws are the formulæ in which the social state of a country is summed up, they are its mirror. Women, as a dependent and subjected sex, make no exception to this rule. The laws are both negative and positive, negative inasmuch as they ignore the existence of the subject class in the distribution of rights, positive inasmuch as they define its position of dependence, and note any possible exceptions.

Our common law is founded on the Roman law, which only recognized man in his capacity of proprietor. But at the same time, the old German law, which took a more liberal view of men and a more dignified view even of women,* has not been without influence. But amongst all Romance nations the Roman conception of law, especially with regard to women, has held its own up to the present day. It is no mere accident that the French language only possesses one word, l'homme, for man and human being. French law only recognizes man as a human being. The same thing applied in Rome. There were Roman citizens and the wives of Roman citizens, but no *citoyennes*.

It is unnecessary to let the whole many coloured map of German common law pass in review; a few specimens will suffice.

According to German common law woman is everywhere in the position of a minor with regard to man; her husband is her lord and master, to whom she owes obedience in marriage. If she be disobedent, Prussian law allows a husband of " low estate " to inflict moderate bodily chastise-

---

* As early as the time of Tacitus there were tribes with women as chieftains, which according to Roman notions was a monstrosity.

ment. As no provision is made for the number or the severity of the blows, the amount of such chastisement is left to the sovereign discretion of the man. In the communal law of Hamburg the regulation runs as follows : " The moderate chastisement of a wife by her husband, of children by their parents, of scholars by their teachers, of servants by their master and mistress, is just and permissible."

Similar enactments exist in many parts of Germany. The Prussian common law decrees further that the husband can determine the length of time during which a woman must suckle her child. All decisions with regard to the children ; rest with the father. When he dies the wife is everywhere under the obligation of accepting a guardian for the children, she is declared to be under age, and incapable of conducting the education of the children alone, even when their means of support are derived entirely from her property or her labour. Her fortune is managed by her husband, and in cases of bankruptcy, is regarded in most States as his and disposed of accordingly, unless a special contract has been made before marriage. When landed property is entailed on the eldest child, a daughter has no rights, as long as husband or brothers are alive ; she cannot succeed unless she has no brothers or has lost them by death. She cannot exercise the political rights which are as a rule connected with landed property, except in some exceptional cases, as for instance in Saxony where communal regulations in the country allow her to vote, but deny her the right of being elected. But even this right is transferred to her husband, if she marry. In most States she is not free to conclude agreements without the consent of her husband, unless she be engaged in business on her own account, which recent legislation permits her to do. She is excluded from every kind of public activity. The Prussian law concerning societies forbids school boys and apprentices under eighteen and women to take part in political associations and public meetings. Until within the last few years women were forbidden by various German codes to attend the public law courts as listeners. If a woman becomes pregnant with an illegitimate child, she has no claim on support, if she accepted any present from the father at the time of their intimacy. If a woman is divorced from her husband, she continues to bear his name in eternal memory of him, unless she happen to marry again.

These examples are enough. In France the condition of the woman is still worse. We have already seen how the

question of paternity is treated in cases of illegitimate birth.
On the same principle, a woman cannot obtain separation
from table and bed, in case of adultery on the part of the
man, unless it has taken place under aggravating circumstances. The husband, on the other hand, can obtain separation at once. The same thing applies in Spain, Portugal
and Italy.

According to section 215 of the Code Civil, a woman may
not appear in court, even though she have a public lawsuit,
without the consent of her husband and of her two nearest
relations. According to section 213 it is the duty of the
husband to protect the wife, and of the wife to obey the
husband. The management of the property is the concern
of the husband, and so on. Very similar regulations exist in
French Switzerland, for instance, in the Canton of Vaud.
There is a characteristic phrase about the manner in which
Napoleon regarded the position of women in France : " One
thing is not French, viz., a woman who can do as she
pleases." *

In England the legal status of woman has been materially
improved since August 1882, in consequence of the energetic
agitation of women themselves among the people and in
Parliament. Up till then the English woman was virtually
the serf of her husband, who could freely dispose of her
person and property. Her husband was responsible for a
crime which she committed in his presence, her condition
being that of a permanent minor. If she injured any third
person the injury was regarded as though caused by a domestic
animal ; the husband had to furnish compensation. By the
law of August 1882 women now enjoy the same civil rights
as men.

Of all European States, Russia is the one in which the
position of women is the freest. In the United States, at any
rate in most of them, women have fought their way to complete equality before the Civil Law,; they have, moreover,
prevented the introduction of the English Contagious Diseases
Act, or of similar enactments against prostitution.

The palpable and tangible civil inequality between women
and men has induced the more enlightened among the former
to claim political rights, with a view to obtaining justice by
means of legislation. It is the same principle as that which
inspired the working classes everywhere to direct their en-

---

* Bridel : " Puissance Maritale." (Marital Power.)

deavours towards the attainment of political power. What was right in the case of the workmen cannot be wrong in the case of the women. Oppressed, outside the pale of the law, invariably set on one side, it is not only their right but their duty to defend themselves and to make use of every available means of gaining a more independent position. Naturally these efforts are greeted by the warning croaks of reactionary frogs. Let us enquire how far their fears are justified.

The great French Revolution which commenced in 1789, bursting old fetters asunder and setting spirits free, in a manner that the world has not yet seen again, brought women too upon the stage. During the last two decades which immediately proceeded the outbreak of the Revolution, many women had already taken active part in the great intellectual struggle which was raging in French society. They flocked in large numbers to the scientific discussions, joined scientific and political clubs, and took their share in preparing the Revolution by which theories were transformed into acts. Most historians have only reported their excesses, which have been monstrously distorted, as is always the case when it is a question of casting stones at the people and rousing indignation against it, in order the better to extenuate the crimes of those in power. On the other hand these historians have disparaged or been silent about the heroism and greatness of soul displayed by many women of this period. As long as the victors alone record the deeds of the conquered, this will continue to be the case. But times change.

As early as October, 1789, the women petitioned the National Assembly " to re-establish equality between men and women, to accord to the latter freedom of labour and occupation, and to appoint them to posts for which they were qualified." The claim for the *re*-establishment of equality between men and women might seem to presuppose that this equality had formerly existed. This is, however, a mistaken notion, which at that time was universally accepted with regard to the past of mankind. Led astray by an inexact study of history, and unacquainted with the laws of human development, people fondly believed that man had once been freer and happier than in the present. This opinion has still a certain number of adherents, but then it was represented and taught by the most influential writers, especially by Rousseau. Consequently reclamations (revendications) played a great part in all political and social discussions, and one still not unfrequently meets with them in the writings of French Radicals.

When the convention proclaimed the Rights of Man in 1793, the clearer headed among the women recognized that the rights of their own sex were not included. Accordingly Olympe de Gouges, Louise Lacombe, and others replied in seventeen articles, entitled the " Rights of Women," and defended these articles before the Paris commune on the 28th Brumaire (20th November), 1793, by the argument that, " if a woman have the right to ascend the scaffold, she must also have the right to ascend the platform." And when the convention, in the face of approaching re-actionary Europe, had declared the " Fatherland in danger," and summoned all sound men to arms for the defence of the country and the republic, enthusiastic Parisian women were ready to do that which twenty years later enthusiastic Prussian women actually carried out against Napoleon—to defend their country in the field. They were opposed by the Radical, Chaumette, who exclaimed : " How long have women been suffered to fore-swear their sex and become men ? How long is it the custom for them to forsake the pious care of their household, the cradle of their children, to crowd together in public places, to make speeeches from the tribune, to join the ranks as soldiers, in a word, to take duties upon themselves which nature has assigned to man alone ? Nature has said to man, ' be a man ! Races, the chase, agriculture, politics, and exertions of all kinds, are thy *privileges* ! ' To woman she has said : ' be a woman ! The care of thy children, the details of the household, the sweet unrest of motherhood, these are thy *tasks* ! ' Foolish women ! Why will you become men ? Is the difference between you not great enough ? What more do you want ? In the name of Nature remain what you are, and far from envying us the dangers of so stormy a life, be content to make us forget them in the midst of our families, by letting our eyes rest on the delicious spectacle of our happy children preserved in health through your care."

The women let themselves be persuaded and went. With-out doubt the Radical Chaumette gave expression to the innermost convictions of many of our contemporaries who would regard all his other opinions with horror. I too consider it an advantageous division of labour to let the men defend their country in the field, while the women undertake the care of house and home. In Russia it is customary in some villages for the entire male population to go in autumn, after the fields are ploughed and sown, to the distant factory towns, and leave the administration of house and community

to the women. For the rest, the poetic effusion of Chaumette
has been sufficiently refuted by the foregoing chapters on
modern family life. His remarks on the agricultural labours
of men are incorrect, for from primæval times up to the
present time the easier part of agriculture has not fallen to
women's share. As to the exertions of the chase, of racing,
and of politics, they may be reduced in the first two cases to
masculine amusements, and in politics there is only danger
for those who swim against the stream ; for all others, political
life is a source of at least as much enjoyment as exertion.
This speech is inspired by manly egotism, but as it was made
in 1793, the speaker may be excused.

To-day things wear a somewhat different aspect. Circumstances have meanwhile undergone an enormous change, and
the position of women has been changed at the same time.
Whether married or unmarried, the existing social and political conditions concern her more closely than at any former
period. It cannot be a matter of indifference to her whether
or not the State keeps yearly many hundred thousand of
strong, able-bodied men in the standing army ; whether the
policy of the Government tends towards war or peace ; what
weight of taxes are to be borne and how the taxes are raised ;
whether the most necessary articles of life are made dear by
indirect taxes, which affect the family all the more nearly the
more numerous it is, and at times when the means of existence are of the smallest. She is concerned too in the system
of education ; it is not a matter of indifference to her how her
sex is educated in the next generation ; as a mother it concerns her doubly.

Further, millions of women are, as we have seen, engaged
in a hundred different branches of industry. All these women
have an interest in the nature of the social legislation relating
to their respective callings. They are as much concerned as
the men in all questions touching the length of the working
day, Sunday and night work, the employment of children, the
form of payment, the length of notice, the introduction of
character-books for the working-classes, protective measures
in factories, the character of the workshops, and similar
important legislative subjects. Workmen know little or
nothing about the condition of many branches of industry in
which women are exclusively or almost exclusively engaged.
It is in the interest of the employers to conceal evils for
which they are responsible ; the inspection of factories does
not extend to many forms of labour, almost entirely carried

on by women; it is, in any case, notoriously insufficient in every way, and yet those branches are probably more in need of protective interference than any others. We need only remind our readers of the work-rooms in which sempstresses, dressmakers, milliners, etc., are crowded together in our great cities. No complaint reaches us from thence, and an investigation rarely find its way thither. The miserable result of the imperial enquête relating to the occupation of women undertaken in the year 1874 is the best proof how little organization has yet accomplished on this ground and how much remains to be done. Finally women who are engaged in trade are concerned in the legislation for the regulation of commerce and duties. There can therefore be no doubt whatever that women are justified in claiming to exercise their influence on the direction of affairs by legislation. Moreover taking part in public life would prove a powerful stimulant and open a number of new vistas to women.

Such claims are met by the short and repellant answer: 'Women understand nothing of politics, and as a rule prefer not to trouble themselves about them; they would not know how to make use of a vote if they had one." This is true and yet not true. It cannot be denied that a very small number of women, at any rate in Germany, have ventured to claim political equality for their sex. One authoress only has, to the best of my knowledge, as yet entered the lists, Frau Hedwig Dohm, but she has done so with energy enough to make up for many laggards.

Nothing is settled by the argument, that woman have hitherto taken but little interest in politics. The fact that women have not yet troubled themselves to follow the course of public events is no proof that they ought not to do so. Did not the same thing once apply to men? The same reasons that are advanced against women's suffrage were made to do service against extension of the suffrage to all male adults in Germany. After its introduction in 1867 all objections disappeared at one blow. I myself was in 1863 one of those who protested against Universal Suffrage; four years later I was indebted to it for my election to the Imperial Parliament. The same thing has happened to thousands. Saul becomes Paul. Although there are still a great many men, who either neglect to make use of their most important political right, or who do so without comprehending its meaning, no one would suggest that

they should be disfranchised on that account. At the elections for the German Reichstag forty per cent. generally
abstain from voting, and these non-voters are recruited from
all classes ; they include the man of science and the
mechanic. And the majority of the sixty per cent. that
takes part in the election votes, in my opinion, as it ought
not to vote, it is understood its own true interests. The
fact that it does not understand them is to be explained by
the want of political education, of which the sixty per
cent. nevertheless possess more than the forty per cent.
who abstain altogether. Of course we must except those
who, because they cannot vote according to their convictions without danger prefer to remain away from the polling
booth.

But political education cannot be provided by shutting out
the masses from public affairs, but only by admitting them to
the exercise of political rights. Practice alone makes perfect.
Hitherto the ruling classes have endeavoured to serve their
own ends by retaining the majority of the people in a state
of political childhood ; and they have as a rule been successful in their attempt. It has, therefore, up to this hour been
left to a minority favoured by circumstances or character to
storm the fortress, to struggle with energy and enthusiasm
for the cause of all, in order gradually to rouse the great
inert mass and carry it along in the same direction. This
has been the history of all great movements, and it is neither
surprising nor discouraging that those of the proletarians and
women form no exception. Previous results prove that
trouble, exertions and sacrifice have been repaid and the
future promises victory.

As soon as women are in possession of political rights they
will awake to the consciousness of their political duties.
When they are called upon to give their votes, they will ask,
" Why, and to whom ? " This will be the starting point for
a number of common interests between husband and wife,
which, far from being detrimental to their mutual relationship will on the contrary materially improve it. The unin-
itiated wife will naturally turn to her better initiated husband
for information. The result will be an exchange of ideas,
and mutual instruction, a state of things which has hitherto
existed only in the rarest cases between man and wife. This
will give an entirely new stimulus to the woman's life. The
change will more and more bridge over the unhappy difference
in culture and powers of perception which we have already

described, which is such a fruitful source of quarrels and disputes, which brings the husband into collision with his various duties and is injurious to the welfare of the community. Instead of a drag the husband will find a helpmate in the wife who shares his opinions, and she will not complain at his fulfilling his public duties, even when other occupations prevent her taking part in them. She will gladly agree to spend a small fraction of his wages in taking in a paper, or for purposes of agitation, for the paper interests and instructs her too, and she comprehends the necessity of the sacrifices made to attain what neither she nor her husband nor her children yet enjoy—a human existence and equal human rights.

Thus the influence of mutual activity for the common good which is so intimately connected with that of the individual is in the highest degree an ennobling and moral influence, and its results are the contrary of those foreseen by short-sighted people or by the opponents of a community based on the equality of all. And this relationship of the two sexes will continue to improve in proportion to the improvement in social conditions, and the liberation of men and women from the burden of pecuniary care and undue labour.

Practice and education will accomplish in this case what they accomplish in all other cases. Without going into the water I shall never learn to swim; without study and practice I cannot master a foreign language. Every one will agree to these propositions, but few people understand that the same argument applies to the affairs of the state and of Society. Are our women more incapable than the negroes of North America who occupy so much lower a position, and on whom nevertheless full political equality has been bestowed? And must we assume that thousands of cultivated women have a worse claim than the rudest, most ignorant man, than an unlettered day labourer from the back of Pomerania, or an ultramontane Polish navvy, simply because the latter happened to come into the world as men? The son has more rights than the mother, from whom perchance he has inherited his best qualities, the mother that has made him what he is? Strange!

Moreover we in Germany are not the first who risk the leap into the dark Unknown, Undreamed of. North America and England have already made a beginning. In some states of North America women possess the same suffrage as men. The results are excellent. In Wyoming Territory the experi-

L

ment of women's suffrage has been made since the year 1869, with what success may be gathered from the following report :—

On the 26th December 1872, Judge Kingman, of Laramie City in Wyoming Territory wrote thus to the Women's Journal in Chicago :—

"Three years ago to-day women obtained the right of electing and of being elected to office in our territory, in the same manner as the other electors. During this period they have exercised the functions of jurors and arbiters ; they have taken part in large numbers at all our elections, and although I believe that some among us oppose the admission of women from motives of principle, no one, I think, can refuse to recognize that their influence on the elections has been an elevating one. It caused them to be conducted in a more peaceable and orderly manner and at the same time enabled our courts of justice to discover and punish various kinds of crime that had until then remained unpunished."

"For instance, when the Territory was first organized, there was scarcely a man who did not carry a revolver and made use of it in the slightest dispute. I cannot remember a single case in which a jury composed of men brought in a verdict of guilty against one of those who had shot with a revolver, but when two or three women were among them, they have invariably attended to the instructions of the court.'

Judge Kingman goes on to say, that women were frequently not to be had as jurors on account of their household duties, much to the regret of the judges, but that when they had undertaken any function they always carried it out with the utmost conscientiousness. They followed the course of the trial with greater attention than the men, they were less influenced by business connections and extraneous considerations, and possessed more delicate scruples with regard to their responsibility.

Further, their presence as jurors and judges had the effect of maintaining order and quiet in the courts, the men had been polite and respectful, the audience had appeared better dressed, the proceedings had assumed a more dignified character, and business had been got through more rapidly.

The same favourable influence had been exercised by women on the general elections. Formerly these elections were accompanied by uproar, tumult, acts of violence of every description and an unfailing contingent of drunken persons, but since the extension of the Franchise to women, they had assumed a totally different aspect. The women who came to give their votes were treated by everybody with the greatest respect, the rioters and brawlers disappeared, and the elections took place as quietly as could be desired. Moreover the women took part in regularly increasing numbers, and not unfrequently voted in opposition to their husbands, without any unpleasant consequences.

Judge Kingman concludes his long letter with the following remarkable words: " I declare most distinctly that while I have seen great advantages and much good for public life arise from this alteration in our laws, I have been unable to detect any evil or disadvantage due to the admission of women, in spite of the bad results which were prophesied by the opponents of the step."

In England too, in a considerable number of municipalities, women who pay the requisite amount of taxes possess the right of voting in municipal affairs. No difficulties have made themselves apparent. Out of 27,946 women who possessed this right in 66 municipalities, 14,415, *i. e.*, over 50 per cent took part in the first election. Out of 166,781 men not quite 65 per cent voted. In Germany also, for instance in Saxony, women have the right of voting ; it is true, only in exceptional cases. According to to the regulations existing for country districts, unmarried women who own landed property may give their votes in communal elections. Supposing that there were a majority of unmarried landed proprietresses in a given district, they could elect two thirds of the parochial representatives for that district, but they must elect men. As soon as a woman marries, she loses her vote, which is transferred to her husband. If the property is sold, he too loses his vote. The suffrage is therefore not an attribute of the person but of the soil. That is extremely characteristic of the dominant State morality, and State conception of the rights of a citizen. Man, you are nothing, if you have neither money nor land. Reason and intelligence are secondary considerations and cannot be taken into account.

A further objection is that it would be dangerous to give women a vote, because of their accessibility to religious influences and of their conservatism. True, but women are religious and conservative only because they are ignorant. Educate them and teach them where their real interest lies. For the rest, the importance of religious influence at elections appears to me exaggerated. The success of the Ultramontane

agitation in Germany was due entirely to the union of
religious with social interests. The Ultramontane chaplains
competed with the Social-Democrats in the denunciation of
social corruption. This was the cause of their influence
with the masses. As soon as peace is concluded in the
Kulturkampf and the demagogic proceedings of these gentlemen are put a stop to, the question will assume a different
aspect, and we shall see how small the purely religious
influence is. The same thing applies to women. As soon as
they hear from the men, in the newspapers and in meetings,
and have learnt by experience where their true interest lies,
they will emancipate themselves from the clergy as quickly
as the men. But even supposing that this did not take place,
would that be a justifiable reason for withholding the
franchise from women?

Probably the most violent opponents of Women's Suffrage
are the clergy, and they know why. Their power would
then be imperilled in their last domain. What would the
workmen say, if the Liberals proposed to abolish Universal
Suffrage which the later find inconvenient enough, because
it is turning out more and more to the advantage of the
Socialists? A valid claim does not become invalid, because
the person who should make use of it has not yet learnt to do
so rightly.

Of course the right of electing must go hand in hand with
the right of being elected, the former would else be a knife
without a blade. "A woman on the tribune of the Reichstag,
that would be a pretty spectacle!" I hear some one exclaim.
We have already accustomed ourselves to see women on
platforms at their own congresses and meetings, in America
in the pulpit and on the jury bench, and why not on the
tribune of the Reichstag? We may be certain that the
first woman who enters the Reichstag will know how to
command the respect of the men. When the first working-
men members appeared there, people also thought they could
make them appear ridiculous, and declared that the workmen
would soon discover what folly they had been guilty of. But
these members very soon made a position for themselves and
now people are afraid that they will become too numerous.
Frivolous jesters object further: "But imagine a pregnant
woman on the tribune, how unæsthetic!" These same
gentlemen think it quite right and proper when women are
employed by hundreds at the most unæsthetic occupations,
in the last stages of pregnancy, at the cost of womanly

dignity, health, and morality. In my eyes the man who is capable of jesting about a woman with child, under whatever circumstances he may see her, is a miserable creature. The mere thought that his own mother was in the same condition before she brought him into the world, ought to send the blood to his cheeks, and the second thought, that this pregnancy was caused by a man and that he himself, the brutal jester, expects the consummation of his highest wishes from a similar condition of his wife, should silence him with shame.

If we are to apply the standard of æsthetic gratification to the external appearance of the people's representatives, many of the present members of the House might stand the test very indifferently. Many are provided with a superfluous corpulence, which they do not owe to a temporary and highly important natural process, but to the excessive care of their own persons, at the expense of their character and their intelligence. Superfluous corpulence is as a rule the sign of a self-indulgent existence, while pregnancy is the sign of physical health, and bears witness to the conscientious fulfilment of a natural vocation. A woman who brings children into the world does the community at least as great a service as a man who defends his country and his home against the attacks of an enemy with his life. Moreover a woman's life is at stake in every case of motherhood; all our mothers have looked death in the face at our birth, and many have succumbed to the act. The number of women who die during delivery or become chronic invalids in consequence of it is probably greater than the number of men who fall or are wounded on the field of battle. This is reason enough to entitle women to complete equality with men especially when the man lays stress on the duty of defending his country as a claim to superiority over the woman. Besides, in consequence of our military system, the majority is never called upon to fulfil this duty; for the greater number it exists on paper only.

All these superficial objections to the public activity of women would be impossible, if the relationship of the two sexes were a natural one, instead of being an artificial antagonism, a position of master and servant, which keeps both socially apart from their earliest years. Christianity is chiefly responsible for this antagonism, inasmuch as it has made one sex a mystery to the other and forbids the free development of confidence and the mutual completion of different characteristics.

It will be one of the first and most important tasks of a rational society to abolish this fatal distinction between the sexes and reinstate Nature in her rights. The sin against Nature begins at school. First, separation of the sexes, and then either bad instruction or no instruction at all with regard to human beings as sexual creatures. It is true that natural history is taught at every moderately good school at the present day ; the child learns that birds lay eggs, and sit upon them ; it learns too when the time of pairing begins, that male and female pair together, that both together build the nest, sit on the eggs and care for the young brood. It learns further that mammals bear live young, it hears of the rutting season, and the fights of the males at that time ; it is told the ordinary number of young, perhaps too the length of pregnancy. But with regard to the origin and development of its own race it is kept entirely in the dark ; everything belonging to that subject remains hidden behind a veil of mystery. And when the child seeks to gratify its perfectly natural curiosity by questioning its parents, for it rarely ventures to question the teacher, it is put off with the silliest inventions, which cannot satisfy it, and the effect of which is all the more injurious when it one day learns the truth in spite of them. And there are very few children that have not learned the truth by the time they are twelve years old. Moreover, in every small town and in the country, from their earliest years the children observe the pairing of the fowls, the copulation of domestic animals in the closest proximity, in the farmyard, in the street, when the geese are driven into the fields. They listen, while their parents, the farm-servants, the elder brothers and sisters discuss the condition of the animals, the gratification of their periodical desires and the act of birth with the most unembarrassed plainness, as a subject of the gravest importance at the morning, mid-day and evening meal. All this arouses doubts in the child with regard to its mother's account of its own entrance into life. The day of understanding comes at last, but quite otherwise than it would have come under a natural and reasonable method of educacation. The child's secret leads to an estrangement between it and the parents, and especially between it and the mother. They have attained precisely the reverse of that which in their folly and short-sightedness they desired to attain. Anyone who recalls his own youth and that of his playfellows knows what the results frequently are.

There is a book written by an American woman in which

the authoress tells us among other things that in order to
satisfy the constant questionings of her little boy of eight
with regard to his origin, and to avoid telling him fables
which she regarded as immoral, she told him the whole truth.
She goes on to say that the child listened with the greatest
attention and from the day on which it heard what pain and
anxiety it had caused its mother, clung to her with an entirely
new tenderness and reverence, and had also shown the same
reverence towards other women. The writer starts from the
correct assumption that a natural education would of itself
suffice to bring about an essential improvement in the relations between men and women, and that one of its inevitable
results would be increased respect and self-control on the
part of the masculine sex towards the feminine.* No one who
is accustomed to think naturally and without prejudice can
come to any other conclusion.

From whatever standpoint we attempt the criticism of the
present state of things we find that the only possibility of
reform is a radical transformation of social conditions and
through it of sexual relationship. But as women left to
themselves would hardly ever reach the gaol, they are obliged
to look about them for allies. Now their natural allies are
the proletarians, themselves an oppressed class of men. The
workmen long since began to storm the fortress, Class-state,
which represents class rule as well as the rule of one sex
over the other. The fortress must be surrounded by trenches
and earthworks from all points, it must be compelled to surrender by artillery of every calibre. The army will find
officers and ammunition on all sides. Sociology and the
natural sciences, combined with modern historical research,
pedagogy and statistics are advancing from various directions,
philosophy does not lag behind, and hastens to announce the
realization of the ideal state in the near future in Mainländer's
" Philosophy of Redemption.'

The final overthrow and renovation of the modern class state
are being facilitated by discord in the ranks of its defenders,
who in spite of their common interest in the struggle against
a common enemy, are continually engaged in quarrelling over
the booty among themselves. The interest of one faction is
opposed to the interest of another. They are further facilitated
by the daily growing mutiny in the hostile troops, whose

---

* " Womanhood ; its Sanctities and Fidelities," by Isabella Beecher-
Hooker. Boston ; Lee and Shepard, publishers. New York ; Lee,
Shepard, and Dillingham, 1874.

soldiers are mostly bone of our bone and flesh of our flesh, who, misled and not recognizing whither they were going, have till now fought against us and themselves, but who are waking up more and more to a sense of their position. And last, but not least, we must mention the desertion from the ranks of the enemy of honers thinkers who have adopted our creed and who are impelled by greater information and larger culture to rise above low class interest and private egotism, and, following their ideal inclination, to join and instruct humanity that is thirsting for deliverance.

But as many do not yet fully recognize the stage of dissolution which State and Society have already reached, in spite of our frequent allusions to the dark spots in the picture, it is necessary to dwell a little longer on the subject. This we propose to do in the following chapter.

STATE AND SOCIETY.

In consequence of the rapid development which the social life of the community has passed through in all civilized countries during the last few decades, and which has caused a proportionately rapid advance in other branch of human activity, all our institutions are in a condition of fermentation and dissolution. Neither States nor individuals feel firm ground under their feet. A sensation of discomfort, uncertainty and discontent has taken possession of all circles, the highest as well as the lowest. There is no doubt about this. The violent efforts made by the ruling classes to patch and mend a state of things which has become intolerable to themselves prove vain and inadequate, and the consequent loss of confidence increases their perturbation and anxiety. No sooner have they set up a prop in the shape of one law or another to support the tottering house, than they discover that at ten other spots a support is still more needed. Meanwhile they are continually engaged in disputes and serious differences of opinion among each other. What seems necessary to one party, as a means of soothing and conciliating the more and more restless masses, is regarded by another as an undue concession, as indefensible weakness and compliance only calculated to rouse the thirst for more.

The Governments,—and not only the German Governments,—tremble like a reed in the wind; they are forced to seek supporters, for they cannot exist without them, and thus they lean sometimes to the one side, sometimes to the other. To-day one party is anvil, the other hammer; to-morrow all is reversed. The one pulls down what the other has with difficulty built up. Confusion is ever on the increase, discontent becomes more and more outspoken, the friction grows, augments, and wears out more workers in a few months than formerly in as many years. At the same time the calls on the private purse, in the shape of rates and taxes have increased enormously, out of all proportion to the increase in the population or in so-called national wealth.

And notwithstanding all this our statesmen appear lulled in remarkable illusions. With a view to sparing the propertied classes, they introduce and go on extending a system of taxation which in their opinion is not oppressive because the public in its ignorance does not clearly recognise its presence. But they forget that these taxes, being principally paid by the working classes, are unjust, and make themselves all the more felt, because they are reckoned by the head. They therefore empty the purse more quickly than an income tax and deteriorate the nourishment of the numbers by making food dearer and encouraging its adulteration. It is a matter of indifference to the treasury whether the father of a family pays 10 pfennige (1¼d.) in small daily instalments, or 365 times as much in the course of the year in much larger instalments. But it is not a matter of indifference to the taxpayer, whether the poor man pays one shilling, corresponding to his income, while the rich man makes up the difference. Instead of which, it is proposed to free the latter from both land and income tax. The influence of such a system must inevitably make itself felt. The discontent of the destitute makes the State responsible when indirect taxation becomes intolerable ; when indirect taxation exceeds certain limits the responsibility is cast on society as a whole, because the evil is felt to be a social one. That is progress. " The gods make blind those whom they doom to destruction."

Meanwhile one new organisation after another is introduced, but no old institution is radically abolished, no new institution is radically carried out. The requirements of civilization, which have grown up out of the national life, demand some consideration, if everything is not to be risked ; even [in a mutilated shape they necessitate the employment of large sums, all the more because our public organization is embarrassed by a crowd of parasites, who skim off the cream for themselves. But at the same time all unproductive institutions, which are in direct opposition to the claims of civilization, are not only retained, uncurtailed, on the contrary, they are proportionately extended, and become the more irksome and oppressive, the more distinctly they are recognized as superfluous by the growing insight of the people. Police, army, legal organization, prisons are being more and more widely spread, are becoming more and more costly ; the same thing applies to the rest of the administrative apparatus, without any corresponding increase in security at home or abroad. Indeed the contrary is the case.

The position of a large percentage of our municipalities is gradually becoming desperate ; they look about them in vain for the wherewithal to meet the annually increasing demands made upon them. This especially applies to the large towns in industrial districts, where the rapid growth of the population necessitates a number of improvements which the mostly poor communities are unable to carry out, without imposing fresh taxes and making fresh loans. The building of schools, the making of roads, gas, drainage, water supply, increased expenses for police and administration continue to absorb more from year to year. In addition to all this, the wealthy minority everywhere makes the most exorbitant demands on the community. It claims upper class public schools, theatres, elegant quarters of the town with corresponding provision for gas, pavements, etc. This preference, which the majority of the population is perfectly right to complain of, is an integral part of the present system of things. The minority has the power, and can seriously injure its opponents if it chooses to do so, inasmuch as it is in exclusive possession of the means of labour, on which the majority is dependant. Moreover, the administration is often far from perfect. The paid officials are frequently insufficient in number, or have not the necessary training for the manifold subjects with which they have to deal and which often require a special preparation. The unpaid officials and town councillors are generally so much engrossed by their own private concerns, that they are unable to devote the necessary time to the fulfilment of their duties towards the town. Such positions are not unfrequently made use of for the furtherance of private interests, to the serious detriment of the community. The consequences are borne by the ratepayers.

It is out of the question for modern Society to attempt any radical alteration of this state of things, such as would appear fairly satisfactory to all concerned ; in this respect it is utterly powerless ; it can do nothing short of abolishing itself, and that it cannot do. In whatever shape it raises taxes, discontent is certain to grow. In a few decades most of these municipalities will be unable to meet the demands made on them in the present form of taxation and administration. Within the limits of local government the necessity for radical reconstruction will make itself much more rapidly felt than in the machinery of central government. The present system is fast approaching bankruptcy. We shall show later on what will and must take its place.

This is a short but accurate sketch of the condition of affairs in state and commune and both are but mirrors and prototypes of the conditions in social life.

    *   *   *   *   *   *

In social life the struggle for existence is daily assuming more gigantic dimensions. The war of all against all has broken out with the utmost violence; it is waged pitilessly, with every weapon that comes to hand. The well known saying: " Ote-toi de là que je m'y mette " is translated into the practice of life with lusty elbowing, pushing, and kicking. The weaker must give way to the stronger. Where physical force, or its synonyms, the power of money and of property will not suffice, the most cunning and rascally means are employed, lies, swindling, deceit, perjury, forgery, and even the worst crimes, such as getting rid of inconvenient witnesses or other hindrances, by false declarations of insanity and murder. And just as individuals contend with each other, in this struggle for existence, so does class contend with class, sex with sex, age with age. Profit and advantage become the only regulators of human feelings and to them every other consideration must give way. Thousands and thousands of working men and women are then turned out of doors, and after they have pawned their last shirt and their last piece of furniture are reduced to accepting public charity, or are forced to quit the country. Troops of workmen journey from place to place, through the length and breath of the land; the longer they have been out of work, the more ragged is their appearance and the more demoralized are they themselves; " respectable people " regard them with terror and disgust. " Respectable people " have not the slightest idea what it means to be compelled to dispense for months with the most primitive requirements of order and cleanliness, to tramp with an empty stomach from place to place, and as a rule to meet nothing but scarcely concealed dislike and contempt from those who are themselves the pillars of this rotten system. Meanwhile the families of the married men suffer the most terrible want, which not rarely drives the parents in despair to commit the most fearful crimes on their children and themselves. The last few years have furnished numerous horrible examples.* Women and

---

* Let us quote one case for many. The copyist S. in Berlin, 45 years of age, married to a still beautiful wife of 39, and father of a daughter of 12, is out of work and near starvation. The wife, with the consent of the

girls are driven to prostitution, crime and demoralization take a hundred different shapes, and all that prospers are the jails, prisons, and so called houses of correction, which can no longer contain the number of their inmates.

The " Leipziger Zeitung " for the 17th April, 1878, gives a dark but perfectly accurate picture of the state of things in the Saxon Voigtland, shewing all the rottenness and help-lessness of our present social system.

" The destitution among our weavers is nothing new; it has very little to do with the present depression of trade ; it is caused by the fact that machinery is supplanting and must supplant hand weaving. The present weaver popula-tion must therefore take up other branches of labour. The weavers who are too old to do this can only be helped by charity. But besides this there is a considerable number of good workmen, partly or entirely out of employment, owing to want of work in weaving. Work must be found for these men ; their faculties must be turned to account, and we hope and trust that industrial employers, incited by the present destitution, will enquire into the case, and consider whether our good and cheap workmen—for the Voigtlandic workman is industrious and easily contented—could not be advan-tageously employed in their factories."

This is a picture of the modern course of development, as sad as it is possible to imagine, and yet it is one sample for a hundred. The work which the industrious and " easily contented " Voigtlandic workman is to get from the capitalist only puts others out of work. That is the circulus vitiosus.

The increase of crimes of every description is intimately connected with the social conditions of the community, little as the latter is inclined to believe it. Society hides its head in the sand, like the ostrich, in order not to be forced to recognize a state of things which bears witness against it, and silences its own conscience and others' with the lying pretence that laziness and love of pleasure on the part of the workmen and their want of religion is accountable for every-thing. This is hypocrisy of the most revolting kind, but it is

husband, resolves to prostitute herself. The police hears of it, and she is inscribed on the register. Shame and despair take possession of the family ; they all three decide to poison themselves, and execute the plan on the 1st March, 1883. A few days before the aristocratic society of Berlin had been celebrating great court festivals, at which hundreds of thousands were squandered. These are the appalling contrasts in modern society but nevertheless we live in " the best of worlds " nevertheless preached with the greatest seriousness. The more unfavourable and depressed the condition of society, the more numerous and grave do crimes become. The struggle for existence then assumes its most brutal and violent shape, it throws man back into his primæval state, in which each regarded the other as his deadly enemy. The ties of solidarity, not too firm at the best of times, become daily looser.*

The ruling classes, who do not and will not recognise the causes of things, attempt to effect a change by employing force against the products of these conditions, and even men whom we should expect to be enlightened and free from pre-judice, are ready to support the system. Professor Häckel, for instance† regards the stringent application of capital punish-ment as desirable, and harmonizes in this point with the reactionaries of every shade, who on all other subjects are his bitterest enemies. According to his theory, hopeless criminals and ne'er-do-weels must be rooted out like weeds, which deprive the more valuable plants of light, air, and soil. If Professor Häckel had occupied himself even to a slight degree with the study of social science, instead of limiting himself exclusively to natural science, he would have discovered that all these criminals could be transformed into useful, valuable members of society, if society offered them more favourable means of existence. He would have found that the annihilation of the criminal has just as little effect on crime, *i.e.*, on the development of fresh crimes, as if on a number of farms the ground were superficially cleared of weeds, while the roots and seeds remained undestroyed. Man will never be able absolutely to prevent the develop-ment of noxious organisms in nature, but it is unquestionably within his power so to improve a social organism created by himself, that it may afford equally favourable conditions of existence and an equal freedom of growth to all ; that no one

---

* Even Plato foresaw the consequences of such a condition of things He writes : " A state in which classes exist is not one but two. The poor constitute one state and the rich another, and both, living in the closest proximity, are constantly on the watch against each other. The ruling class is finally unable to go to war, because to do so it requires the services of the mass, which, when armed, inspires it with more terror than the enemy."—Plato, " Republic." And Aristotle says : " Wide-spread im-poverishment is a disadvantage, inasmuch as it is hardly ever possible to prevent such people from becoming agitators."—Aristotle, " Politics."

† " Natürliche Schöpfungsgeschichte." (Natural History of Creation.) Fourth, revised edition, Berlin, 1873, pp. 155-6.

may be forced to gratify his hunger or his desire of possession or his ambition at the expense of some one else. People only need to investigate the causes of crime and to remove them, and they will abolish crime itself.*

Naturally those who seek to abolish crime by abolishing its causes cannot take kindly to measures of brutal suppression. They cannot prevent society from protecting itself against crime in its own way, but they demand all the more urgently the radical reformation of society, *i.e.*, the removal of the causes.

Now the reason for the untenability of our social conditions is the capitalistic system. Whoever is in possession of large pecuniary means rules over all those whose means are smaller or who possess nothing. He buys the labour of the destitute, as an article of trade, at a price which is regulated, like that of any other article of trade, by the law of supply and demand. This price is subject to slight oscillations, being sometimes higher and sometimes lower than the cost of production ; the surplus value of the labour product goes into the pocket of the capitalist, in the shape of interest, undertaker's profits, house and ground rent. With the help of this surplus value, extracted from the workman, which gradually crystallizes into capital, the manufacturer buys fresh workmen, and, armed with a more complete division of labour, with machines, with technical improvements, in short, with a well organized system of production, he advances against his less wealthy competitor like a knight in full accoutrement against an un-armed foot soldier and crushes him. This unequal struggle is gaining ground on all sides, and women's labour, the cheapest, next to the labour of children, is playing a more and more important part in it. The result of this state of things is the increasing separation between a small minority of powerful capitalists and a large majority of destitute individuals of both sexes who depend for their subsistence on the daily sale of their labouring power. The position of the middle classes is meanwhile becoming more and more critical. One branch of production after another, which was hitherto the domain of petty industry, is becoming the prey of capitalists among themselves. Small, independent artisans are being crushed and forced into the class of day labourers,

---

* Plato remarks on this subject :—" The causes of crimes are want of culture, bad education, and the bad institutions of the State." We see that he knew more about the nature of Society than his learned successors twenty-three hundred years later. Hardly a subject for congratulation.

unless they are able to take refuge in some other independent branch, which is daily becoming more difficult if not impossible. All attempts to escape from the process of absorption, which acts with the force of a natural law, by the help of institutions and apparatus from the lumber-room of the past, are ridiculous child's play. The well-meant, often repeated counsel to ward off fate by the exercise of greater artistic skill or the application of cheap motor powers only shows want of comprehension for the situation. The perfected machine replaces the skilful hand, whose products moreover are too dear for a large market; and the application of cheap motor power only increases the competition of small producers among each other, and hastens their ruin. In December, 1882, 414 industrial and trading establishments were announced in München as having ceased, and only 315 as having commenced, in other words, a reduction of 99 independent establishments in one town in one month. And the condition of the existing small establishments is illustrated by the fact, that in ten cases of death, nine proprietors are proved to have died insolvent, but their bankruptcy is rarely published, because no one has an interest in the publication. There is nothing to be had. For the same reason the ruin of many living proprietors takes place unnoticed and unregistered.

That which has escaped the devouring force of capital is finally crushed by the gluts which occur from time to time. These gluts become more frequent and more intense in proportion to the increasing power and influence of production on a large scale, and the danger of over-production, the result of blind production *en masse*. This danger is a constantly growing one and recurs at shorter and shorter intervals. Both the moderately well-to-do and the struggling manufacturer, with their small capacities for holding out, cannot but succumb rapidly to a glut.

The gluts arise because there are no means of estimating the real demand for an article at a given moment. In the first place the customers are spread over a wide area, and their purchasing power, on which their power of consumption depends, is modified by a number of factors, which the single producer is entirely unable to ascertain. In the second place, besides himself there exists a number of other single producers, with regard to whose powers of production, both in respect to quantity and quality, he is also quite in the dark. Each one of these makes every exertion of which he is capable—cheap prices, enormous advertisements, long credit, the employment of commercial travellers, or even the underhand and fraudulent depreciation of his competitor's productions, a weapon which is made considerable use of in critical times—with a view to driving the others from the field. Thus is our entire production at the mercy of chance, and the personal judgment of the single producer.

But this chance proves just as often unfavourable as favourable. Every single producer is obliged to sell a certain amount of wares, under which he cannot exist. But he endeavours to sell a much larger quantity, firstly because this ensures him much larger profits, and secondly because the probability of triumphing over his competitors and finally maintaining the field is thereby increased. For a time his sale is assured, possibly it is growing; this induces him still further to enlarge his business, to produce still greater masses than before, The good times, however, do not influence him alone, but induce all competitors to make similar exertions. Suddenly it becomes apparent that the market is overstocked with goods. The sale falls off, the price sinks, production is slackened. Lessening the production in any branch means lessening the number of workmen, lowering the wages, and limiting the consumption on the part of those affected. A depression of production and sale in other branches is the necessary consequence. Small artisans of every kind, tradesmen, eatinghouse keepers, bakers, butchers, etc., whose customers are workmen, lose their customers and with them their lucrative trade.

One industry provides another with its raw materials ; one depends upon the other, consequently one must suffer from the depression of the other. The circle of those who are affected and injured becomes wider and wider. A number of obligations undertaken in the hope that the previous state of things might be of longer duration, cannot be fulfilled ; thus the crisis feeds itself, and assumes larger dimensions from month to month. An enormous mass of stored up wares, implements, and machines becomes pretty well worthless. The wares are got rid of at ruination prices ; the ruin does not touch only the single producer, but a dozen others who are now also compelled, by his reckless sale, to throw away their goods under cost price. During the glut the methods of production are being constantly improved, as the only means of meeting the heightened competition, and this again becomes the source of fresh and more extensive gluts. After the glut has lasted for years, and the over-production has been gradually relieved by a sale at all costs, by the limitation of production and the annihilation of the smaller manufacturers, society slowly begins to recover. The demand increases, and production increases at the same time. At first, gradually and cautiously, but with the apparent permanence of the good times, the old story begins anew, everyone wishes to make good what he has lost, and hopes to save himself before a fresh crisis breaks out. But as all producers are impelled by the same desire, and each improves his means of production in order the better to compete with the others, the catastrophe is conjured up again, more rapidly than before and with more destructive results. Numberless existences come up like bubbles and burst, and this constantly changing play presents the terrible picture which we witness in every glut. And these gluts becomes more numerous, as we have already said, in proportion to the increase of pro-duction *en masse*, and to the increasing violence of the competitive struggle, raging not only between individuals but between entire nations. The fight both for customers on a small scale, and for empire in the markets of the world, is constantly growing more bitter, and involves gigantic losses. And while enormous quantities of wares and victuals are stored up, the great mass of humanity suffers hunger and want.

One can hardly imagine a more final condemnation of this social condition than the remark made by most men of business during such periods ; " We have too many competitors ; half of them must be ruined, if the others are to exist." In speaking thus, each one takes for granted, as a good christian citizen should, that his competitor will be ruined and he himself rescued. The same cynicism is contained in the serious assurance of the newspapers that, for instance in the European cotton industry, there are at least fifteen million spindles too many and that those must be destroyed before the remainder can be sufficiently employed. And the same people tell us that our iron and coal works are twice as numerous as they ought to be, to ensure a lucrative business. According to these doctrines then, we have too much trade, too many producers, too good means of production, and too many wares, and yet all complain of want. Is it not apparent that our social organization suffers from serious infirmities ? How can there be a question of over-production when there is no lack of consuming power, properly so called, *i. e.*, of needs. Clearly it is not the production itself, but the form in which we produce, and still more the manner in which we distribute the products which causes this vicious and contradictory state of affairs.

$*$ $*$ $*$ $*$ $*$ $*$

In human society all individuals are bound together by a thousand ties, which become the more numerous in proportion to the higher state of civilization which a nation attains. When a disturbance occurs, it makes itself felt at once by all members of the community. Disturbances in the present form of production react on distribution and consumption and *vice versâ*. The characteristic of modern production is its tendency to become concentrated in fewer and fewer hands and in increasingly large productive establishments. In distribution an apparently opposite tendency seems gaining ground. The man who is erased from the list of independent producers by annihilating competition makes desperate efforts in nine cases out of ten to edge himself in as trader between producer and consumer, and thus gain a scanty subsistence.

Hence the remarkable fact of the enormous increase of middlemen, who do business on a small, often on the pettiest scale, of tradesmen, little shopkeepers, hucksters, dealers, brokers, agents, publicans, ginhouse keepers, etc. The majority of these persons among whom there is a large contingent of women as independent proprietors of shops, leads an anxious and miserable life, in which there is more appearance than reality. Many, in order to exist at all, are compelled to speculate on the lowest of human passions, and to further them by all the means in their power. Hence too the spread of a revolting system of advertizing especially in all those branches the object of which is the gratification of sensual appetites.

It cannot be denied that the desire for greater enjoyment in life is deeply implanted in modern society, and regarded from a higher point of view, this tendency is only calculated to awaken satisfaction. People are beginning to comprehend that a human being has a claim to the decencies and comforts of life, aud they give expression to this recognition conformably to their social standard of enjoyment. But society has become much more aristocratic under the growth of its wealth than it was at any former period. The gulf between the richest and the poorest is greater to-day than ever before, while on the other hand society

has become much more democratic in its ideas and laws.*
But the mass demands greater equality, not only in theory
but also in practice, and in its ignorance, it seeks to
attain this equality, in imitation of the upper classes, in
procuring every enjoyment within its reach. A thousand
artificial stimulants are provided for the purpose of turning
this impulse to account, and the consequences are apparent
everywhere.

The gratification of a natural instinct, perfectly justifiable
in itself, leads in numerous cases to trouble and crime, and
ruling society intervenes in its own way, because it is unable
to do so in a more reasonable way, without undermining its
own present existence.

The daily increasing number of middlemen has other evils
in its train. Although this numerous class as a rule leads an
extremely hard and overworked life, it is nevertheless throughout all its ranks a class of parasites, *whose activity is unproductive
and which lives from the products of others' labour, just as much as
the capitalist class does.*

As an inevitable consequence articles of clothing and of
food rise in price to an altogether disproportionate extent, till
they often cost the purchaser twice and three times as much
as the producer received for them.† And when it is not
advisable or possible to raise the price materially, depreciation
and adulteration of the necessaries of life, false measure and
weight are the means of making the profits that cannot be
had in any other way.‡   Thus have swindle and fraud

---

* Prof. Adolf Wagner expresses the same thought in his revised edition
of Rau's "Lehrbuch der Politischen Œkonomie" (Handbook of Political
Economy.) He says, p. 361 : "The social question is the recognized contradiction between our economic development and the social principle of
development in the form of freedom and equality, which hovers above us
as an ideal, and which is already attaining realization in political life."

† Dr. E. Sachs, in his work "Die Haus industrie in Thüringen"
(Domestic Industry in Thüringen) informs his readers among other things,
that in the year 1869 the production of 244½ millions of slate pencils
represented 122,000 to 200,000 florins (£10,370 to £17,000) labour wages for
the producers, but that the final price at which the pencils were sold by
the last dealers rose to 1,200,000 florins (£102,000) *i.e.*, at least six-fold as
much as the producer received.

‡ The chemist Chevalier tells us that among the very various kinds of
adulteration of food which exist, he is acquainted with 32 for coffee, 30 for
wine, 28 for chocolate, 24 for flour, 23 for brandy, 20 for bread, 19 for
milk, 10 for butter, 9 for olive oil, 6 for sugar, &c., &c. The Wesel
Chamber of Commerce reported in 1870 that the chief fraud in the sale of
weighed goods takes place in the shops of small shopkeepers, who give 24

become an inevitable social institution as much as prostitution, and certain State regulations, such as high indirect taxes and finance taxes are the immediate means of promoting them. No laws against the adulteration of food will be of much avail. In the first place, stringent measures only force the adulterators to employ more cunning in their methods, and in the second, a thorough and strict inspection cannot be expected under present conditions. Most respectable and influential circles of our ruling classes have their interests engaged in the system of deception. Accordingly every really serious control is rendered illusory by the objection, that it could only be carried out by an extensive and expensive executive apparatus under which legitimate business would suffer as much the adulterators. And wherever such laws and measures of control are really brought to bear, the result will be a considerable rise in the price of unadulterated goods, because only adulteration made the lower prices possible.

The co-operative companies are of very little use ; their business management is generally deficient, and they do not touch those who are most in need of help, the working classes. The so-called Housewives' Associations for obtaining unadulterated and cheaper goods by purchasing on a large scale have the same tendency. They are merely a symptom of the recognition that is gaining ground among large classes of women, that the intervention of the tradesman, and I might add trade altogether, is useless and injurious. It is certain that the best form of society would be one in which the products reached the consumers in as direct a manner as possible. The next step would be, not only to purchase the goods in common, but also to prepare them on a large scale for a common table.

*   *   *   *   *   *   *

The foregoing remarks on our social organization have reference only to the condition of trade and industry ; the condition of agriculture remains untouched. This too has

---

or 26 ounces instead of 30 to a pound, and thus manage to indemnify themselves doubly for a reduction in price. Workmen and poor people who are obliged to buy on credit, and therefore to hold their peace, even when this cheating is carried on before their eyes, are the victims of the system. Disgraceful deception with false weight and adulterated flour is especially practised among bakers.

been already influenced to a large extent by our modern development. The crises in trade, commerce and industry make themselves felt in the country as well as in the town. Many members of farmers' families are partly or entirely occupied in trading or industrial establishments, and this kind of employment is becoming more and more common. The large landed proprietors find it extremely profitable to transform an important part of the produce of the soil into industrial products on their own ground. In the first place they save the considerable expense of carriage for the raw material, for instance, potatoes for spirit, beetroot for sugar, grain for flour, or brandy, or beer, etc., etc., in the second place, labour is cheaper and the labourers more amenable to authority than in the towns or the industrial districts. Factories and rents are also considerably cheaper; rates and taxes are lower, the landed proprietor in the country being to a certain extent at once lawgiver and executor of the law, and wielding the all-important police power. Hence the fact that the number of factory chimneys in the country increases from year to year, and that the connection between agriculture and industry is becoming more and more intimate. The advantages of the change are at present only reaped by the large landed proprietor.

It requires no particular sagacity to discover, that when the landed proprietor finds himself in the agreeable position of being able to improve his income on his own ground, his appetite for the property of his poorer neighbour grows. This neighbour occupies the same position towards him as the small handicraftsman towards the capitalistic manufacturer.

Moreover the country has not remained untouched by our growing civilization, even in its remotest corners. We have already mentioned that when the peasant's son returns home to the far-off country village after three years spent in town and barracks, the atmosphere of which he has hardly found impregnated with higher morality, he frequently comes as the bearer and spreader of venereal disease. On the other hand he has become acquainted with a number of new ideas and requirements of civilization, which he desires to gratify in the future as far as possible. The extended and improved means of traffic are another factor in the spread of civilization. The countryman sees the world and receives all kind of fresh impressions. Then again the peasants feel the pressure of higher taxation in State, province and parish. For instance

the communal taxes of country districts in Prussia, which in
1849 amounted to 8,400,000 thaler (£1,260,000), had risen to
23,118,000 thaler (£3,466,500) in 1867. The contributions of
town and country parishes for provincial, district, and communal purposes had risen from 16,000,000 to 46,000,000 thaler
(£2,400,000 to £6,900,000) within the same time. The
average sum of local expenses had risen from 2.96 marks
(2s. 11¼d.) to 7.05 mark (7s. ¾d.) per head. And since then
these amounts have been considerably raised.

It is true that the produce of the soil has also risen considerably in value during the same period, but not in proportion to the increase in rates and taxes. Moreover the
peasant does not receive the price which the town pays for
his products; indeed he receives far less than the large
landed proprietor. The jobber or dealer who travels through
the country on particular days or at particular seasons, and
as a rule sells again to other dealers, must have his profit;
besides it is much more trouble for him to collect a number
of small quantities than for the large proprietor to sell his
own produce. All this affects the price. The peasant
mortgages a portion of his land to gain money for improvements; he has no great choice of creditors and is accordingly
unable to make favourable conditions. High interest and
fixed times for repayment fill him with constant anxiety, a
single bad harvest, or a false speculation in the crop for
which he has reckoned on a good price, bring him to the
brink of ruin. Frequently the purchaser of the ground
produce and the lender of capital is one and the same
person, the peasant is therefore at the mercy of his creditor.
The small proprietors of whole villages and districts are
often in the hands of a few creditors, for instance a large
number of the hop, vine, and tobacco growers in South
Germany, the vegetable gardeners on the Rhine. The
mortgagee drains them to the last drop, and leaves them as
mock possessors on the little piece of land that in fact no
longer belongs to them. The capitalistic vampire finds it
more convenient and more profitable to do business in this
way than to take possession of the land and cultivate or sell
it. Thus many thousands of proprietors figure in our
official lists, who in reality are proprietors no longer. It is
true, many a large proprietor who does not understand his
business also becomes the prey of a blood-thirsty capitalist.
The capitalist becomes master of the soil and divides it into
smaller plots, with a view to making double profits, inasmuch

as a large number of small proprietors pay better than one large one. In the same way houses in the town with many small dwellings bring in the highest rent. There is always a number of small proprietors who take advantage of the occasion. The beneficent capitalist is willing to let them have the land in return for a small payment in ready money ; the remainder is left as a mortgage at a good rate of interest to be paid off by degrees. This is the secret of the transaction. If the small proprietor has luck, if he succeed, with the greatest exertions, in getting profitable harvests, or, very occasionally, in borrowing the money cheaper elsewhere, he may save himself ; if he cannot, he suffers the fate already described.

The death of one or more sheep or cows is a very serious loss ; if his daughter marries, his debts are increased, and he loses a cheap servant ; if a son marries, he claims his piece of land ; necessary improvements cannot be carried out ; if the cattle do not provide sufficient manure, which is hardly ever the case, the crops become scanty, for manure is too dear to buy ; he can rarely afford to purchase a better and more productive seed ; he must dispense with the use of machines ; a change of crops, corresponding to the chemical composition of his soil, is frequently beyond his reach. He is equally unable to apply the advantages offered by science and experience to improving the condition of his animals. Want of suitable fodder, want of proper stalls, want of all the necessary arrangements make it impossible. We see there are many causes which bring the peasant proprietors of middle sized and small farms into debt, which place them at the mercy of the capitalistic extortioner or of the large proprietor, and finally ruin them altogether.

The assertion which some people are fond of supporting by statistical figures, that the increasing concentration of landed property is a fiction, inasmuch as there are at present more proprietors than formerly, proves nothing against the foregoing arguments. In the first place, we have already called attention to the fact that thousands of persons who have ceased to be proprietors are still registered as such, and secondly, the increase in the population and the consequent subdivision of the land which occurs in cases of death must be taken into account in dealing with the numbers in question. But those very subdivisions contain the germ of ruin for the proprietor, the smaller a property is, the greater being the difficulty of existing upon it. Since the introduction of freedom of trading, the number of small master workmen has also increased considerably in many branches, but it would be a mistake to conclude from this that their prosperity had increased correspondingly. On the contrary, only the competition among them has increased, and facilitated their annihilation and absorption by large capital.

Therefore if there are sometimes two or three proprietors at present where there was formerly but one, this is very far from signifying that the two or three are better off than the one was before. We may always take the contrary for granted. The unfavourable conditions which we have described, and which are inseparably connected with the circumstances of the case, doom such proprietors to speedy decline. Moreover we must not forget that subdivision is carried on to a great extent in the neighbourhood of large towns where arable land is converted into gardens or building plots. This may be an advantage to solitary proprietors, and of course it increases the number of proprietors, but such changes have no influence on the position of the mass. Again, such pieces of land frequently pass into the hands of speculating capitalists, before the original owner is able to rescue his property or has any idea of its real value.

It is evident that this process of development must be especially disadvantageous to women in country places. The prospect open to them is that of exchanging the position of the independent proprietress or housewife with that of the maid-servant, or cheap factory hand in the agricultural or industrial employ of the large landowner. As a sexual being she is on the whole even more exposed to the illegitimate desires and claims of the master and his employés than in town factories, although there too at the present day a Turkish harem system has established itself in the midst of Christian Europe, and the right of possession in labour is frequently extended to the right of possession in the whole person. In the country the woman is far more isolated than the woman in the town. The court of justice is represented by her employer or a friend of his, there are no newspapers and there is no public opinion to which she could turn for protection, and the workmen themselves are mostly in a state of degrading servility. Heaven is high and the Czar far off.

But the condition of the country and of agriculture is of the very highest importance in the development of our entire civilization. The whole population depends in the first place on the soil and its produce. The soil cannot be increased at will. All the more serious is the question as to how it may be best cultivated and turned to the greatest advantage. We have already reached a stage at which a considerable yearly importation of bread and meat has become inevitable, if we are to prevent a still greater rise in price than that which has already taken place.

We have to deal with two important antagonistic interests, that of the agricultural and that of the industrial population. It is an essential interest of the industrial population, in fact of the entire non-agricultural population to have cheap food ; upon this depends not only the welfare of the human beings which compose it, but the prosperity of these human beings as trading and industrial individuals. Every rise in the price of food either entails a still greater deterioriation in the nourishment of a large portion of the community, than that already existing, or wages and consequently the price of industrial products are so far raised that the sale falls off on account of the increased difficulty of competing with foreign countries. The matter has quite another aspect for the agriculturist. Just as the manufacturer desires to make as large profits as possible out of his factory, the agriculturist desires to do the same out of his land and labour, or the labour of his workmen, and it is all the same to him which product best serves this end. If the importation of foreign corn or foreign meat prevents him from obtaining the prices which he considers desirable or necessary from the cultivation of grain or the breeding of cattle, he gives up cattle-breeding and grain-growing and devotes his soil to the cultivation of some other product which is of more advantage to himself. He plants beetroot for the manufacture of sugar, potatoes, and rye for spirit, instead of wheat and rye for bread. He sacrifices the most fertile fields to the growth of tobacco, instead of using them for vegetable and garden produce. Then again thousands of acres are turned into pasture land for horses, because horses fetch a high price for military purposes. On the other hand large tracts of forest, that might easily be made arable, are reserved for the hunting sport of aristocratic gentlemen, mostly in districts in which a few hundred acres of wood might be cleared and converted into cultivated soil without any detrimental effect on the rain supply of the neighbourhood.

With regard to the rain supply the most recent investigations of the Forest Department, based on extensive practical experiments, make it questionable whether the influence of woods on the development of moisture is so great as has been assumed. It is now stated that woods should only be preserved on a large scale in districts in which the nature of the soil excludes the growth of useful crops, or where it is a question of covering hilly or mountainous land with some kind of cultivation which has an economic value and prevents the water from flowing off too rapidly. If this view be correct, many thousand square kilometres of fruitful soil might still be devoted to agricultural purposes in Germany. But this conversion does not coincide with the interests of a well-paid body of officials, or with the hunting interests of the large landowners, who refuse to sacrifice their hunting grounds and their sport.

The practical aspect which these conditions have gradually assumed may be gathered from the following facts, which refer specially to Germany and Austria. In 1861 there were in the old Prussian provinces:

18,289	estates of	600 Morgen* and more, together	40,921,536	Morgen
15,076	,,	300—600 ,,	,,	6,047,317	,,
391,586	,,	30—300 ,,	,,	35,914,889	,,
424,951				82,883,742	

O.1 the other hand :

617,374	estates of	5—30 Morgen, together	..	8,427,479	Morgen
1,099,161	,,	under 5 ,, ,,	..	2,227,981	,,
1,716,535				10,655,460	

Thus we see that 424,951 proprietors were in possession of eight times as much land as 1,716,535 proprietors.

In this calculation the State figures as the owner of 1,156,150 morgen excluding the forests, while the province of Westphalia, with 143,498 town and country estates, and 2,959,890 morgen is not included. The table shows the enormous preponderance of middle-sized and large estates in Prussia, which, in fact, represent the greatest part of the entire land. This distribution was re-adjusted by the annexations of 1866, still more in favour of the large land-owners, for in the province of Hannover there were in 1867 no fewer than 13,100 estates of more than 120 morgen each, and in Schleswig-Holstein there were alone 300 estates in the possession of noble families without counting the landed property of rich peasant proprietors. In Saxony, in 1860-70,

---

* The Prussian Morgen equals 3,917 hectares.—Translator.

there were 228,36 square miles* in the hands of private owners; 942 noble owners possessed 43.24 square miles, *i.e.*, nearly a fifth of the entire area, again without counting the peasant farmers. In Mecklenburg-Schwerin matters are even worse. Out of 244 square miles of land the domanium and seven cloisters possess 107.78 square miles, and forty town territories and crown-lands amount to 26.45 square miles. Among 15,685 landowners (over 6,000 hereditary tenant-farmers and over 6,000 cottagers); there are only 630 free proprietors. In Bohemia the Church has more than 106,000 Joch† in its possession, and 1,269 large feudal owners together have 3,058,088 Joch, *i.e.*, one-third of the entire country. Nevertheless they contribute only 4 millions to the land-tax, which amounts to 14 million florins (£1,190,000). More than half the land possessed by noble families s divided among 150 owners, the property of Prince Schwarzenberg alone covers 29½ square miles. The forests of the country amount to 260 square miles, and 200 square miles are in the hands of the aristocracy. They consist of magnificent, far-famed hunting grounds. Similar conditions obtain in Silesia, Poland, the province of Prussia, &c. Emigration is taking place, *en masse*, especially from Bohemia and the German provinces on the Baltic; these populations are for the most part poor, while fertile land is lying waste or as good as waste, because it is the property of a private person, who can afford to squander the riches of his soil. Other landlords again make workmen superfluous by the introduction of machines or by the conversion of arable land into pasture.

The extent to which " hands " are in fact becoming super-fluous in agriculture and the industries connected with it, is shown among other things by the report of the Brunswick Factory Inspectors for 1881, in which it is stated that in spite of the considerable increase in the production of sugar, the number of workmen employed has been reduced by more than 3,000, solely in consequence of improved methods of production. The same experience is being made wherever agriculture is carried out on a large scale. The growing use of machinery, the planting of large areas with the same crop effects a considerable economy in the workmen's time, the farm-servants are reduced to the number indispensable for attending to the farmyard and the cattle, and the day

---

* A German geographical mile equals 7.4 kilometres.

† The Austrian Joch (Yoke) equals 0.57 hectare.—Translator.

labourers are dismissed. At harvest time these day labourers are called together from all parts of the country, overworked for a short period and again dismissed. Thus a country proletariat of the worst kind is being developed in Germany, precisely like that which already exists in England. If these labourers demand high wages, because they are sought after, and on account of their short employment, people are indignant at their presumption ; after their dismissal, when they wander about hungry and on the outlook for work, they are called vagabonds, abused, often driven from the yard with dogs, given over to the police as idlers who refuse to work, and and accordingly sent to the workhouse. A pretty " order " of things.

The application of the capitalistic system to the land leads to a capitalistic state of affairs in another direction. Many of our great landowners, for instance, have for years made enormous profits out of the cultivation of beetroot and the production of sugar. Moreover the mode of taxation* favours exportation. These results did not pass unnoticed ; the experiment was quickly repeated. Many hundred thousand hectares of land, which had hitherto been devoted to the cultivation of grain and potatoes, were turned into beetroot fields, factories were built everywhere, and are still being built, and the necessary consequence will be a tremendous glut which must inevitably occur sooner or later. Further, the beetroot cultivation causes a rise in the price of land, the result is that a number of small properties, whose owners were too poor to join the game, were bought up. While the ground is being thus placed at the service of industrial speculation, grain and potatoes are restricted to soil of inferior quality and the natural consequence is the increased importation of food from abroad. The supply grows with the demand. The enormous importation of foreign produce, and the cheap carriage permit a system of low prices, at which the landowners at home, with his burden of mortgages and taxes, his inferior soil, his frequently faulty organization and deficient farming is simply unable to exist. The next step is to tax the foreign importation, a process which benefits the rich agriculturist alone. The small agriculturist has no advantage whatever from this taxation, which presses heavily on the non-agricultural population.

---

* Taxation of home consumption, sugar bounties on exported sugar, the latter higher than the former.—Translator.

The advantage of the few is the injury of the many, and the small proprietor continues his retrograde course as though nothing had happened. No elixir can be found for him. The benefits which the large landowner gets from protection, prohibited importation, and restrictive measures of all kinds enable him to buy up the small proprietor with all the more ease, while the latter. who generally produces for his own needs alone, profits little or nothing from these measures. In Cisleithanian Austria, with the exception of Dalmatia and Vorarlberg, the number of estates sold in consequence of bankruptcy amounted in 1874 to 4720. It rose in 1877 to 6977, and in 1879 reached the considerable height of 11,272. More than 90 per cent. were farms. In 1874 4413 peasant properties were sold in Cisleithanian Austria, in consequence of bankruptcy, with an average of 3136 florins (£266) debts each. In 1878, 9090 properties were thus sold, with an average of 4290 florins (£364) debts each. The sum of mortgage claims which remained unpaid on account of insufficient returns amounted in 1874 to 4,679,753 florins (£397,779), 33.8 per cent. of the whole debt. In 1878 the loss had aisen to 20,366,173 florins (£1,731,128) or 52.2 per cent. of the whole debt. In Hungary, as early as 1876 no fewer than 12,000 estates were sold in consequence of bankruptcy, and the number of the population occupied in agriculture had sunk from 4,417,574 in 1870, to 3,669,117 in 1880, i. e., in ten years 748,457, or 17 per cent. And this took place in spite of a considerable increase in the area of cultivated land during the same period. The soil passed into the hands of large capitalists and magnates, who employed machines instead of men. The men became superflous. Quite Irish conditions.

According to the report of the Minister of Finance in the Bavarian Parliament on the 24th February 1881, in the year 1878, 698 properties with 27,000 Tagwerken* were sold by auction, in other words the cultivation of these properties had not covered their expenses. In 1880, the number of properties sold by auction in Bavaria was 3722, representing 5000 hectares of arable land. In consequence of these conditions a great deal of land remains uncultivated. In Bavaria, for instance, in 1879, there were 698 properties, together 8043 hectares, and in 1880, 953 properties, together 6000 hectares lying entirely uncultivated. It is hardly

---

* A Bavarian Tagwerk equal 2,935 hectares.—Translator

necessary to point out that all over-mortgaged land will be most inadequately attended to.

But whatever the landowner desires to do with his land is his own affair, his right, in the era of "sacred" private property. What does the community and its welfare concern him ; he has to attend to himself—so clear the way. The manufacturer acts on the same principle, when he makes obscene pictures and immoral books, or builds whole factories for the adulteration of food. These and many other employments are injurious to society ; they undermine morality and feed corruption. But what does it matter. There is more money to be made by them than by moral pictures, scientific books, or the honest sale of unadulterated goods. The manufacturer wants to make money, and as long as he can avoid detection by the keen eye of the police, he may carry on his disreputable trade in peace, with the assurance that he will be envied and respected by society on account of the money thus earned.

Nothing characterizes the Mammon-Worship of our age in this direction better than the Exchange and the business carried on there. The produce of the soil, manufactures, means of transport, the condition of the weather and of politics, want and superfluity, the destitution of the mass, accidents, public debts, inventions and discoveries, the health, sickness and death of influential persons, wars and rumours of wars, often invented solely for this purpose, all this and a great deal more is made the object of speculation, of exploitation, of mutual fraud and extortion. The matadores of capital here gain a decisive influence on the well being of the entire community, and heap up enormous riches, thanks to their powerful connections and the pecuniary means at their disposal. Ministers and governments become puppets in their hands, and must dance when the wires are pulled behind the scenes. It is not the State that controls the Exchange, but the Exchange that controls the State. Against his will, the minister must water and foster the poison-tree, that he would rather tear up by the roots.

All these things, which daily become more obvious, as the evil increases daily, cry to heaven, to use a common expression, and demand a speedy and radical reform. But modern society is impotent to help ; it stands before the question as certain animals before the mountain,* it keeps going round in

---

* " Wie die Ochsen am Berge,"—" Like the oxen at the foot of the hill," is a German proverb.—Translator.

a circle like a horse in a mill, hopeless, idealess, a picture of wretchedness and imbecility. Those who want to help are still too weak, those who ought to help do not comprehend the situation, those who might help will not ; they put their trust in force and think, if the worst come to the worst, with Madame Pompadour, " *après nous le deluge.*" But what if the deluge come in their time ?

People answer us with the exclamation : " Propose something, show us what we must do to be saved." That would be very unnecessary trouble. The best proposals we could make would be more vehemently opposed than any others, for nothing can be done till privileges and monopolies of all kinds are sent down to Orcus, and this is exactly what people refuse to do, in spite of all their fine phrases. Yes, it would be well if we could cure a sick world with sentiments and assurances.

We have the best example of the impossibility of this in the so-called Social Reform in Germany. What has been proposed there ? Things, which under existing circumstances have not as much significance as the dot on an "i" suffice to keep the whole ruling class in a state of excitement for years, because the execution of the proposals would require this class to open a chink in its money bags. And after years have gone by, and mountains of paper have been covered with talk and printers' ink, there appears at last a little miniature mouse. Whether it will live is doubtful. But the social question is a Chimborazo, which must be climbed. That costs much trouble, sacrifice and sweat.

The measures to be taken in each of the various phases of development, must be determined when the time comes ; it is useless to dispute about them to-day. The most powerful minister is compelled to adapt himself to circumstances, and does not know what step the coming year may oblige him to take. We too must await the course of events and act as the occasion demands.

I maintain, that within a given time all the evils described will have reached a point at which their existence will not only be clearly recognised by the vast majority of the population, but will also have become unbearable ; that a universal irresistible longing for radical reformation will then take possession of almost the whole community, and make the quickest remedy appear the most opportune.

If, therefore, our argument be proved, that all evils without exception have their origin in the social order of things, which at present rests on the capitalistic basis, in the private possession of all the means of production—viz., land, machines, implements, means of traffic, as well as on the private possession of the sources of food and the articles of food, *then the whole of this private property must be converted into common property by one great act of expropriation.*

" Expropriation takes place now through the action of the laws immanent in capitalistic production, through the concentration of capital. One capitalist devours many other capitalists. Hand in hand with this concentration, or the expropriation, of many capitalists by a few, the co-operative form of production is developing, on a continually growing scale, the conscious technological application of science, the systematic cultivation of the soil by combined labour, the transformation of implements into such as can only be used in common, and the economizing of all the means of production by their employment in common for combined social work. Along with the constantly decreasing number of large capitalists who usurp and monopolize all the advantages of this process of transformation, the mass of misery is growing, the mass of oppression, of subjugation, of degradation, of exploitation, but at the same time the indignation of the working-classes, classes which are always on the increase, and have been trained, combined, and organised by the mechanism of the capitalistic system itself. The monopoly of capital is becoming the fetter of the capitalistic process, which has developed along side of it and beneath it. The concentration of the means of production and the association of labour are reaching a point at which they become incompatible with their capitalistic garment. The garment is rent. *The death knell of capitalistic private property is sounding. The expropriators are expropriated.*[*]

Society assumes all the rights and duties involved in this general expropriation, and regulates and arranges everything in the interests of the community, which now no longer clash with the interests of the individual.

---

* Karl Marx, "Das Kapital" (Capital); second edition, pp. 792 and 793.

The Socialization of the Community.

The expropriation of all the private proprietors of the means of production being effected, society starts on a new basis. The conditions of existence and labour for both sexes, industry, agriculture, traffic, education, marriage, science, art, and intercourse, in short, of human life altogether are changed. The State organisation as such gradually loses its foundation. The State is the organisation of force for the maintenance of the existing relations of property and social rule. But as the relations of master and servant disappear with the abolition of the present system of property, the political expression for the relationship ceases to have any meaning. The State expires with the expiration of a ruling class, just as religion expires when the belief in supernatural beings or supernatural reasonable powers ceases to exist. Words must represent ideas; if they lose their substance, they no longer correspond to anything.

" Yes," a startled reader reader with capitalistic tendencies will perhaps object, " that is all very well, but what right has society to carry out this change ? " The right is the same as it always was, when changes and reforms were proposed, namely, the public welfare. The source of right is not the State but society; the State is nothing but the official whose function it is to administer and dispense right. Society has hitherto only been a small minority, but it acted in the name of society at large (the people) when it assumed the title of Society, much as Louis XIV. assumed the title of the State, "*l' état, c'est moi.*" When our newspapers tell us : " The season is beginning, everyone is coming up to town," or " the season is over, everyone is going into the country," they do not mean the nation but the upper ten thousand, who are "everybody, because they represent the State. The nation is plebs, canaille, vile multitude, the " common people." Consequently, everything which history records as having been carried out by the State and by society " for the good of the community," never failed to be for the good of the ruling classes, in whose interest the laws were made and administered. " *Salus reipublicæ suprema lex esto* " (let the welfare of the community be the highest law) is a well-known fundamental principle in old Roman legislation. But of what did the Roman community consist? The subjugated nations? The millions of slaves? No, of the altogether disproportionately small number of Roman citizens, chiefly the nobility, who lived at the expense of the subjected classes.

When the nobles and princes of the Middle Ages stole common property, their right was founded on the public welfare. When the French Revolution expropriated the aristocracy and clergy, it did so in the name of public welfare, and seven millions of peasant proprietors, the support of modern bourgeois France, are the result. In the name of public welfare Spain has frequently taken possession of Church property; and Italy has confiscated it altogether, amid the plaudits of the warmest advocates of "inviolate property." The English nobility has been robbing the English and Irish people for centuries of its property, and took "legal" possession of not less than 3,511,710 acres of public land, between 1804 and 1831. And when in the great North American War of Emancipation, millions of slaves, representing property that had been bought and paid for, were declared free without any compensation to their owners, this was done in the name of the public welfare. The whole of our great middle class development is an uninterrupted process of expropriation and confiscation, in which the manufacturer ejects the artisan, the large landowner the peasant, the merchant the shopkeeper, and at last one capitalist the other, in short in which the smaller inevitably falls a prey to the larger. And our bourgeoisie tells us that this is all for the " public welfare," for the " good of society." The Napoleons " saved " society on the 18th Brumaire and on the 2nd December, and society congratulated them. If society at some future time saves itself, it will accomplish its first reasonable action, for it will not oppress one in the interests of another, but give to all equality in the conditions of existence, it will place the decencies and comforts of life within the reach of all. It will be the morally purest and grandest measure which human society has ever carried out.

If we now proceed to enquire into the transformations which this measure will involve in the principal branches of human activity, we naturally cannot pretend to mark out impassible barriers, or set up unalterable rules. No one can determine to-day the details of the institutions which will best fulfil the needs of a future generation. Everything in society as in nature is exposed to constant change, one thing comes and another passes, what is old and lifeless is replaced by that which is new and full of vitality. Innumerable inventions, discoveries and improvements of the most various kinds are being made, and, when turned to practical account, in proportion to their importance, transform or revolutionize human customs and society altogether.

We, therefore, merely propose to demonstrate general principles, whose deduction follows as a matter of course from the previous postulates, and whose realization can be predicted with approximate certainty. Even under existing circumstances society is the reverse of an automaton which can be guided by the will of single persons. Although this may often have appeared to be the case, those who thought they directed the course of the stream were in reality borne along by it. Society has always been an organism which developed in accordance with definite, immanent laws. If this has been true of the past, how much more will it be impossible for one person to usurp authority and exercise control over others in the future. Society will then have discovered the secret of its own existence, it will have found out the laws of its own development, and will apply them in full consciousness of the aim in view.

         *   *   *   *   *   *   *

After society has entered into exclusive possession of all the means of production, *the equal duty of all to labour, without distinction of sex, will become the first fundamental law of the Socialistic community*, inasmuch as needs cannot be satisfied without a corresponding amount of labour, and no healthy person, capable of work, has a right to expect that others should work for him. The assertion of malicious opponents, that Socialists refuse to work, and, in fact, intend to abolish work altogether, is an absurdity upon the face of it. Idlers can only exist as long as others work to support them. This admirable condition of things is the one in which we live, and hose who profit by it most, are the most declared enemies of Socialism. On the contrary, Socialists maintain that he who will not work has no right to eat. But by work they do not understand mere activity, but useful, *i.e.*, productive work. The new society demands, therefore, that each of its members should execute a certain amount of work in manufacturing, in a handicraft or in agriculture, by which he contributes a given quantity of products for the satisfaction of existing needs. *Without work, no enjoyment, and no work without enjoyment.*

But when all are under the obligation of working, it will be the interest of all to fulfil three conditions in working. Firstly, that the amount of work be moderate, that no one be worked too hard or too long; secondly, that the work be as agreeable and as full of variety as possible; and thirdly, that the work be as productive as possible, because by this the measure of enjoyment is limited. All three conditions depend upon the quality and quantity of the productive forces at disposal, and on the manner of life which society is content to lead. As the Socialistic community does not constitute itself in order to lead the life of proletarians but in order to abolish the proletarianism of the majority, and to bring the largest possible measure of tbe amenities of life within the reach of all, the question arises, how high will society place its average claims.

To decide this question the institution of an executive comprising all branches of social labour is requisite. The single communes form a suitable basis for such an institution, and where they are too large to allow of the convenient transaction of business, they can be divided into districts. All adult members of the commune, without distinction of sex, take part in the necessary elections, and determine to what persons the conduct of affairs shall be entrusted. At the head of the local executives is the central executive, not a government, be it noted, with supreme power, but a business executive, in the exact sense of the term. It is of no interest to us to decide now whether this central executive will be appointed direct by the nation or by the communal executives. No particular importance will be attached to such points as these, as it will not be a question of filling a post with which peculiar honour, greater power, or higher income is connected, but merely a confidential post to which the most efficient person, whether man or woman, is appointed, dismissed and eventually reelected, according to the needs and wishes of the community. These posts are only filled by each delegate for a time. The character of an official does not attach to the delegates, inasmuch as the appointment is neither permanent nor affords the possibility of advancement. There is no such thing as an hierarchical system. For the same reason it is an indifferent matter whether any intermediate body shall be established between the central and local executives, for instance, provincial executives. If they appear necessary, when the time comes, they will be established, if they are superfluous, they will not be established. The practical necessity decides. When more advanced development has made old forms of organization obsolete, they will be abolished, without any flourish of trumpets or violent disputes, as the question touches no personal interests, and a new organization will be introduced with just as little trouble. One sees, this executive is as far removed from our present system as the heavens are from the earth. What quarrels in the newspapers, what a war of tongues in our parliaments, what piles of documents in our offices, when even a slight change in the administration has to be effected.

The chief question will then be to determine the nature and amount of forces at our disposal, and the nature and amount of the means of production, such as factories, workshops, the soil, its previous fertility, the existing stores ; then to calculate the demand for the various kinds of food, by the average consumption of the population. In all these things statistics play the most important part ; they become the principal auxiliary science in the new community, inasmuch as they provide us with a standard for all social labour.

Statistics are already employed on a large scale for similar purposes. The budgets of the empire, of the state, and of the commune are based on a large number of statistical reports, which are annually drawn up by the various departments of the executive. Long experience and a certain stability in the current requirements facilitate the process. Moreover every proprietor of a large factory and every merchant is able, under normal circumstances, to estimate with exactitude the demand of the next three months and to arrange his manufactures and purchases accordingly. Unless quite unforeseen changes occur he is able to carry out his plans with ease.

The experience that gluts are caused by blind production, *i. e.*, production without knowledge of the stores, of the sale, and of the demand for various articles in the general market has induced the traders in iron in different countries to combine for the purpose of making out an accurate statistical report of their ready goods, their capabilities of production, and the probabilities of sale, and for determining in accordance with this report how much each single factory may produce during the subsequent months. An infringement of the regulation involves a heavy conventional fine and expulsion from the society. The employers conclude these treaties for their own advantage, but without consideration for their workmen, who are first overworked and then thrown out of work altogether, In the same way commerce already possesses extensive statistics. Week by week the great trading houses and harbours publish reports on the stores of petroleum, coffee, cotton, sugar, corn, etc., reports, which, it is true, are frequently incorrect, because it is in the interest of the owners to conceal the truth, but which, nevertheless taking them all in all are fairly accurate, and enable those concerned to form a tolerably just estimate of what the conditions of the market is shortly likely to be. All advanced States have also begun drawing up statistics of the harvests, so that, if it is known how much land is sown with a given seed, the average returns of the crop and from them the price can be calculated with approximate accuracy.

Now as in a socialized community all society is organized, as everything will be reduced to system and regulated by plan and order, the estimation of the demand for the various articles of consumption can be accomplished with ease and after a certain amount of experience has been gained, the whole organization will go on like clockwork.

The average measure for the daily social labour required is obtained by comparing the statistics of demand, made under different districts and at different periods, with the actual productive power of society.

Everyone decides for himself in which branch he desires to be employed ; the large number of various kinds of work will permit the gratification of the most various wishes. If a superfluity of workmen occur in one branch and a deficiency in another, it will be the duty of the executive to arrange matters and readjust the inequality. In proportion as all the members become accustomed to their duties, the wheels will go smoother and smoother. The different branches and divisions elect their foremen who undertake the direction. These foremen are not slavedrivers like the majority of inspectors and head men at the present day, but the peers of all the other workmen, who exercise the executive function entrusted to them in place of a productive function. It is therefore by no means impossible, that with more advanced organization and higher culture of all members, these functions may become simply alternating ones to be undertaken

in turn by all those engaged in the branch, without distinction
of sex.

It is evident that labour thus organized on principles of
perfect freedom and democratic equality, in which one
represents all, and all one, must awake the highest sense of
solidarity and a spirit of cheerful activity, and call forth a
degree of emulation such as is nowhere to be found in the
present industrial system. And this spirit must react on the
productivity of labour and the growing improvement of the
product.

Moreover both the individual and the community, inasmuch as each works mutually for the other, are interested
not only in making the work as substantial and complete as
possible, but also in getting through it as quickly as possible,
either with a view to reducing the time of labour, or to gaining
time for the manufacture of new products, for the gratification
of higher claims. This will induce all to devote their
ingenuity to *the improvement, simplification and acceleration of the
process of production. The ambition of inventors and discoverers will
be stimulated to the highest degree, each will endeavour to outdo his
fellows in propositions and ideas.**

Thus the very contrary of everything predicted by the
adherents of the bourgeois system takes place. How many
inventors has the bourgeois world let perish ? How many
has it turned to account and then thrust on one side ? If
talent and genius were to take the lead in the bourgeois world,
the greater number of employers would have to give place to
to their workmen, foremen, technical assistants, engineers,
chemists, etc. These are the people who in ninety nine cases
out of a hundred make the discoveries, inventions and improvements which the man with the large money bag knows
how to profit by. How many thousands of discoverers and
inventors have failed, because they found no one ready to
advance the necessary sums; how many have been crushed in
the germ by the social misery of daily life ? These are things
that can never be ascertained. Not the people with clear
brains and acute powers of reasoning, but those with large

---

* "The power of emulation, in exciting to the most strenuous exertions
for the sake of the approbation and admiration of others is born witness
to by experience in every situation in which human beings publicly
compete with each other, even if it be in things frivolous, or from which
the public derive no benefit. A contest who can do most for the common
good, is not the kind of competition which Socialists repudiate." John
Stuart Mill. "Political Economy."

means are the lords of the world, though we are far from denying that occasionally clear brains and a full purse may be united in one person. The exceptions prove the rule.

Everyone who has had any experience of practical life knows with what mistrust the workman regards every improvement, every new discovery which is introduced. And he is perfectly right. He has no benefit from it but only his master; he has every reason to fear that the new machine will turn him out of doors to-morrow as superfluous. Instead of gladly welcoming an invention which is an honour, and is supposed to be an advantage to humanity, he has an execration and a curse upon his lips. That is the natural consequence of the conflict of interests.*

This condition of things is completely changed in a socialized society. Everyone develops his faculties to benefit himself, and in doing this he benefits the community as well. To-day personal egotism and public welfare are two contradictory things which exclude each other; in the new society these contradictions are done away with, personal

---

* Von Thünen: "Der Isolirte Staat" (The Isolated State) says: "The conflict of interests is the reason why Proletarian and Possessor must remain the irreconcilable opponents of each other, as long as this conflict is not put an end to. It is true, the national wealth is not increased only by the prosperity of the employers, but also from time to time, by industrial discoveries, by the building of high-roads, and railways, by the formation of new commercial connections. But all those things do not affect the workman under our present social system, his position remains what it was, and the increase of wealth falls to the share of employers, capitalists, and land-owners." Is not this last sentence almost a verbal anticipation of Gladstone's declaration in the English Parliament, where he asserted in 1864:—"This intoxicating increase of wealth and power" (which had taken place in England within the last twenty years) "is exclusively limited to the propertied classes." And on page 207 of the "Isolated State" von Thünen says:—"The evil lies in the separation of the producer from his products."

Plato, "Republic": "A State in which classes exist is not one but two; one consists of the poor, the other of the rich, who living in close proximity, are constantly on the watch against each other. The ruling class is at length unable to carry on war, because, to do so, it must take the multitude into its service, and it fears the people in arms more than the foe."

Morelly, "Principles of Legislation": "Property divides us into two classes, the rich and the poor. The former love their property and have no inclination to protect their country; the latter cannot love their country, to which they owe nothing but misery. But every one loves his country in a socialistic community, for through it he receives life and happiness."

egotism and public welfare become synonymous and inter-
changeable expressions.*

The incalculable effect of such a moral condition is apparent.
The productivity of labour will be enormously increased, and
thereby the gratification of higher claims facilitated.

Further, labour is to be made more and more agreeable.
This demands workshops arranged with regard both to convenience and beauty, so far as possible the prevention of all
danger, of unpleasant smells, vapours, smoke, &c., in short
of all injurious and disagreeable accessories.

At first the new society will carry on production with the
means received from the old. But however perfect these
may now appear they will then prove insufficient. The
number of scattered workshops and factories is deficient in
every respect ; the number of implements and machines
which we now possess in every grade of perfection, from the
most primitive to the most finished, will be too small for the
number of workers, and inadequate with regard to convenience
and ease of handling.

The most urgent need is, therefore, the provision of a considerable number of large, well-lighted, and well-ventilated
factories, artistically built within and without, and fitted up
with every requisite for production.

Art, technical skill, brain and hand labour here find at once
a wide field of activity. Every branch for the construction
of machines and implements, every branch of architecture,
and every branch connected with the interior fittings of
buildings has full employment. Everything that man's in-
ventive spirit can create in the way of commodious and
artistic edifices, ventilation, lighting, heating, mechanical and
technical apparatus, water supply, etc., will be turned to
account. Economy of motor power, heat, light, time, convenience of labour and living require the advantageous concentration of all the workshops at given points. Dwelling-
houses will be separated from workshops and factories, and
freed from all the disagreeables connected with the latter.
These disagreeables, on the other hand, will be reduced to a

---

* When counting up the advantages and disadvantages of Communism
John Stuart Mill says, in his " Political Economy " :—" No soil could be
more favourable to the growth of such a feeling than a communistic association, since all the ambition, and the bodily and mental activity, which
are now exerted in the pursuit of separate and self-regarding interests, would
require another sphere of employment, and would naturally find it in the
pursuit of the general benefit of the community."

minimum by suitable appliances and preventive measures of all kinds, and will in part be altogether done away with. We know that technical improvements have already succeeded in stripping some of the most perilous callings, for instance that of the miner, of their dangers. And there can be doubt that the disagreeables which are still connected with mining might be got rid of by a different method in boring, by powerful ventilation, by lighting, by considerably shorter hours, by a frequent change of workmen, etc., etc. The consumption and prevention of smoke, soot, dust, and smells has also been made possible by chemical and mechanical appliances. Wherever the factories and workshops of the future may be, either over or under the earth, they will be as different from the present ones as light from darkness. But all these things are a question of money under the present private system ; the first consideration is: can the business afford it ? will it pay ? If it will not pay, the workman must be sacrificed. Capital holds aloof from everything by which no profits can be made. Humanity has no rate of exchange on the Bourse.

In no trade is this trifling with human life in the interests of the money bag so apparent as in the shipping business and marine traffic. The startled world had its eyes opened to the fearful unscrupulousness of English capitalists by the indiscretions of Plimsoll, as we have already said, about 1870. People were indignant, horrified, and yet just the same thing is happening everywhere. The English capitalists are not the only ones who know how to do business, and leave the devil to take care of their consciences, in place of which they have a stone.* And what has the State yet done in this direction ? At some of the most dangerous points, at the entrance to rivers and harbours, it builds lighthouses and stations signal-ships, but with those exceptions the entire coast is unprotected. The rest is left to private benevolence, thanks to which a considerable number of lifeboat stations have been erected, and many a life rescued. But those very

---

* "Capital, says the *Quarterly Review*, avoids tumult and disputes and is of a timid disposition. That is very true, but not the whole truth. Capital abhors the absence of profit, or a very small profit, as much as Nature abhors a vacuum. With sufficient profit, capital becomes daring. Ten per cent. certain, and it can be had everywhere ; 20 per cent. and it becomes lively ; 50 per cent., positively rash ; for 100 per cent. it tramples all human laws under foot ; 300 per cent. and there is no crime which it will not venture to commit, even at the risk of the gallows. If tumult and disputes are profitable, it will encourage them both."—Karl Marx, " Das Kapital " (Capital), Second Edition, note 250.

inadequate provisions only extend over a comparatively small portion of the coast, and still less has been done to anticipate cases of shipwreck on the open sea. A glance at our emigrant ships teaches us enough. Steamers, which when packed full contain 1,000 to 1,300 passengers, have nutshells of boats, which altogether, at the outside, can hold 200 to 250 persons, that is to say, in the most favourable case, they suffice to rescue a fourth or fifth of the crew, supposing that it is possible to get them loosened and properly filled in time. This is almost always an impossibility. Three-fourths to four-fifths of the passengers have no help but the so-called swimming-belts, which at best keep them a few hours above water, if they do not die in the meanwhile. If the accident happen at night, the belts are useless, and if it happen by day, equally so, unless a ship chance to pass close by within a few hours after the wreck. For a ship at a distance sees the human heads on the water as little, as for instance, any-one on the banks of the Rhine would see 400 or 500 corks, that had been thrown into the river from the bridge at Cologne. Under these circumstances the means of rescue become the means of prolonging a terrible death-struggle. When such catastrophes occur as the foundering of the *Cimbria* in January 1883, the whole world cries out, every one demands a remedy and measures of precaution against such accidents as these. But the only really effective measure is not thought of, viz., to make it illegal for any ship to carry more passengers than it can with ease take into its boats in case of need. In other words, either the number of passengers must be considerably reduced, or the size of the ships must be increased to allow of their carrying more boats. Both of these propositions come into collision with the most powerful of all interests, *the interests of capital.* Shipping would cease to be a good investment, and therefore we may be assured that bourgeois society will never adopt such a plan. It is hardly necessary to add that various other regulations would have to be made besides those alluded to. This is a field in which the future solidary union of all civilized nations will celebrated the greatest triumphs.

The profit question will cease to play any part in a socialistic society, which knows no other considerations than the well-fare of its members. What benefits or protects them must be introduced, what injures them must be avoided ; in no case will any one be forced to join a dangerous undertaking against his will. When expeditions are fitted out, in which there is a prospect of danger, more than enough will join them voluntarily, all the more as the object of such expeditions will never be destruction, but the spread of civilization.

The appliance of motor power on a grand scale, perfected machines and implements, division of labour carried into the smallest detail and an appropriate combination of all the labouring forces will bring production to such a state of development, that it will be possible considerably to reduce the time necessary for producing the necessary articles of consumption. The capitalist lengthens the working day wherever he can, even during a glut, in order to sell the product cheaper by extorting more surplus value from the workman. In a socialistic community the advantages of increased production are shared by everyone, each receives a larger portion of produce, and the time claimed by society for purposes of labour is curtailed.

Among the motor powers in question, electricity will probably take the leading and most important place. Bourgeois Society has already begun to enlist its services in all directions. The more extensively and successfully this is done, the better. The revolutionizing influence of this mightiest of all natural powers will hasten to burst the fetters of the bourgeois world, and to clear the road for Socialism. But electricity will attain its fullest development and its most widespread application in the socialized community. If only a part of the prospects which already appear opened for its use are realized, and we cannot doubt that this will be the case, it will contribute enormously to the amelioration of human conditions of existence. Electricity excels every other motor force by the fact that we do not need to manufacture it, like gas, vapour, heated air, but that it is everywhere present in nature. All our water-courses, the tides of the sea, the wind, properly turned to account, represent innumerable horse powers. Through the discovery of the so-called Faure Batteries it has already been proved, that great quantities of force, which like tides, wind, mountain streams are only at our disposal periodically, can be bound, and applied at any given place or at any given time. But all these discoveries and inventions are still embryos, whose full-grown shape we can surmise but not wholly foresee.

Thus we perceive vistas opening for the future, in which the quantity, quality, and variety of products will increase to an enormous extent, and the pleasures of life be correspondingly multiplied for coming generations.

The desire for freedom of choice and for change of occupation is deeply implanted in human nature. Just as constant and regular repetition without variation will at length make the best food disliked, an employment that is daily repeated becomes as monotonous as a treadmill; it blunts and relaxes. The man performs a given task, because he must, but without enthusiasm or enjoyment. Now everyone possesses a number of capabilities and inclinations, which only require to be roused, developed, and put into action to give the most satisfactory results and enable their possessor to unfold his whole and real being. The socialistic community will offer the fullest opportunity for gratifying this need of variety, as we shall see later on. The enormous increase in productive power, combined with growing simplification in the process of production will permit, as we have said, a considerable limitation in the time of labour, while it faciliates the acquirement of mechanical skill in a number of different branches.

The old apprentice system is obsolete, it no longer exists anywhere but in old-fashioned, retrograde forms of production, such as small handicrafts, and can exist nowhere else. When these handicrafts have disappeared in the new community, all the institutions peculiar to them will disappear also, and be replaced by new institutions. We see already in every factory how few workmen there are who still pursue a calling to which they have been apprenticed. The workmen belong to the most heterogeneous categories; a short time suffices to accustom them to any one of the various divisions of labour. Under the present system, it is true, they are then tied to the machine, without change or regard to their inclinations, during an immoderately long working day, till they become machines themselves.* But this state of things will be rendered impossible by a different organization. Abundant time will remain for the execution of work requiring dexterity of hand and artistic skill. Young and old will have ample opportunity of learning with ease one or more handicrafts in large workshops arranged for this purpose, and fitted out with every requisite in the way of comfort and technical appliances. There will be chemical and physical laboratories, corresponding to all the demands of science, and a proportional staff of teachers. Not till then will people become aware

---

* "The generality of labourers in England and in most other countries have as little choice of occupation or freedom of locomotion, are practically as dependant on fixed rules and on the will of others as they could be on any system short of actual slavery." John Stuart Mill.

what a world of instincts and capacities the capitalistic system of production has either crushed altogether or only permitted to attain a stunted development.*

It will therefore not only be possible to take this desire for change into account, it is in fact the object of society to realize it in the case of each individual, because on this his harmonious development depends. The stamp of one's calling in one's face, by which our present society is characterized, whether the "calling" consists in the fulfilment of one monotonous task or another, or in a life of luxury and idleness, or in forced inactivity, will disappear more and more. How extremely small is the number of people who at the present day possess or make use of the possibility of change. Very occasionally we come across such cases, which, favoured by peculiar circumstances or character, retire from the monotony of their daily task, and after they have paid their tribute to physical labour, seek recreation in mental employment. On the other hand we sometimes find brain workers who occupy themselves with some manual labour, such as gardening, etc. Every hygienist will allow that the alternation of mental and physical activity, carried out with moderation in proportion to the strength, is the only condition that conforms to natural laws.

Well, the community of the future will have scholars and artists of every kind, and in very considerable numbers, who will devote a small portion of each day to assiduous physical toil, and spend the remainder of their time according to their tastes, in the pursuit of their studies or arts.†

---

* "A French workman, on his way home from San Francisco, writes:— 'I should never have believed that I was capable of working at all the different trades which I have carried on in California. I was firmly persuaded that I was good for nothing but printing . . . But once in the midst of this world of adventurers, who change their trade more easily than their shirts, ma foi, I did as the others did. As the business of mining did not prove profitable enough, I gave it up and went to town, where I was type-setter, tiler, lead-founder, etc., by turns. Thanks to this discovery that I am always good for something, I feel myself less of a mollusc and more of a man!" Karl Marx, "Das Kapital" (Capital).

† What men can become under favourable conditions of development may be seen for example in Leonardo da Vinci, who was a great painter, first rate sculptor, an architect and engineer of repute, an admirable military builder, a muscian and an improvisor. Benvenuto Cellini was a celebrated goldsmith, an excellent modeller, a good sculptor, a well known military architect, a first rate soldier and a trained musician. One would not go far wrong in asserting that the calling of most people does not correspond to their faculties, because the choice was not dictated by their free-will but by the force of circumstances. Many a bad professor would make good shoes, and many a good shoemaker would be a good professor as well.

The antagonism which exists to-day between hand and head work and which the ruling classes have done their best to accentuate, in order to monopolise head word for themselves, will thus be abolished.

It is evident from the foregoing remarks that periods of glut and want of work will be impossible in the new community. We saw that gluts had their origin in individualistic, capitalistic production, in which the producers, stimulated by the prospect of personal profit, and guided only by this consideration, without means of estimating the chances of sale in the general market, overfill it by the manufacture of goods for which there is no demand. The nature of products as wares under the capitalistic system makes consumption dependant on the purchasing power of the population. Now this purchasing power is limited in the case of the vast majority that is insufficiently paid for its labour, and whose work ceases altogether as soon as it no longer represents surplus value in the shape of profits for the employers. Power of purchasing and power of consuming are therefore two very different things. Millions require new clothes, shoes, furniture, linen, meat and drink, but they have no money and accordingly their requirements, *i.e.* their power of consumption, remain unsatisfied. The market is overstocked and the people hungry. They are willing to work, but they find no one who will buy their work, because the capitalist can earn nothing by the transaction. " Canaille, you can die, go to the dogs, become vagabonds or criminals; I, the capitalist, cannot help it." And the man is quite right from his point of view.

The new society will do away with this contradiction. The new society will not produce " wares," with the intention of buying and selling, but it will produce requisites, to be used and consumed, this being the only object of their production. The power of consumption will therefore be no longer limited by the purchasing power of the individual, but by the productive power of the community. As long as the means of production and the time for production suffices, every desire can be gratified ; satisfaction becomes the only limit of the consuming power of society.

As therefore there are no " wares " in the new community, neither will there be any money. Money is the representative of wares, and yet at the same time a ware itself; it is the social equivalent of all other wares. But the new society possesses no wares, only objects of necessity, of use, whose making requires a certain amount of social working time. The working time which the making of an article requires is therefore the only scale by which its social value can be measured. Ten minutes of social work in one branch, are exchangeable for ten minutes of social work in another, neither more nor less. For society is not intent on earning, its task consists only in effecting the exchange of articles of equal quality and equal use-value among its members. If society finds for instance that three hours work a day is necessary for the production of the requisite quantity of goods, it will appoint three hours as the length of the working day.* If society increases and the methods of production are so far improved, that all requisites can be made in two hours, then the working day will be fixed at two hours. If on the other hand the majority demands the gratification of higher needs, than those which, despite the increase in number and the greater productivity of labour, can be provided for in two or three hours, it can lengthen the working day to four. Its will is its paradise.

It will be easy to calculate how much social working time each single product requires.† The relation of part of the working time to the whole is fixed accordingly. Any kind of certificate, a printed piece of paper, gold or brass is a receipt for the time spent in work, and enables the possessor to ex-

---

* We must remember that production will then be organised to the highest degree of technical perfection, and that the whole community is productively employed. Under these circumstances, a three hours working day may rather appear too long than too short. Owen calculated in his time—the first quarter of the century—that two hours would suffice.

† " It is by no means necessary to make a circuitous calculation of the amount of social labour represented by a product ; daily experience will suffice to show how large the average amount is ; society can easily ascertain how many working hours are contained in a steam-engine, in a hectolitre of last year's wheat, in a hundred square metres of cloth of a given quality. It will therefore never dream of expressing these amounts of work, which are contained in the products, and which it knows with absolute certainty by a relative, varying, insufficient measure, which it formerly used for want of a better, a measure which is itself a third product, instead of by the natural, adequate, absolute measure, viz., time. . . Society must arrange its plan of production, with regard to the means of production, especially to the producers. The value of the different objects of use in relation to each other, and to the amount of time necessary for their production will finally regulate the plan. People will then arrange everything very simply, without the intervention of the celebrated money-value." Fr. Engels : " Herrn Eugen Dührings's Umwälzung der Wissenschaft " (Mr. Eugen Dühring's Revolution of Science).

change this token for articles of the most various kinds. If he finds that his requirements are less than those covered by that which he receives for his work, he can work a correspondingly shorter time. If he prefers to give away his superfluity, no one can prevent him ; if he is foolish enough voluntarily to work for another who spends his time in cultivating the dolce far niente and prefers sharing the earnings of his neighbour, to working himself, it is his own concern. But no one can compel him to work for another, and no one can deprive him of a part of his claims for the work done. If a suit of clothes in fine cloth costs twenty hours of social labour, and he prefers to have one for eighteen, he can do so. And so on and so on. We see, every one will be able to satisfy all legitimate desires, but not at the expense of others. Every one will receive from society the equivalent of his labour, neither more nor less.

" And what becomes of the difference between the industrious and the idle, the intelligent and the stupid ? " I hear some one ask. There will be no such differences because that which we associate with these conceptions will have ceased to exist. The reward of industry and the punishment of idleness in bourgeois society reminds one of the position which intelligence occupies in the social scale. An idler, in the phraseology of society, is a man thrown out of work against his will, and forced to become a vagabond, who at length in fact becomes one, or who goes to the dogs because he is brought up in the midst of vice. But the gentleman with private property, who lounges away his time in luxury, would be very much offended if he were called an idler ; he is a " thoroughly good fellow." And with regard to intelligence we have already shewn how the question lies.

What then will be the state of affairs in a free community ? As all will carry on social labour under conditions of perfect equality, and each will be occupied with the kind of work for which his tastes and faculties best qualify him, it is evident that the differences in the quality of the work done will be extremely small.* The whole moral atmosphere of society, which incites each one to emulate the achievements of others,

---

* " All well organised human beings are born with very much the same amount of understanding, but *education, laws* and *circumstances cause them to vary later on*. The interests of the individual, rightly understood, coincide with the public interests, or the interest of the community. Helvetius : " Ueber den Menschen und dessen Erziehung." (Man and his Education).

exercises an equalising influence. If any one feels that he is unable to do as much as others in any branch, he chooses another branch, which harmonises better with his powers and capacity. Under such circumstances what right has one to be privileged before another? And if any one be so badly treated by nature that in spite of the best intentions he is unable to do as much as his fellows, society cannot make him responsible for the faults of nature. If on the other hand anyone has received talents from nature which place him above his fellows, society is under no obligation to reward that which is no personal merit.

When Goethe made a study of the Cologne Cathedral on a journey up the Rhine, he discovered in the documents of the building that the old master-builders paid all their workmen only by the time, with a view to obtaining good and conscientious work. It was reserved to bourgeois society to ruin the quality of its workmen by piece-work, in buying the workman as a ware. It was bourgeois society that introduced the system of piece payment which forces the workmen to mutually overwork each other, and it does so, in order the better to regulate the under-pay and the depression of wages.

The same thing applies to so-called brain work as to physical labour. Everyone is the product of the time and circumstances in which he lives. Goethe,—to abide by this example—born under equally favourable conditions of existance in the fourth instead of the eighteenth century, instead of becoming a great poet, and an inquirer into natural laws, would have become a great father of the Church, and possibly have put St. Augustine into the shade. Goethe, born in the eighteenth century as the son of a poor cobbler in Frankfurt instead as the son of a rich patrician, would never have become grand ducal minister at Weimar, but would most probably have remained a shoemaker all his life, and have died as a respectable shoemaker master. If Napoleon I. had been born ten years later, he would never have become Emperor of France. If the clever child of intelligent parents is placed among savages, it becomes a savage, though an intelligent one. Society has made everyone that which he is. Ideas are not a product of the brain of any one individual, sprung from nothing, or implanted by a divine inspiration from above, but a product of social life and action, an outcome of the spirit of the times. An Aristotle could not have the ideas of a Darwin, and a Darwin cannot but have other ideas than an Aristotle. Each one thinks as the spirit of the times and his surroundings force him to think. Thence the experience that so often different people have one and the same idea at the same time, that one and the same discovery or invention is made contemporaneously at two different spots, far apart from each other, that an idea, expressed fifty years too soon, roused no enthusiasm, but repeated fifty years later in the right form, sets the world on fire. The Emperor Sigismund could venture to break his word to Huss in 1415, and to have him burnt in Constance. Charles V., although a much greater fanatic, was obliged to let Luther depart un-molested from the diet of Worms in 1511. Ideas are the product of co-operating social factors. Without modern Society we should have no modern ideas. That is clear and indisputable. Moreover, in the new community the means of culture which everyone makes use of are the property of the community, and Society cannot be expected to pay a higher price for that which it receives from itself, which is in fact its own product.

So much on the different qualifications for physical and so-called mental labour. By the same process, we arrive at the conclusion that there can be no distinction between higher and lower class physical labour. At present, for instance, a mechanic thinks himself infinitely superior to a day labourer, who works on the road, or has some similar employment. Inasmuch as society only undertakes work that is useful to the community, every form of work which fulfils this con-dition is equally valuable to it. If unpleasant or disgusting work cannot be performed by the help of machines or chemistry, or by their means be transformed into an agreeable process, which we shall in time doubtlessly succeed in accomplishing, and if the necessary number of voluntary labourers is not forthcoming, then it becomes incumbent on each member of society to perform his share of such work in turn. Here is no place for false shame and imbecile con-tempt of useful labour. These things are only possible in our community of drones, in which idleness is regarded as an enviable lot, and the labourer is the more looked down upon, the harder, more laborious and more unpleasant his work is, and the more indispensable it happens to be for society. In-deed we may regard it as the rule, that the most disagreeable work is that which is worst paid, because, owing to the per-petual revolutionizing of production there is always a reserve army of superfluous hands at starvation's door, ready, for the sake of keeping soul and body together, to undertake the

vilest work at such prices that it would be unprofitable for the
bourgeois world to replace them by machines.   For instance,
stone-breaking is proverbially one of the worst paid and most
disagreeable kinds of work.   Nothing could be simpler than
to have stones broken by machines, as is done in North
America, but we have such an amount of cheap labour, that
the machine would not "pay."*   From a rational point of
view a workman who clears out cesspools and thereby saves
people from the influence of noxious gases, is a very useful member of society, while a professor who teaches falsified history in
the interests of the ruling classes, or a theologian, who seeks
to cloud men's brains with supernatural and transcendental
doctrines is an extremely pernicious and dangerous person.
The class of scholars which at present fills our professional
chairs represents for the most part a guild, paid for the express purpose of defending the supremacy of the ruling
classes by the authority of science, of proving this supremacy
to be justifiable, beneficial and necessary, and of upholding
existing prejudices.   That is false science, brain-poisoning,
the enemy of civilization, a sale of spiritual gifts in the
interests of the bourgeoisie and its clients.†   A form fo
society which makes the further existence of such a privileged
guild impossible will perform an act of liberation for humanity.
      On the other hand, genuine science often necessitates the

---

* "If the choice were to be made between Communism with all its
chances and the present state of Society with all its sufferings and
injustices; if the institution of private property necessarily carried with
it as a consequence, that the produce of labour should be apportioned as
we now see it, almost in an inverse ratio to the labour,—*the largest portions
to those who have never worked at all, the next largest to those whose work is almost
nominal, and so in a descending scale, the remuneration dwindling as the work
grows harder and more disagreeable, until the most fatiguing and exhausting bodily
labour cannot count with certainty on being able to earn even the necessaries of life ;
if this or Communism were the alternative, all the difficulties, great or small, of Communism would be but as dust in the balance.*" Mill took the greatest pains to reform
the bourgeois world and bring it to reason, naturally to no purpose, and thus
he at last became a Socialist, like every other logical person acquainted
with the actual condition of things.   He did not venture, however, to acknowledge it during his life, but waited till after his death, when his auto-
biography proclaimed his Socialistic confession of faith.   His case was the
same as Darwin's, who also objected to be known as an atheist during his
life.   That is the comedy which bourgeois society forces thousands to
play.   The bourgeoisie wears the mask of loyalty, religion and dogmatic
belief, because on them its authority partly rests.

† "Scholarship is as often the hand-maid of ignorance as of progress."
Buckle: "History of Civilization."

most disagreeable and revolting work, for instance, when a doctor examines a corpse in a state of putrefaction, or operates on suppurating wounds; or when a chemist analyses excrements. Thus we see that the most unpleasant work is often the most useful, and that our conception of agreeable and disagreeable work, like so many other conceptions of the present day, is false, superficial, and founded on externals alone.

*   *   *   *   *   *

When the entire production of the new community has been placed upon such a basis as the one described, it no longer produces "wares," but only objects of use, for the actual requirements of Society. This is equivalent to the cessation of commerce, which has no *raison d'être* except in a society founded on the production of wares. An enormous army of persons of both sexes and of all ages is thus set free for productive labour. Millions will become producers, who have hitherto lived like parasites on the products of others' labour, notwithstanding their hard working and anxious lives, which we are far from leaving out of account. No single person is responsible for that which Society has made out of him. In the place of the dozens, hundreds and thousands of shops and trading establishments of all kinds which every town in proportion to its size now possesses, we shall have large communal depots, storehouses, elegant bazaars, whole exhibitions, whose management will require a comparatively small number of persons. This transformation alone represents a revolution in all our previous arrangements. And as the entire system of modern commerce is replaced by a central distributive administration, our whole system of traffic will undergo a corresponding change.

Telegraphs, railways, posts, sea and river ships, trams, and whatever other vehicles are employed as means of public communication, are the property of society. The fact that many of these institutions, such as the post, the telegraph, and most of our railways, are already in the hands of the State, will considerably facilitate their conversion into property of the community. In these cases there can no longer be any question of injuring private interests. If the State continues to work in this direction, so much the better. But this State administration is very far from being the same as a Socialistic administration, as is sometimes erroneously sup-

posed. The State administration is just as much a system
of capitalistic exploitation as if the institutions in question
were in the hands of private undertakers. Neither the
officials nor the workmen have any particular advantage from
their position. The State treats them just as any private
undertaker would do ; as, for instance, when the Imperial
Marine issues the regulation for all its departments, that no
one over forty years of age need apply for an appointment.
When such measures as these proceed from the State as
employer they are much worse than when they proceed from
a private undertaker, inasmuch as the latter is comparatively
a small employer of labour, and another may give the employment which he refuses. The State on the other hand, as
a monopolistic employer, can cause at one blow the misery of
thousands by such maxims as these. This method of action
is therefore, as we said before, not Socialistic, but thoroughly
capitalistic, and Socialists protest energetically against the
confusion of the present State administration with Socialistic
administration. In Socialistic administration there are no
employers, no superiors, no oppression ; all are equals and
enjoy equal rights.

As therefore large central establishments take the place of
all the various tradesmen, middlemen and private producers,
the entire transport of products will assume a correspondingly
simplified character. The millions of small separate packages
now sent to as many purchasers, will become great waggon
loads which take their way to the communal depots, and
the central places of production. Here, too, everything will
be simplified to a very large degree, time, labour, material
will be enormously economised, the physiognomy of our
means of communication, and especially of our dwellings,
will assume a perfectly different aspect. The nerve-destruc-
tive noise, the crowding and hurrying in our large places of
resort with their thousand vehicles of every description, will
not only be considerably modified, but to a large extent totally
changed. The building of streets, the cleansing of streets,
the manner of living will be changed at the same time.
Hygienic measures can then be carried out with ease and
simplicity which at present are either altogether unfeasible,
or can only be accomplished imperfectly and with great
expense, and often enough only for the richer quarters of the
town. The " common people " do not need them ; they can
wait till the money is to be had, a condition which is rarely
fulfilled.

As a matter of course the means of communication will be extended to their utmost limits, and carried out with all the appliances of growing science. Roads and rails are the blood vessels through which the circulation, *i.e.*, the exchange of products of the entire community, flows ; they are the means of personal and mental intercourse of men and women with each other, and are therefore a most important factor in establishing an equality of well-being and culture throughout society. Their development and ramification as far as the remotest spots in the remotest districts is a necessity and a matter of general interest to the community. In this direction as well as in all others, tasks are awaiting the new society far surpassing those which present society is capable of dealing with. This perfected and extended system of communication will, moreover, favour the decentralisation of the large populations and of the means of production at present crowded together in great towns and centres of industry, and lead to their dispersion over the whole country. Such a change must be of the greatest significance, both with regard to health and to the spiritual and material advance of civilisation.

*   *   *   *   *   *

One of the chief means of labour and production in manufactures and exchange, is the soil as basis of labour and fundamental condition of all human existence and of society. Society re-appropriates at the most advanced stage of its development that which belonged to it from the beginning. We find that common property in land existed among all the peoples of the earth, as soon as they attained a certain degree of civilisation. This common possession was the basis of every primitive society, which would have been impossible without it. Not until the appearance and development of the various forms of supremacy was common property put an end to and usurped as private possession, an act which gave rise to the most violent struggles, which have continued down to our own time. The theft of the land and its conversion into personal property was the origin of bondage, which has passed through all possible phases from slavery to the "free" workmen of our day, till at length, after a development covering thousands of years, the land will be reconverted into common property by the bondsmen themselves.

The recognition of the importance of the land for the existence of the race has made it the chief object of contention in all the social struggles of the world, in India, China, Egypt, Greece (Kleomenes), Rome (the Gracchi), in the Christian Middle Ages (religious sects, Münzer, Peasants' War), among Azteks and Incas, down to the present day, and even men such as Adolph Samter, Prof. Adolph Wagner, and Dr. Schäffle, who, in other directions, are prepared to make the greatest concessions and to accept half measures of social reform, regard the common possession of the land as a justifiable claim. *

The profitable cultivation of the land is therefore a question of primary importance for the prosperity of the population. It is eminently the interest of all to raise its fertility to the highest possible degree. We have already shewn that this is impossible in the form of private property, either on small or middle-sized farms, or on large estates. Moreover, the highest state of cultivation does not depend on the care bestowed on small portions of the land, but on factors with which neither the largest land owner nor the most powerful farming association can reckon, factors which extend beyond our present national boundaries and which are only capable of international treatment.

In the first place society will have to enquire into the nature of the land as a whole, i.e., with respect to its topographical character, its mountains, plains, woods, rivers, pools, moors, bogs, and marshes. The topographical character

---

* Even the Popes and Fathers of the church in former ages, at a tim when the tradition of common possession was still in existence and thef of land had already assumed large dimensions, could not refrain from zealous expostulations in an altogether communistic tone. This tone is foreign to the syllabus of the nineteenth century ; the popes of Rome have become the subjects of bourgeois society, like everyone else, much against their will. Pope Clement I. says : " The use of all things in this world is to be common to all. It is an injustice to say, ' this is my property, this belongs to me, that belongs to another.' Hence the origin of contentions among men." Bishop Ambrosius Milan, about 374, says : " Nature bestows all things on all men in common, for God has created all things that their enjoyment might be common to all, and that the earth might become the common possession of all. Common possession is therefore a right established by Nature, and only unjust usurpation has created the right of private property." Pope Gregory the Great, about 600, says : " Let them know that the earth from which they spring and of which they are formed, belongs to all men in common, and that therefore the fruits which the earth brings forth must belong to all without distinction." And one of the moderns, Zacharias says : " All evils with which civilized nations have to contend can be traced back to individual property in land as their source." —" Forty Books on the State."

exerts a distinct influence on the climate and the composition of the soil. These investigations will open out not only a most comprehensive field of activity, but also one in which a mass of experience must be gathered and a number of experiments made. The state has hitherto done very little in this direction. For one thing, it applies only small sums to the solution of such problems of civilization, and even if it desired to take any decided steps in the matter it would be prevented doing so by the large landed proprietors who have the casting vote in our legislature. The present State could effect nothing without making very considerable encroachments on private property. But as its existence depends on the preservation of private property as a sacred institution, and these great landed proprietors are its principal support, it naturally has neither the power nor the will to proceed in the manner described. The new society will therefore have to undertake the improvement of the soil on a gigantic and comprehensive scale.

Another question of extreme importance is that of providing an extensive and systematic network of rivers and canals, carried out and regulated on scientific principles.

The question of cheap carriage by water, important as it is for society at present, will not have to be taken into account in the new community. On the other hand, rivers and canals will play a most important part through their effect on the climate, their value as a means of irrigation, and their influence on the fertility of the soil.

It is well known that dry countries are much more exposed to cold winters and hot summers than well watered countries, for instance, that coast districts are either free from the extremes of temperature, or at any rate are only visited by them for short periods of the year. Now these extremes are neither beneficial nor agreeable either for plants or animals. An extensive canal system, combined with the above-mentioned measures for the cultivation of forests, would, without doubt, moderate their intensity. At the same time, such a network of canals in connection with large reservoirs would serve to collect and retain the water when the rivers are swollen by the melting of snow or by heavy rains, and overflow their banks. Floods and the devastations which they cause would then become impossible. Probably also the extensive water surface with its considerable evaporation would occasion more regularity in the fall of rain. In districts in which the water supply was at times insufficient for the cultivation of the soil, there would be no difficulty in erecting hydraulic machines and pumping works to provide the necessary quantities.

Large tracts of land which were hitherto entirely or almost entirely sterile, might be turned into fruitful plains by means of artificial irrigation. In places where at present sheep barely find a scanty meal, and where at best a few wretched pines stretch out their thin branches to the sky, luxuriant harvests might thrive and a dense population find food in abundance. Again this canalization would drain extensive bogs and marsh land and make them accesssible to cultivation,—for instance, in North Germany and Bavaria. These numerous currents of water might further be turned to account on a large scale for the breeding of fish, and would thus prove a fertile source of nourishment, while in summer they would afford suitable bathing places for districts without a river.

The few following examples may serve to shew to what an extent irrigation affects the fertility of the soil. In the neighbourhood of Weissenfels 7½ hectares of well irrigated meadow land yielded 480 cwts. of grass at the second hay harvest, while 5 hectares of adjoining meadow with a similar soil, but without irrigation, only yielded 32 cwts., *i.e.*, the former yielded in proportion tenfold the amount. Near Riesa, in Saxony, the irrigation of 65 acres raised the net profits from 5,850 marks (£292 10s.) to 11,100 marks (£555), notwithstanding the considerable expenditure incurred. There are in Germany whole provinces whose soil, consisting chiefly of sand, only yields even a moderately good harvest after an unusually rainy summer. If these provinces were intersected with canals and irrigated, they would in a short time produce five and ten times as much as they now do. There have been cases in Spain in which the harvest of well irrigated land was thirty-seven times as great as that of not irrigated land. Then give us water, and we can conjure fresh stores of food out of the ground.

Where are the private land owners, and where are the States capable of going to work on such a scale as that which appears both necessary and feasible? When a State, after years of most bitter experience, in which millions' worth of property has been destroyed, at length gives way to the urgent demands of those who have been ruined by one calamity after another, how slowly it does so, with what circumspection, with how much calculation. It is so easy to do too much : the State runs the risk of heedlessly sacrificing the sums required for building new barracks, or maintaining several regiments of soldiers. And then, when too much is done on one side, people come from all other sides and demand help as well. " Man, help yourself, and God will help you," is the bourgeois creed. Everyone for himself and no one for all. Consequently hardly a year passes without the occurrence of floods of more or less importance, once, twice, and oftener, caused by rivers and streams in various provinces and states. Large regions of the most fertile soil are swept away by the violence of the current, or covered with sand, stones and rubbish. Trees are torn up, houses, bridges, roads, embankments washed away, railways undermined, cattle drowned, not unfrequently human life sacrificed, improvements of the land destroyed, the crops ruined. Moreover, a large extent of country which is exposed to the danger of frequent floods is cultivated as little as possible, and sown only with inferior crops to avoid a double loss.

On the other hand, unscientific corrections of the beds of large rivers, undertaken in the one-sided " interests of trade and commerce," the only interests which induce the State to make any efforts in this direction, serve to increase the danger of inundation. This danger is rendered still greater by the laying waste of large tracts of wood on the mountains, chiefly by their private owners. This mad sacrifice of forest, for the sake of " profit," is said to be cause of the appreciable deterioration of climate and decline in the fertility of the soil in the provinces of Prussia and Pomerania, in Styria, Italy, France, and Spain.

Frequent inundations are the consequence of stripping high ground of trees. The inundations of the Rhine and Vistula are chiefly attributed to the devastation of forest land in Switzerland and Poland. The climate of Trieste and Venice is said to have been perceptibly deteriorated by the extent of wood laid bare in the Carnian Alps, and Madeira, large parts of Spain, extensive, once luxuriantly fruitful countries of Asia have to a great degree lost their fertility from the same cause.

Naturally the new community will not be able to solve all these great problems at once, but it will apply itself to them at once, with all the means within its reach ; inasmuch as its only aim is the fulfilment of these and similar tasks, and their fulfilment without let or hindrance. In the course of time it will accomplish public works, and solve problems of public interest, which it would make present society giddy even to think of, tasks which present society neither could nor would dream of undertaking.

The entire cultivation of the soil will therefore be very considerably improved under the new organisation, by the measures alluded to and others of a similar nature. To the means already mentioned for increasing the fertility of the soil, the following may be added. At present many square miles* of land are planted with potatoes, to be converted into huge quantities of brandy, which are almost entirely consumed by the destitute and miserable portion of the population. Brandy is the only stimulant, the only soother of care within its reach. For the civilised man of the new community brandy will have ceased to be an article of consumption ; the potato and grain now cultivated for this purpose, in other words, land and labour will be set at liberty for the cultivation of nourishing forms of food. We have already seen to what an extent our most fertile cornfields are sacrificed to the beetroot speculation. Our standing army, our unorganised methods of production, means of transport and agricultural system necessitate the employment of many hundred thousands of horses, and consequently extensive tracts of land are required for the pasturage and breeding of foals. The complete transformation that will take place in all these conditions will make the greater number of these horses superfluous and again a large amount of land and labour will be gained for other purposes of civilisation.

The wide field of agriculture has already become the subject of discussion of a very comprehensive scientific literature. No branch has been left untouched ; the cultivation of forests, irrigation and drainage, the growth of cereals, of leguminous and tuberous plants, of vegetables, fruit trees, flowers and ornamental plants, fodder for cattle, the treatment of meadows, rational methods of breeding cattle and poultry, the application of their excrements, natural and artificial manure, the profitable use of refuse, the chemical examination of the soil, its fitness and preparation for various kinds of crops, machines and implements, the nature of seed, the most appropriate manner of erecting agricultural buildings, the succession of crops, the conditions of the weather— all these things and some others have as we said been made the subject of scientific treatises. Hardly a day passes

* A German geographical mile = 7·4 Kilometres. Transl.

without some new discovery, some new invention, which surpasses the improvements already made in one branch or another. Agriculture has become a science since the day of J. v. Liebig, and one of the chief and most important sciences; it has attained a greater significance and larger dimensions than any other department of productive activity. If however we compare this immense progress with the actual condition of agriculture in Germany we discover that so far only a very small minority of private proprietors has been in a position to profit by these improvements to any appreciable extent, and naturally no one has paid attention to any consideration but his private interest without regard to the general welfare. By far the greater part of our agriculturists and gardeners (one may safely say 90 per cent.) is totally unable to make use of the advantages opened out by science. Here the new community will find a field for its activity, both theoretically and practically well prepared, which it only needs to take in hand and organize to obtain far higher returns than any hitherto achieved.

The concentration of agriculture, when carried to the utmost extent, is another source of considerable advantages; much new land can be gained by the removal of hedges, roads and footpaths between the scattered properties; the use of large agricultural machines, combined with applied physics and chemistry, will convert land that is at present entirely incapable of cultivation, of which much still exists everywhere, into fertile soil. Scientific manuring of the fields, in addition to thorough ploughing, irrigation and drainage will considerably increase the returns of every kind of land; a careful choice of seed and protection from weeds, a point in which there is much room for improvement, will effect still more in the same direction. All sowing, planting, and the succession of crops, will of course be arranged with a view to obtaining as large a quantity of nutriment as possible. The cultivation of fruit and vegetables will be developed to a degree hardly thought possible at present, and its returns be multiplied accordingly. The concentration of stalls, storehouses, manure depots, fodder, &c., all arranged with regard to the greatest advantage, will increase the returns of cattle-breeding, and facilitate the collection of manure which is so important to the agriculturist. All machines and implements will be provided in a state of the greatest possible perfection. Animal products, such as milk, eggs, meat, honey, wool, will be obtained and employed according to scientific principles. The preparation of the fields for sowing and the gathering in of the crops will be carried on by whole armies of workmen, who can therefore take advantage of favourable weather in a manner which is at present utterly impossible. Large drying houses will allow of the crops being cut even in bad weather, and prevent the losses which under present circumstances are unavoidable.

Recent attempts to apply electric light in order to promote the growth of plants by night have had results which open out quite new perspectives in another direction, and the employment of artificial warmth in large greenhouses will make it possible to cultivate fruit and vegetables at seasons and weathers at which this has hitherto only been feasible on a very limited scale.

But as the cultivation of the land can only reach its highest development and be maintained at this height if the ground receives a sufficient amount of manure, the question of obtaining and storing the latter becomes one of the most important social problems.*

Manure is precisely the same to the land as food to man, and every kind of manure is just as far from being of the same value for the land as every kind of food is from being equally nutritive for man. The ground must receive exactly the same chemical ingredients as those which have been extracted from it by the previous crops, and it must especially receive those chemical ingredients which the crop to be next

---

* " There is a prescription for securing the fertility of the fields and perpetual repetition of their produce; if this prescription be consistently carried out it will prove more remunerative than any which has ever been applied in agriculture. It runs as follows:—' Let every farmer like the Chinese coolie who carries a sack of corn or a hundredweight of rape, or carrots, or potatoes to town, bring back with him as much or more of the ingredients of his field products than he took with him, and restore it to the field whence it came; he must not despise a potato paring or a straw, but remember that one of his potatoes still needs a skin and one of his ears of corn a stalk. The expense of this importation is slight, the outlay secure, a savings bank cannot be securer, and no investment brings in a higher rate of interest; the returns of his fields will be doubled in ten years; he will produce more corn, more meat and more cheese without expending more time or labour, and he will not be driven by constant anxiety to seek for new and unknown means, which do not exist, to make his ground fertile in another manner. . . . All bones, soot, ashes, whether washed out or not, the blood of animals and refuse of all kinds ought to be collected in special storehouses and prepared for use. The different governments and the town police should take precautions for preventing the loss of these materials by a suitable arrangement of drains and closets.' " Liebig: " Chemische Briefe." (Chemical Letters).

sown requires. This is a field in which the study of chemistry and its practical application will develop to an extent unknown at present.

Animal and human refuse and excrements principally contain the chemical ingredients which are the most appropriate for the reconstruction of human food. It is therefore desirable to obtain this manure to as large an extent as possible. This rule is being constantly transgressed at the present day, especially in large towns, which receive enormous quantities of food, but only restore a small portion of the valuable refuse and excrements to the land.* The consequence is, that all farms at a distance from the towns to which they annually send the greater part of their produce, suffer considerably from want of manure; that obtained from the human inmates and from the cattle of the farm is insufficient, because they consume only a small portion of the crops, and a ruinous system of cultivation ensues, by which the soil is impoverished, the harvests lessened, and the price of food raised. All those countries which principally export produce of the soil, but receive no materials for manuring in return, are being gradually but inevitably ruined, Hungary, Russia, the Danubian Principalities, and America. It is true, artificial manure, especially guano, replaces that of men and cattle, but few farmers are able to buy it in sufficient quantities on account of its price, and in any case it is reversing the natural order of things to import manure from a distance of many thousand miles, whilst that which one has close at hand is wasted. The great difficulty at present is the building of suitable and capacious reservoirs, and the costs of carriage. It is comparatively dearer to procure manure from the town than to fetch guano from the far distant transmarine guano

---

* Every Coolie (in China) who carries his produce to market in the morning brings home two buckets full of manure on a bamboo rod in the evening. The appreciation of manure goes so far, that every one knows how much a man produces in a day, a month, and a year, and the Chinaman considers it more than rude, if a guest leaves his house carrying with him a benefit to which his host thinks himself justly entitled as a return for his hospitality. . . . Every substance derived from plants or animals is carefully collected and used as manure by the Chinese. . . . To complete the idea of the importance attached to animal refuse, it will suffice to mention the fact that the barbers carefully collect and trade with the hairs cut from the head and beards of the hundred millions of customers whom they daily shave; the Chinese are acquainted with the use of gypsum and chalk, and it not unfrequently occurs that they renew the plaster in their kitchens merely for the purpose of using the old plaster as manure." Liebig: " Chemische Briefe." (Chemical Letters.)

fields, which however are naturally becoming exhausted in proportion to the necessarily increasing demand.

The sums expended at the present day for manure are enormous. Germany pays annually 70—100 million marks to foreign countries,* while four times this amount is being wasted at home. We only need to consider that a town of 100,000 inhabitants produces about 45,000 cwt. of solid and ten times as much liquid manure, and that this quantity is in many cases carried into the rivers, which are thus made impure and dangerous. If we consider further, that one person produces very nearly as much manure yearly as is required for manuring a field on which food sufficient for one person can be grown, the prodigious loss is evident. To human and animal excrements we must add the refuse of the kitchen and of factories, which might be turned to account in the same way, and which is to a large extent thoughtlessly wasted.

Assuredly the new community will find ways and means of solving a problem of such vital importance as completely as possible. What is ˌbeingˌ done at present in this direction is patchwork, inadequate in every respect. For instance, the excessively expensive drainage and sewage fields of the imperial capital, which were acknowledged to be defective to the last degree, long before they were completed. The new community will find other and simpler measures for dealing with this question, and one of the first will be gradually to abolish large towns and decentralize their population.

No one can regard the development of our large towns as a healthy product. The present industrial and economic system is constantly attracting great masses of the population thither. There we find the manufacturing and commercial centre, there is the junction of the great roads of communication, there are the large incomes, the central police courts, the military headquarters, the highest courts of law. There, too, are the great universities, the centres of culture, amusement, recreation, picture galleries, exhibitions, museums, theatres, concert halls, etc. Thousands are drawn by their occupations, thousands in search of pleasure, and thousands more by the hope of easy earnings and an agreeable manner of life.

But the growth of these large towns reminds one of a man

---

* Carl Schober: "Vortrag uber landwirthschaftliche, kommunale und volkswirthschaftliche Bedentung der Städtischen Abfallstoffe, etc." (Lecture on the agricultural, communal and economic significance of Town Refuse, etc.) Berlin, 1877.

whose body is always getting fatter and his legs thinner, till
at last the latter are no longer able to bear the weight of the
former. All round the towns and immediately adjoining
them, the villages are also assuming the character of towns,
and an enormous mass of proletariat is collecting within
them. The parishes, which are as a rule entirely devoid of
means, are forced to tax the ratepayers to the utmost possible
extent, and are nevertheless unable to meet the demands
made upon them. Meanwhile the villages increase in the
direction of the town and the town in the direction of the
villages, until at length they fall into the town, like planets
that have come too near the sun. But their mutual conditions of existence are not improved thereby ; on the contrary. These aggregations of masses, these centres of
revolution as one might call them, were necessary during the
present phase of development ; when the new community is
constituted, their object will have been fulfilled. Their
gradual dissolution becomes inevitable ; the current of population will then set from the towns towards the country, and
there form new communes, befitting the new conditions,
where industrial and agricultural occupations can be combined.

As soon as the town population is able to transplant its
accustomed means of culture to the county, as soon as it
there finds its museums, theatres, concert halls, reading
rooms, libraries, clubs, schools, etc., it will commence the
migration without delay. Life will then have all the advantages offered by great towns without their disadvantages.
Dwellings will be healthier and pleasanter. The country
population will take its share in industrial, and the town
population in agricultural production.

Here, too, the bourgeois world is preparing the way for the
future transformation, by establishing year by year a greater
number of industrial undertakings in the country. The unfavourable conditions of life in the large towns, the high
rents, and higher wages, force the employers to take this
step ; the large landed proprietors, too, become manufacturers (of sugar, brandy, beer, paper).*

It will then be an easy matter to apply refuse in all its
forms to the soil, especially owing to the concentration of
production and of the establishments for preparing food.
Each commune forms, so to speak, a zone of civilization, in

---

* Bismarck has erected a paper mill on his estate.—Transl.

which it grows a considerable portion of that which it requires for its own uses. Particularly gardening, perhaps the most agreeable of all practical occupations, will be brought to the highest degree of perfection. Flowers, shrubs, vegetables, fruit, present an inexhaustible field for human activity, and this is work which must be carried out in detail, and excludes the employment of machinery on a large scale.

Through the decentralization of the population, the distinction between town and country inhabitants, which has existed for thousands of years, disappears.

The peasant, this modern helot, who, in his isolation in the country, was cut off from all possibility of higher culture, will then become a free man, * a wish expressed by Prince Bismarck, to see the large towns annihilated, will be fulfilled.

*   *   *   *   *   *

If we look back on the previous argument we find that with the cessation of private property in the means of work and production, and hand in hand with their conversion into social property, the crowd of evils has disappeared, which present society disclosed at every step we took. As society itself labours, guides, and controls at the same time, every pernicious form of activity, whether proceeding from individuals or from whole classes, ceases as a matter of course. Swindle and fraud of every kind, the adulteration of food, the transactions at the Exchange, have the ground taken from under their feet. The halls of Mammon's temples are empty, for all consols, shares, pledges, mortgages, etc., will have become waste paper. Schiller's words, " Unser Schuldbuch sei vernichtet, ausgesöhnt die ganze Welt " (Our book of debts be cancelled, the whole world reconciled), will have

---

* Prof. Adolph Wagner remarks in the work already quoted : " Lehrbuch der Politischen Œkonomie von Rau " (Handbook of Political Economy, by Rau) : " Small peasant properties form an economic basis, which can be replaced by no other, for a very important portion of the population, an independent race of peasants, with its peculiar position and function in social politics." If the author does not make a point of glorifying the peasant proprietor à tout prix, out of consideration for his conservative friends, he must acknowledge, after all that has been said on the subject, that the small proprietor is one of the most miserable of men. The peasant is, under present circumstances, beyond the reach of culture ; he is unable to improve his position, and therefore becomes a check to civilization. Those who love stagnation and darkness, because they find it profitable to do so, may approve of these conditions ; a friend of civilization cannot.

been translated into practical reality, and the words of the Bible, " In the sweat of thy brow shalt thou eat bread," will apply to the heroes of the exchange as well as to other mortals. But they will not be overwhelmed by their labour, and their bodily health will be considerably improved. The present state organization will have vanished too, leaving no void behind.

" The State was the official representative of the whole community : it was its union in a visible body, but only inasmuch as it was the State of that class which represented to it the entire community. By actually becoming the representative of the whole community, it becomes superfluous. When there is no longer any class of society to be held in subjection, as soon as the supremacy of caste and the struggle for existence, based on the present anarchic form of production, have ceased, and along with them the collisions and excesses to which they give rise, there will be nothing left to repress worth any special repressive measures. The first act in which the State appears as the actual representative of the entire community, viz., the appropriation of the means of production in the name of society, will be at the same time its last act as State. The Government of Persons is re-placed by the Administration of Things, the Management of Productive Processes."*

The representatives of the State will have disappeared along with the State itself,—Ministers, parliaments, standing armies, police and gens-d'armes, law courts, lawyers, and public prosecutors, prisons, rates, taxes, and excises,—the entire political apparatus. Barracks and other military buildings, prisons, palaces of justice and administration, will then await a better destination. Tens of thousands of laws, ordinances, regulations, have become so much waste paper, possessing only historical value as curiosities and antiquities. The great, and yet so petty, parliamentary struggles, in which the heroes of the tongue flatter themselves that they rule and lead the world by their speeches, have disappeared and given place to administrative colleges and administrative delegations, whose function it is to settle the best methods of production and distribution, the necessary stores and advantageous innovations. These are all practical, tangible things, which each member of society will consider objectively, because he is influenced by no strong personal motives.

---

* Friedrich Engels : "Herrn Eugen Dühring's Umwälzung der Wissenschaft." (Mr. Eugen Dühring's Revolution of Science).

The many hundred thousand former representatives of the State have taken up the most various occupations and help to increase the productive wealth of the community. Neither civil nor political crimes or offences are known any longer. There are no more thieves, because in the new society every one can gratify his desires with ease, like all his neighbours, by honest work. Neither will there be any more vagabonds and tramps. Murder? Why? No one can enrich himself at the cost of another. Perjury, forgery, deception, legacy-hunting, fraudulent bankruptcy? There is no room for these crimes where there is no private property. Incendiarism? Who will find pleasure or satisfaction in it, since society gives him no reason for hate. Crimes against the mint? Why, money is a chimæra; the trouble would be in vain. Blasphemy? Let us leave the almighty and beneficent God to punish those who insult him, supposing that people still continue to dispute about the existence of a God.

Thus all the foundations of the present " order " of things become myths. Parents will tell their children about them, as they now tell them fairy tales of old times, and the little ones will shake their heads and not be able to understand. And the tales of the persecution and tyranny to which the men of new ideas are exposed to-day, will sound to them as the burning of witches and heretics sound to us. All the names of these " great " men, who now distinguish themselves by their persecution of the new ideas and are applauded by their narrow-minded contemporaries for their prowess will be forgotten, will have passed away like the wind, or at best come in the way of the historian, when he turns over old books. I will suppress the remarks that will then rise to his lips, as, alas, we do not yet live in these fortunate times, in which mankind can breathe freely.

And religion will share the fate of the State. It will not be " abolished," God will not be dethroned, religion will not be " torn out of the people's hearts," nor will any other of the phrases be put into effect, of which the atheistic Social-Democrats are accused. Social-Democracy leaves all such foolish attempts to the bourgeois ideologists who tried to realise them in the French Revolution, and naturally came to grief. Religion will disappear by itself, without any violent attack.

Religion is the transcendental image of the condition of society at any given period. The religion of society changes in the same measure as society changes and as its development progresses. The ruling classes seek to preserve it as a means of upholding their supremacy. This business becomes an important official function, exercised by a caste formed for the purpose of supporting and enlarging the edifice with all the subtilty at its command, and thereby assuring its own power and prestige.

At first Fetishism, at the lowest stage of civilisation under primitive social conditions, religion becomes polytheism at the next stage, and monotheism with the advance of culture. It was not the gods who created men, but men who made gods for themselves. "And he made god in his own image, in the image of man made he him," and not *vice versâ*. Even monotheism is already dissolving and evaporating into a Pantheism that embraces and penetrates all matter. Natural science has made a myth of creation ; astronomy, mathematics and physics have converted heaven into airy space, and the stars on heaven's tent where the angels sat enthroned, into fixed stars and planets, whose nature quite excludes the presence of such beings as angels. The ruling class, which sees its existence threatened, clings to religion as the support of all authority, a dogma which all rulers have upheld up to the present day.* The bourgeoisie believes nothing ; it has itself destroyed all belief in religion and authority by its own process of development, and by science, to which it has given birth. Its belief is a farce, and the church accepts the help of this false friend because it needs help. "But," says the bourgeoisie, "religion is necessary for the common people."

---

* The opinion of the Ancients on this matter is shown by the following quotations :—"The tyrant (as the supreme ruler was called in ancient Greece) must preserve the appearance of paying the greatest deference to religion, for the subjects do not fear illegal treatment so much from a ruler whose conduct they regard as god-fearing and pious, and on the other hand they do not so easily rise up against him, believing that he has the gods on his side." Aristotle; "Politics." Aristotle was born 384 B.C. at Stagira in Macedonia and is therefore frequently called the Stagirite.

"The Prince must possess all good and humane qualities, or better still, he must appear to possess them, and above all he must seem all piety, all religion. Even though some few detect the dissimulation, they will hold their peace, for the majesty of State protects the prince, who, thanks to this protection, can assume a different attitude when his interest requires it. The bulk of his subjects will believe that he is an honourable man even when he neither keeps faith nor respects religion, because he maintained the appearance of godliness on many occasions when it cost him nothing to do so. Moreover, the prince must pay the greatest attention to the support of divine service and of the hierarchy." Machiavelli, in his celebrated book : "The Prince," 18th chapter. Machiavelli was born at Florence, in 1469.

For the new community no such considerations exist. Human progress, and genuine unadulterated science is its motto, and it will act up to this motto.

Those who still have religious needs can satisfy them in the company of fellow believers. Society will not interfere. The priest must perform his share of social labour, and as this is full of instruction for him as well as for others, perhaps the time will come for him too in which he recognises that the highest aim in life is to be a human being.

Morality and ethics have nothing to do with religion ; those who assert the contrary are either fool or hypocrites. Morality and ethics are the expression of conceptions which regulate the actions of men and their relations towards each other ; religion regulates the actions of men towards supernatural beings. But ideas of morality are the fruit of the social conditions of mankind at a given period, just as religion is the fruit of those conditions. Cannibals consider it highly moral to eat men, Greeks and Romans considered slavery moral, the feudal lord of the Middle Ages considered serfdom moral, and the modern capitalist considers wage labour the essence of morality, with its demoralisation of women and children by factory and night work. Four phases of society and four moral conceptions, each higher than the preceding one, but none of them the highest. The highest state of morality is unquestionably that in which men are in a position of freedom and equality towards each other, in which the first principle of ethics, " Do unto others as ye would that they should do unto you, " becomes, through the organisation of society, the inviolable rule of human relationships. In the Middle Ages a man was esteemed for his genealogical tree, in modern times he is esteemed for his money, in the future he will be esteemed for himself. And the future is the realisation of Socialism.

*   *   *   *   *   *

Some years ago Dr. Lasker gave a lecture in Berlin, in which he arrived at the conclusion, that it was possible for all members of society to attain to the same level of culture.

Now Herr Lasker was an anti-Socialist, a stolid adherent of private property, and of the capitalistic form of production, and the question of culture is at the present day, eminently a question of money. It is difficult to understand how an equal level of culture is possible under such circumstances. A few energetic people, favoured by circumstances, can attain a higher degree of culture, but the mass can never do this as long as it lives in dependence.*

In the new community the conditions of existence will be the same for everyone. Needs and tastes will be different, but everyone will be able to live and develop in harmony with his own character. The uniform similarity which people are fond of attributing to Socialism is, like so much else, a calumny and an absurdity. If Socialism really desired it, Socialism would be unreasonable ; such a system would be a direct contradiction to human nature and would have to resign all hopes of seeing human society develop according to its principles. Even if it were possible to take society by surprise and force it into an unnatural form, in a very short time such bonds would be burst asunder, and Socialism condemned once and for ever. Society must develop out of itself, according to its own immanent laws. As soon as it recognises those laws and the laws of human development, it will act in harmony with them, and above all adapt the education of its offspring to them, as the foundation of all further development in a similar direction.

Every child that is born, whether boy or girl, is a welcome addition to the community, inasmuch as the community sees in the child a continuation of itself, its own prolonged existence ; it is therefore a matter of course that it accepts the duty of providing for the new being to the fullest extent of its power. Accordingly, the mother that suckles the child is the first object of its care. An agreeable dwelling, hygienic surroundings, every arrangement required at this stage of motherhood, attentive nursing for herself and her child are primary conditions. Naturally the child must be left at the mother's breast as long as is possible and necessary. Moleschott, Sonderegger, all hygienists and doctors agree

---

* " A certain degree of civilisation and prosperity is a necessary external condition for the development of the philosophical mind. Thence we find that only these nations begin to philosophise, that had obtained a considerable degree of civilisation and prosperity." Tennemann. Note in Buckle's " History of English Civilisation." First vol. page 10.

" Material and intellectual interests go hand in hand. One cannot exist without the other. There is a union between both similar to that between body and soul; if they are divided, death ensues." V. Thünen : " Der Isolirte Staat." (The Isolated State).

" The best kind of life for the solitary individual as well as for the whole State, is one in which virtue is so far provided with worldly goods that it can take an active part in useful and beneficent works." Aristotle ; " Politics."

that no other form of nourishment is capable of entirely replacing the mother's milk.

As soon as the child is old enough, he joins the games of children of his own age, under the care of common guardians. Again everything is provided that human knowledge and intelligence can supply for the development of mind and body. In addition to the halls for play comes the Kindergarten, and later on, as a combination of play and work, the introduction to the elements of knowledge and of human activity. Mental and bodily work, gymnastics, exercise in the playground, skating, swimming, marching, wrestling, for both sexes succeed each other by turns, and form together an educational whole. The object in view is the training of a healthy, hardy race, normally developed in mind and body. Step by step the growing child is made acquainted with tne different forms of practical activity, with manufacturing, horticulture, agriculture, with all the technical appliances of production. Meanwhile his mental training in the various branches of knowledge will not be neglected.

Moreover the same process of purification and improvement which takes place in the methods of production will also take place in the system of education, and a large number of obsolete and superfluous subjects of instruction, which instead of furthering only restrain both mental and physical growth, will be abolished. The knowledge of natural things, presented to a natural understanding will prove a very different incentive to the love of learning than an educational system in which one subject of instruction contradicts and cancels another, as for instance, religion and natural science. The schools, class-rooms, educational apparatus and means of instruction will be in accordance with the high degree of civilisation which society has attained. Books, instruments, clothes and food being provided by society, no pupil will be worse off than his fellows.* The number and capacity of the

---

* Condorcet makes the following demands in his plan of education: "Education must be free, it must be the same for all, and open to all; it must be bodily, mental, industrial and political, and must aim at real and actual equality."

Rousseau demands the same in his "Political Economy." "Above all education must be public, general and mixed, and its object, the training of men and citizens."

Aristotle, too, says: "As the State has only one object, it must provide one and the same education for all its members. It is the business of the State and not of private persons to make the necessary provisions for such an education."

teachers will be on a par with everything else. An ideal condition will at last be reached when we have provided educators for the growing generation in the same proportion as subaltern officers are at present provided for the army, where, as we know, one is allowed for every group of ten " common " soldiers.

Thus will education be the same for all, *and for both sexes*. The sexes will be separated only in cases in which functional differences make it absolutely necessary. And this system, strictly regulated and systematised and carried out under the control of persons fitted for the post, up to the time at which society declares its members of age, will enable the youth of both sexes to fulfil the duties and enjoy the rights which the community imposes on and accords to its mature members, and to do this the fullest extent and in every direction. Society may then rest assured that it has trained only capable and fully developed beings, men and women to whom no natural facts are strange, who are acquainted with the laws of their own existence as well as with the essence and condition of the society into which they enter.

All the faults and extravagances of the youth of the present generation, which increase from day to day, and are but the inevitable consequence of the rottenness and dissolution of society will have disappeared. The unmannerly behaviour, want of discipline, the immorality, the love of vulgar pleasures, which are called forth and fed by the disorder and restless-ness of family life, by the poisonous influences of social life, demoralizing books, shameless stimulants to lust, ambiguities of all kinds in the press, the factory system, over-crowded dwellings, the complete want of control as well as of inde-pendence at an age at which a young man or woman is most in need of checks from without and of training to self-discipline, all these and many other evils can be avoided with ease by the future community without the exercise of force or tyranny. The social atmosphere will make them im-possible.

The same thing applies in Sociology as in Nature. Diseases and organic destruction can only occur where a process of dissolution is going on by which soil for their development is provided.

No one can deny that our whole system of instruction and education labours under great and serious drawbacks, which affect the higher class schools and colleges even more than the lower. A village school is a picture of moral health in comparison with a gymnasium (public school), a sewing school for poor children a model of morality in comparison with a large number of expensive boarding schools. We need not look far for the cause. In the upper classes of society every effort towards higher humanitarian aims is crushed; there is nothing left to strive for; owing to the absence of ideals and of any ennobling activity applied to clearly recognized objects, an unbounded thirst for pleasure, and excesses of all kinds with their physical and moral consequence increase and spread. How can a generation growing up under such conditions be other than it is? Coarse material pleasures without measure or limit is the only aim in life that it sees and understands. Why should it exert itself, since the wealth of the parents makes every exertion appear superfluous? The height of culture for our middle-class young men consists in passing the examination for one-year military service. When this is attained, they fancy they have climbed Pelion and Ossa, from whence they descry Olympus and feels as gods of the second order. And when they have the commission of a reserve officer in their pocket their pride and arrogance know no bounds.

The daughters of our middle-class families are trained as dolls, fools of fashion, and ladies who can grace a drawing-room; they rush from one amusement to another, till at length, surfeited with pleasure, they fall a prey to ennui and all sorts of real and imaginary diseases; when old, they becomes models of piety, turn up their eyes at the corruptions of the world and preach morality and religion.

As for the lower classes, we are endeavouring to restrict their education. The mob might grow too clever, get tired of its servile condition and rise in mutiny, against its gods.

Thus we find modern society as helpless with regard to the question of education and training as with regard to all other social questions. What are its resources? It calls for the stick and beats, preaches religion in every shape, and founds reformatories regulated by a religious spirit to receive the worst elements. Having done this, its pedagogic wisdom is at an end.

After the community has educated the young up to a given age on the principles laid down, it can leave them to decide their further training for themselves, in the certainty that every one will gladly take advantage of the opportunities given him for continuing the development of the germs that have been tended so far. Each will practise and carry out those occupations for which his capacities and tastes qualify him, in the company of those who have made the same choice as himself. One will apply himself to some branch of natural science, which meanwhile assumes grander and grander dimensions, anthropology, zoology, botany, mineralogy, geology, physics, chemistry, or prehistoric investigation; another will apply himself to history, philology, or the study of art; a third will become an enthusiastic musician; a fourth, painter; a fifth, sculptor; a sixth, actor. The narrow artists' guilds of the present day will have ceased to exist, along with the like guilds of scholars and artisans. Thousands endowed with brilliant talents that have been suppressed hitherto, will attain development, receive recognition and be of service to society through their scholarship and capacities when occasion offers. There will be no musicians, actors, artists and scholars by profession, but *by spontaneous choice, by right of talent and genius*. And what they accomplish will probably as far excel what is at present accomplished in these various branches, as the industrial, technical and agricultural results of the future community will excel those of the present.

It will be the commencement of an era for science and art such as the world has not yet seen, and the creations which it brings forth will be worthy of it.

The metamorphosis and new birth which art will undergo when human society has become humane was recognized and put into words by no less a person than Richard Wagner, as early as 1850, in his book " Kunst und Revolution " (Art and Revolution). This book is especially remarkable on account of its appearing immediately after the suppression of a revolution in which Wagner had taken part, and which was the occasion of his being obliged to flee from Dresden. In this book Wagner clearly perceives what the future will bring and appeals directly to the working classes to assist artists in laying the foundations of true art. Among other things he says:—" When our freemen of the future are no longer compelled to make the support of life the object of life, when the realization of a new faith, or rather of a *new knowledge, assures to all the means of livelihood in return for congenial and useful labour*, in short, when industry is no longer our mistress but our handmaid, *we shall discover that the object of life is joy in living*, and seek to train our children to the full capacity of enjoyment. Education, starting with the development of strength and of physical beauty, will assume an artistic character, from unimpeded love to the child and delight in its growing charms, and *every human being will become an artist in truth in one direction or another. The variety of natural tastes will lead to the development of the most manifold talents to an unprecedented extent.*" These words are entirely Socialistic in spirit.

       ❋   ❋   ❋   ❋   ❋   ❋

Social life will in the future become more and more public; the tendency in this direction has already made itself apparent, and most clearly in the totally altered position of women in comparison with earlier times. Household life will be reduced to the narrowest possible limits, and the widest field will be opened for the gratification of social instincts. Large places of meeting for lectures, debates, and the discussion of all social concerns, which will then be decided by the sovereign voice of the entire community, halls for games, eating and reading rooms, libraries, concert halls, and theatres, museums, playgrounds, gymnasia, parks and public works, baths, schools and universities, laboratories, hospitals for the sick and invalided, and all these institutions arranged and fitted out with the greatest possible perfection, will perform the objects for which they are intended, and offer abundant opportunity for every kind of recreation, as well as for art and science.

How small our own much lauded epoch will look beside such an era; this cringing for favour and smiles from above, this fawning attitude, this envious struggle for the best place with the lowest weapons of malice; this suppression of the real convictions, the concealment of good qualities that might offend, this castration of the character, this hypocritical display of untrue feelings and opinions. All that elevates or ennobles a man or woman, real self-reliance, independence, incorruptibility of thought and conviction, a free confession of opinion, is regarded under present circumstances as so many failings and weaknesses. They are characteristics that inevitably ruin their owner, unless he suppress them. The explanation why so many do not feel their degradation is that they are accustomed to be degraded. The dog sees nothing remarkable in having a master who lets him taste the whip when out of temper.

Along with all these gigantic changes in social life, our entire literary production will as a matter of course assume a totally different aspect. Theological literature which at present forms the largest contingent in the yearly list of literary novelties, will disappear altogether; the same thing will apply to legal works and to the literature dealing with all former State and Social institutions, except inasmuch as they are valuable for historical research. The mass of shallow literary productions, the publication of which is only made possible by perverted tastes, patronage, or the vanity of the author who prints them at his own expense, will vanish from the scene. Judging from present conditions, one may affirm without exaggeration that at least four fifths of all the literary wares in the market might disappear without the slightest loss to civilization or culture, so great is the amount of superficial and pernicious productions or of absolute rubbish.

The press will be overtaken by the same fate as light literature. It is impossible to conceive of anything more dreary, more devoid of intellect or shallower than our modern newspaper literature. If the contents of our ordinary papers were to be made the criterion for the condition of civilization and scientific progress, the latter would seem to be at a low ebb indeed. The actions of persons and the condition of things are judged from a stand point belonging to past centuries, which science has long since proved to be ridiculous and untenable. This is not remarkable. A considerable number of our newspaper literati, are people who have "missed their calling," but whose education and claims on remuneration suits the bourgeois interest from a business point of view. At the same time it is the function of the daily papers and of the majority of belletristic periodicals to favour the lowest speculation and fructify burgeois morality in their advertisement sheets; their money and exchange articles are enlisted in the same service on another field.

Belletristic literature is on the whole no better than newspaper literature; its object is mainly the treatment of sexual subjects with all their excesses; it represents sometimes shallow enlightenment, sometimes the most imbecile prejudices and superstititions. The *raison d'être* of the whole thing is to make the bourgeois world appear as the best of all worlds, in spite of small failings, whose existence must be conceded.

On this large and important field the future community will undertake very radical reforms. The ground will then be occupied only by science, truth, art, the conflict of opinions of those who seek the best, and everyone who is capable of taking part in the contest will have the opportunity of doing so. The author will no longer be a slave to the favour of the bookseller, to the prospects of profit, or to prejudice, but will depend on impartial and qualified judges, whom he himsel helps to appoint.

  ❊   ❊   ❊   ❊   ❊   ＊

If the development of the individual is to be complete, and if the object of this development is a social one, no one must remain chained to the soil on which he happens to have been born. Though he makes the acquaintance of men and the world through books and papers, the acquaintance can never be thorough. This is only possible through personal inspection and practical study. Future society would be insufficiently organized if it did not allow of travelling at least to the same extent as at present, when the cause is frequently business necessity. *The need of change in all the surroundings of life is deeply implanted in human nature.* This impulse is one of the indwelling instincts of all organic beings towards attaining perfection. The plant growing in a dark room will stretch itself towards a light that falls through a chink, as though it did so consciously. And man acts in precisely the same way. And every innate, natural instinct must be gratified.

The gratification of this instinct for change, far from being prevented by the state of the new community, will be brought for the first time within the reach of all. It will be facilitated by a highly developed system of communication, it will be necessitated by international connections. Then everyone will be in a position to have his " holiday trip," which it will be an easy matter to organize satisfactorily. Everyone will be able to visit foreign lands and continents, and to join expeditions and colonizing settlements of all kinds, of which there will be no lack, in return for a corresponding service rendered to society.

It will be the duty of the executive bodies to provide stores of all the requisites of life, sufficient to satisfy the needs of all. We have already shown that this task will not be difficult to fulfil. Society will regulate its working hours by circumstances; they will be shortened or lengthened, according to the claims of its members and the demands of the season. At one period of the year labour will be more agricultural, at another more industrial in its character; the workers will be

distributed as the necessity of the moment dictates. Thanks
to this combination of large numbers of workers, with perfected technical appliances, society will be able with ease to
execute undertakings which at present appear impossible.

A community which provides for its children, will certainly
not neglect the aged, the sick and the invalid. Society is
under the obligation of caring for those who from one cause
or another are incapable of working. Such cases will be
treated with every possible attention and consideration ;
hospitals and convalescent houses, arranged on the most
advanced scientific and technical principles, will provide the
means of soon restoring a worker to society, or of soothing
the close of his life, when he has grown old and weak. His
days will be poisoned by no thought that others are waiting
for his death to take possession of his property, he will suffer
no anxiety from knowing that, when old and helpless, he
will be cast on one side like a squeezed out lemon. He will
depend neither on the charity and support of his children nor
on the beggarly pittance of the parish.*

The moral and physical condition of society, its provisions
for employing, housing, nourishing and clothing its members,
the social intercourse which it facilitates will all combine to
reduce accidents, premature disease and decrepitude to a
minimum. Natural death, the gradual loss of vitality will
become more and more the rule, and the conviction that
heaven is on earth, and that death means the cessation of
existence will induce all to live as nature directs.

The first conditions of a natural manner of life are rational
food and drink. Friends of the so-called natural way of
living often ask why Social-Democracy is so inaccessible to
vegetarianism. These frequent questions are the cause of
our devoting a few words to the subject here. Vegetarianism,
i.e. the doctrine that plants are the only fit nourishment is a
doctrine that was first ventilated among people who were in
the agreeable position of being able to choose between
vegetable and animal diet. The question does not exist at
all for the vast majority of humanity, that is forced to live as
it can, and whose poverty limits it exclusively or nearly so to

---

* " A man who has spent his life up to old age in hard and honest work
must not depend in his last days either on the favours of his children or on
those of society. An independent old age, free from trouble and care, is
the most appropriate recompense for unceasing labour in days of health
and strength." V. Thünen : " Der Isolirte Staat." (The Isolated State).
But what do we see in bourgeois society to-day ?

vegetable diet, often of the least nourishing description. In large districts of our working population, in Silesia, Saxony, Thüringia, and all industrial neighbourhoods, potatoes are the principal means of subsistence, bread occupies a secondary place, and even the worst quality of meat hardly ever appears on the table. The greater part of the agricultural population exists almost entirely without meat ; the peasants are obliged to sell the cattle which they breed, to purchase other requisites with the money thus earned.

For all these involuntary vegetarians a substantial beefsteak or a good leg of mutton would be a decided improvement in diet. Vegetarians are right when they protest against the undue importance attached to meat, they are wrong when they represent its consumption as injurious and dangerous. Their reasons are partly sentimental ones, such for instance as natural feeling forbidding us to kill animals, to eat of a corpse, etc. The desire of living agreeably and undisturbed compels us to declare war against a considerable number of organisms in the shape of vermin and to destroy them, and we are obliged to kill and exterminate wild beasts, if we do not wish them to exterminate us. And if we allowed the " the friends of man," domestic animals, to increase unhindered, in half a century we should be blessed with so large a number of these friends, that they would eat us up by depriving us of nourishment. The assertion that vegetable diet induces gentleness of character is exaggerated. The beast awoke in the mild, rice-eating Hindu, when the cruelty of the English roused him to revolt.

Sonderegger hits the nail on the head when he says : " There is no order of rank for the importance of different kinds of food, but an immutable law according to which they must be combined." It is perfectly true that no one can live on meat alone, whereas he can live on plants, supposing he exercises a proper choice. On the other hand, no one can be satisfied with one kind of vegetable diet, even the most nourishing. For instance, beans, peas and lentils contain more nourishment than any other kind of food. But it would be intolerable although possible to subsist entirely on them. Karl Marx quotes a case in point in his " Capital." " The mine-owners in Chili force their workmen to eat beans from one year's end to another because this gives them more strength, and enables them to carry greater weights than any other kind of food. The workmen often refuse the beans, but they receive nothing else, and have no choice but to eat them." Q

It is evident that increasing civilization is introducing vegetable diet more and more in place of the almost exclusive meat diet common to races of hunters and herdsmen. The manysidedness of plant cultivation is a sign of higher general culture. Moreover, a given area of land produces much more vegetable nourishment than can be extracted from the same area by breeding cattle on it. This fact lends a growing importance to the question of vegetable diet. For the importation of meat, which is being carried on at present, thanks to the wastefulness of foreign countries, especially South America, will come to an end within the next few decades. On the other hand, we must not forget that animals are not bred for their flesh alone, but on account of their wool, hair, bristles, skins, milk, eggs, etc., and that they provide materials for various branches of industry and for many articles of food. Further, a considerable amount of manufacturing and household refuse can be turned to no better account than in feeding animals. Finally, the sea will open its enormous storehouses of animal food to men in the future on a very different scale to the present one. Vegetarianism as the exclusive mode of subsistence in the new community is therefore neither probable nor necessary, nor even possible.

The quality of food is much more important than the quantity. The quantity avails very little unless the quality be good. Now the quality can be considerably improved by the mode of preparation. It is therefore quite as necessary to apply science to the preparation of food as to any other form of human labour, in order to make it as profitable as possible. To accomplish this we require knowledge and the requisite apparatus. That women, to whom the preparation of food chiefly falls at the present day, neither are, nor can be, in possession of the necessary knowledge has already been fully shown. Neither do they possess the necessary apparatus. But machines for boiling, roasting, etc., in the greatest technical perfection, *i. e.*, arranged according to scientific principles, may already be seen at work in the kitchen of every large hotel, in barracks and hospitals, and even at cookery exhibitions. The question to be solved is how to attain the best results with the smallest expenditure of power, time, and material. This question is of especial importance when applied to human nourishment. The small private kitchen in the individual household is therefore an obsolescent institution, in which time, power, and material are thoughtlessly and extravagantly wasted. The entire preparation of food will be undertaken by society in the future; the greatest attention will be devoted to perfecting cookery, which will then be carried out in the most profitable and appropriate manner. The private kitchen will disappear. The nutritive value of food will be increased by its increased ease of assimilation, which will be the criterion of excellence. * A system of nourishment in accordance with natural laws will therefore only be possible in the new community.

Cato boasts of ancient Rome that, up to the sixth century after its erection (200 B.C.), there were learned men possessing a knowledge of medicine; but there was no occupation for those desirous of practising their art. People lived so soberly and simply that diseases rarely occurred, and death from old age was the usual form of decease. Not till gluttony and idleness had extended, till dissipation had appeared on the one hand and misery and oppression on the other, did a total change take place. "Who eats little, lives well" (*i.e.*, long), said the Italian Cornaro in the sixteenth century, as Niemeyer quotes.

Again, chemistry will teach us how to prepare new and better articles of food in the future, to an extent quite unknown at present, To-day science is abused to facilitate adulteration and deceit; but unquestionably a chemical compound, possessing all the properties of a natural product, answers the same purpose as the latter. The source from whence an article of food is obtained, or the manner in which it is prepared, is irrelevant so long as the product fulfils the demands made on it.

When, in addition to these central kitchens, we have central washing establishments, in which clothes are washed, dried, bleached, and ironed by the help of machinery, and if we take into account that besides all this there will be central heating and lighting, a supply of cold and warm water laid on, a sufficient number of baths, and that all our clothing and underclothing will be manufactured in central factories, we find our whole household life radically changed and simplified.†

---

* "The ease with which food can be assimilated by the individual is the measure of its worth." Niemeyer: "Gesundheitslehre." (Theory of Hygiene.)

† "Without servants, no civilization!" exclaims Prof. v. Treitzschke, in comic pathos, in a polemic against Socialism. It is certainly new that our servants are the "pioneers of civilization," The learned and professorial brain of Herr v. Treitzschke is just as incapable of imagining

The servant, that domestic slave of all the caprices of the "mistress," has disappeared, and the "lady" along with her.

---

anything outside the bourgeois world, as Aristotle was, twenty-two centuries ago, of imagining anything outside the Greek world. Society seemed impossible to Aristotle without slaves. And Herr von Treitzschke is evidently disturbed and anxious in his mind as to how he should get his shoes blacked and his clothes brushed, and we must allow that this is at present an " unsolved problem." Well, more than ninety per cent. perform these tasks at present for themselves, and in the future the remaining ten per cent. can do the same, unless the matter has been settled meanwhile by the introduction of machines, or unless the Herr Professor finds a sympathetic youth willing to help him out of his difficulty, for I trust he will live to see the new era. Moreover, work is no disgrace, not even that of blacking boots. Many an army officer with a long genealogical tree, who ran away from his debts to America and there became porter or shoe-black, has already made this discovery.

Woman in the Future.

This chapter can be very short. It merely contains the conclusions with regard to the position of women which follow from the foregoing remarks and which everyone can easily draw for himself.

In the new community woman is entirely independent, no longer subjected even to the appearance of supremacy or exploitation ; she is a free being, the equal of man.

Her education is the same as that of man, except where the difference of sex makes a deviation from this rule and special treatment absolutely unavoidable ; she develops all her mental and physical powers and capabilities under natural conditions of existence ; she can select such fields for her activity as her wishes, tastes and faculties may direct. She works under exactly the same conditions as a man. Having performed her share of social labour in some branch of industry, the next hour she becomes educator, teacher, or nurse, later on she devotes herself to art or science, and afterwards exercises some executive function. She enjoys amusements and recreation with her own sex or with men, exactly as she pleases and occasion offers.

In the choice of love she is free just as man is free. She wooes and is wooed, and has no other inducement to bind herself than her own free will. The contract between two lovers is of a private nature as in primitive times, without the intervention of any functionary, but it is distinguished from the primitive contract by the fact that the woman no longer becomes the slave of a man who obtained her as a gift or by purchase, and can cast her off at his pleasure.

Human beings must be in a position to act as freely, where their strongest impulse is concerned, as in the case of any other natural instinct. *The gratification of the sexual impulse is as strictly the personal affair of the individual as the gratification of every other natural instinct.* No one has to give an account of him or herself, and no third person has the slightest right of intervention. Intelligence, culture and independence will direct and facilitate a right choice. Should incompatibility, disappointment, and dislike ensue, morality demands the dissolution of a tie that has become unnatural and therefore immoral. As men and women will be fairly equal in number, and all other causes that have hitherto condemned a large proportion of women to celibacy or prostitution will have disappeared, men will no longer be in a position to assert any superiority. On the other hand the state of society will have removed the many drawbacks and disturbing elements which, as already shown, influence the married life of to-day and so often prevent it reaching its full development.

All these checks, all these contradictions to nature in the present condition of women have led even persons who are not disposed to accept the farther consequences of change in our present social state to recognise the justifiability of a perfectly free choice in love, and if need be, of an equally free dissolution of the relationship, without any external hindrance. Mathilde Reichardt-Stromberg, for instance, expresses herself as follows in a polemic against the Women's Rights agitation of the authoress Fanny Lewald :

" If you (F. L.) claim the complete equality of women with men in social and political life, George Sand must necessarily be also right in her struggles for emancipation, by which she demanded nothing more than that of which man has long been in uncontested possession. There is absolutely no reasonable ground for admitting the head but not the heart of woman to this equality, and not leaving her to give and take as freely as a man. On the contrary ; if woman has by nature the right and consequently the duty (for we will not bury the talent entrusted to our keeping) of exerting her brain to the uttermost in the race with mental Titans of the other sex, she must also have precisely the same right to preserve her equilibrium by quickening the circulation of her blood in whatever way seems good to her. We all read without the slightest moral indignation for instance how Goethe—to exemplify by the greatest—again and again wasted the warmth of his heart and the enthusiasm of his great soul on one woman after another. Every reasonable person regards this as perfectly natural, precisely because a great soul is difficult to satisfy and only the narrow minded moralist stops to blame him. But why then do you ridicule the " great souls " among women ?   .   .   .   Let us suppose

for example that the whole female sex consisted of great
souls like George Sand, that every woman were a Lucretia
Floriani, that all her children were children of love, but that
those children were all brought up with true motherly
devotion as well as with intelligence and good sense. What
would become of the world under such circumstances ?
Doubtless the world would go on as before, and progress as
before, and would possibly have remarkably little to complain of."

The authoress is perfectly right. What Goethe did was
and is done by many thousand of others, who resemble
Goethe in no other respect, without the slightest loss of caste
or prestige in society. All that one requires is a good position and everything else arranges itself. It is true the women
of these circles often allow themselves considerable liberty,
but on the whole their position is a far more unfavourable
one than that of the men, and then women with the character
of a George Sand are extremely rare at present. And in any
case such a condition is regarded as immoral, inasmuch as it
trespasses against the moral laws laid down by society and is
opposed to the nature of our social state. The compulsory
marriage is the normal marriage in bourgeois society, the
only " moral " union of the sexes, and every other sexual
union is, from this point of view, under all circumstances
immoral. This is quite consistent. The bourgeois marriage
is a consequence of bourgeois property. This marriage
standing as it does in the most intimate connection to property and the right of inheritance, demands "legitimate"
children as heirs ; it is entered into for the purpose of obtaining them, and the pressure exercised by society has enabled
the ruling classes to enforce it in the case of those who have
nothing to bequeath.*

But as in the new community there will be nothing to
bequeath, unless we choose to regard household furniture as

---

* Dr. Schäffle says in his book : " Bau und Leben des Socialen
Körpers," (Structure and Life of the Social Body) : " A loosening of
the marriage tie by facilitations for divorce is certainly not desirable ;
it is opposed to the ethical aims of human pairing, and would be injurious
to the preservation of the population and the training of children."
After what I have already said on this subject, it is hardly necessary to
remark, that I not only regard this view as incorrect but am strongly
inclined to consider it " immoral." But in any case Dr. Schäffle will
allow that we cannot imagine a society at a much higher stage of civilisation than the present one introducing or maintaining an institution that
is in opposition to its own conceptions of morality.

a legacy of any importance, compulsory marriage becomes unnecessary from this standpoint as well as from all others. This also settles the question of the right of inheritance which Socialism will have no need to abolish formally.

Woman is therefore entirely free, and her household and children if she has any, cannot restrict her freedom, but only increase her pleasure in life. Educators, friends, young girls are at hand for all cases in which she needs help.

Possibly there will be men in the future who will agree with Humboldt, when he says:—"I was not made to become the father of a family ; moreover, I consider marriage a sin, and the begetting of children a crime." What does it matter ? The force of natural impulses will preserve equilibrium, and we need not allow ourselves to be disturbed at this time of day by the philosophical pessimism of Mainländer, and von Hartmann, who prophesy the self-extinction of humanity in the ideal State.

Fr. Ratzel, on the other hand, is perfectly right when he says : "*Man must cease to regard himself as an exception from natural laws ; he must at length begin to search for the guiding laws in his own actions and thoughts and seek to direct his life according to them. The result will be that he will no longer regulate his relations to his fellows, i.e., to family and State, by the rules of former centuries, but by the reasonable principles of natural sense. Politics, morals, principles of right and wrong, which are at present fed from all possible sources will then be determined in accordance with the laws of nature alone. A human life worth living, of which fables have been told for thousands of years, will at length have become reality.*"*

---

* Quotation in Häckel's " Natürliche Schöpfungsgeschichte" (Natural History of Creation).

INTERNATIONALITY.

———

A human life worth living is not the manner of life of a single privileged nation only. However admirable the institutions of this nation might be, it could neither found nor uphold them in an isolated position, inasmuch as they are the product of the co-operation of international forces and relationships. Although the national idea still possesses all heads, and is used as a means of supporting the existing social and political supremacy, which is only possible within national boundaries, we are nevertheless already deep in internationalism.

Treaties of commerce and of navigation, postal unions, international exhibitions, congresses on the laws of nations and on an international system of geographical measurement, other international scientific congresses and societies (not least, workmen's societies) international expeditions of discovery, our trade and commerce, all these things and many others prove the international character which the relationships of the various civilised nations have assumed, in spite of a national exclusiveness, which they are already throwing off. We already speak of a Universal Economy in distinction to National Economy, and attribute greater importance to the former, because on it the welfare and prosperity of single nations depend, to a very considerable degree. A large proportion of home products are exchanged for the products of foreign countries, without which we could no longer exist. And just as one branch of industry suffers, when another declines, the national production of one country is lamed when that of another falls off. The relations of one country to another are constantly becoming more intimate in spite of all temporary disturbances, such as wars and national hatreds, because material interests, the strongest that exist, overrule all other considerations. Every new line of communication, every improvement in the means of locomotion, every advance or discovery in the process of production, leading to the cheapening of goods, strengthens the intimacy of these connections. The ease with which personal intercourse can be kept up between far distant lands is a new and important link in the chain of communication. Emigration and colonization are other powerful factors. One nation learns from another, and each seeks to out-do the other in the competitive race. Alongside of the exchange of every kind of ware, an exchange of mental products is going on at the same time; millions find themselves obliged to learn foreign languages; and nothing is better adapted to remove unfounded antipathies than material advantages in union with comprehension of the language and mind of a foreign nation.

The consequence of this international process is that the social conditions of different countries are becoming more and more alike. In the case of the most advanced and therefore most important civilized nations, this similarity is already so great, that if we are acquainted with the social structure of one people, we are acquainted with that of the others as well, in all its principal points, much as animals of the same genus have the same bony organization and structure, although the different species may vary in size, strength and other secondary matters.

A further consequence is that where similar social conditions exist, the effects caused by these conditions will also be the same. These effects are the accumulation of great riches, and its counterpart, proletarianism of the masses, wage slavery, bondage of men to machines, dominion of the few over the many, and all that results therefrom.

And in fact we see that the same class conflicts that are undermining Germany are agitating all Europe and the United States. From Russia to Portugal, from the Balkan, Hungary and Italy to England and Ireland, we find the same spirit of discontent, the same symptoms of social fermentation, of universal disquiet and dissolution. Externally different in its appearance, according to the character of the populations and the political forms under which they live, essentially it is everywhere the same; everywhere we see a deep social gulf yawning between class and class; every year that passes must deepen it, must drive the members of the social body more and more asunder, till at length an apparently trifling cause will bring about the catastrophe, that will spread with the speed of lightning through the whole civilized world, a signal summoning all to arms on one side or the other.

The revolt of the new world against the old has broken out. The stage is crowded with actors, the struggle will be carried on with an amount of intellect such as the world has seen in no struggle before and will see in none after. For it will be the last social struggle. The 19th century will hardly end before the contest is decided.

Thus will the new community be built up on an international basis. The nations will fraternize together, will shake hands over old quarrels, and unite in gradually extending the new state over all the peoples of the earth.* They will approach foreign races, not as foes who come to spoil and oppress, not as the representatives of a strange faith which they force upon others, but as friends who seek to raise these races to their own level of civilization.

When civilized nations are united in a great federation, the time will have come in which "the storms of war are hushed." The eternal peace is no dream, as the uniformed lords of the earth believe and persuade others. The time will then have come in which the nations recognise their real interests, which cannot be attained by war and strife, by armaments that ruin whole countries, but by the very opposite of these things. Thus the last weapons will find their way into the collections of antiquities, to tell future generations how earlier peoples rent each other like wild animals for many thousands of years, until at length man triumphed over the beast within him.

These future generations will then realize with ease undertakings which have long occupied the best brains of the past, and whose execution has been attempted but without success.†

---

* "National interests and human interests are at present the opponents of each other, At a higher stage of civilization both these interests will coincide and become one." V. Thünen : "Der Isolirte Staat." (The Isolated State).

† For instance, Condorcet, one of the French Encyclopædists of the last century, had, among other ideas, that of a universal language ; he demanded, too, the entire equality of women.

"As commerce, education, and the prompt transmission of thoughts and matter by telegraph and steamer have changed everything, I believe that God is preparing the world to become one nation, to speak one language, and to attain to a state of perfection in which armies and fleets of war will be no longer needed," Passage from an address of the Ex-President Grant. That a full-blood Yankee can only imagine God playing this part is not surprising. Hypocrisy flourishes nowhere more than in the United States.

Each advance in civilization will prompt another, will provide humanity with new tasks, and cause it to attain to a
continually higher stage of development.

The less the organisation of the State permits it to press upon the masses,
the more must this be done by religion. Consequently the bourgeoisie is
always most pious in countries where the State is most lax; next to the
United States, in England, Belgium, Switzerland.

Overpopulation.

From the international standpoint which we have now eached, we can form an impartial opinion on another " burning " subject of the present day, or rather one which is regarded as such by a certain number of persons, namely that of the increase of the population. Indeed, this subject is sometimes treated as the most important of all questions, on the solution of which the solution of all others depends. The law by which the population increases has become a constant matter of debate since the time of Malthus. In his celebrated and notorious work : " Essay on the Principles of Population," which Karl Marx designates as an immature, superficial, pompous, and priestly plagiarism on Sir James Stewart, Townsend, Franklin, Wallace, etc., " not containing a single sentence thought out by himself," Malthus lays down the proposition that human beings have the tendency to increase in geometric progression (1, 2, 4, 8, 16, 32, etc.), while food can only increase in arithmetical progression (1, 2, 3, 4, 5, etc.), consequently the numbers of the population must very soon be out of proportion to the amount of food, and want and starvation ensue. It is therefore necessary to practise abstinence in the procreation of children, and no one must marry without sufficient means, else there will be no place for his offspring at Nature's table.

The fear of over-population is very old. It has been already mentioned in this book, among the remarks on the social conditions of the Greeks and Romans, and towards the end of the Middle Ages. It is a characteristic fact, worthy of close attention, *that this fear always appears during periods in which the state of society is in decline and decay*. That is easily explained. All states of society up to the present day were based on class supremacy, and the principal means of class supremacy is possession of the land. The land passes out of the hands of a large number of proprietors into the hands of a small number, who cultivate it to an altogether insufficient degree. The masses have neither property nor means of existence, their share of food, therefore, depends on the good-will of the ruling classes. These classes meanwhile are quarreling among each other. The form which the contest takes depends upon the state of society, but it ends in a further concentration of the land in a still fewer number of hands. Under such circumstances every addition to the family is felt to be a burden by the rest, the spectre of over-population makes its appearance, and gains ground in pro-portion to the decrease in the number of proprietors, to the neglect of agriculture, and to a mode of cultivation in which the pleasure of the owner ranks higher than the productivity of the soil. At no time were the agricultural returns of Rome and Italy smaller than when the entire land was in the possession of about 3,000 proprietors; thence the cry of alarm, "The great estates are ruining Rome!" The land was turned into extensive hunting grounds and magnificent pleasure gardens, or was often left uncultivated because its cultivation by slave labour was dearer than the importation of corn from Sicily and Africa. This state of things offered every encouragement to a most shameless system of usury among corn-dealers. Consequently the impoverished Roman citizen, and the nobility, that as a rule was also impoverished, preferred to give up marriage and fatherhood, and thus arose the laws setting a premium on matrimony and parentage as a means of preventing the growing reduction of the ruling classes.

The same thing occurred towards the close of the Middle Ages, after the nobles had spent centuries in robbing the numerous peasants of their possessions, and in appropriating the common land to themselves, by every measure of force and stratagem, and, after the peasants had risen up in re-bellion and been crushed, had continued their predatory occupations on a larger scale, and had encroached on the property of the Church. Never was the number of robbers, beggars, vagabonds greater than shortly before and after the Reformation. The expropriated country population streamed to the towns, but there the chances of obtaining a subsistence had, as we have already shown, become more and more precarious, and "over-population" made itself felt on all sides.

The appearance of Malthus coincides with the period in English industry, in which, owing to the inventions of

Hargreaves, Arkwright and Watt the mechanical and technical conditions of production, especially in the cotton and linen branches, had been revolutionised and the workmen engaged in these branches thrown out of employment by tens of thousands. The concentration of capital and of landed property assumed enormous dimensions at this time in England, and hand in hand with the rapid accumulation of wealth on the one side went the growing wretchedness of the masses on the other. At such at time the ruling classes, who had every reason to be satisfied with the world as it was, were forced to look about them for an explanation of such contradictory facts as the pauperisation of the people in the midst of increasing wealth and a flourishing industry. For this purpose nothing could be more convenient than to seek the cause in the too rapid growth of workmen's families, rather than in the capitalistic process of production and the accumulation of land in the hands of large landlords, by which the workmen were made superfluous. Under such circumstances the " immature, superficial, pompous and priestly plagiarism " published by Malthus was a book which gave drastic expression to the most secret thoughts and wishes of the ruling classes, and justified their course of action before the world. Thence the unlimited approval which it met on the one hand, and the violent opposition which it called forth on the other. *Malthus had spoken the right word at the right moment for the English bourgeoisie, and thus, although his book " did not contain a single sentence thought out by himself," he became a great and celebrated man* and founded a school called after his name.

The state of affairs by which Malthus was induced to utter his warning and to proclaim his brutal doctrine (for it was chiefly directed to the working classes and added insult to injury) has not ceased since then, but has grown worse from decade to decade, and not only in that part of the United Kingdom where Malthus was born—he was a Scotchman like Adam Smith—but in all the countries of the world where the capitalistic process of production, the system of robbery in land, the enslaving of the masses and their treadmill labour in the factories have taken root and spread. The system consists, as already proved, in separating the producer from his means of production in the shape either of land or of implements, and in the concentration of these means of production in the hands of the capitalists. It continually creates new branches of industry, which it develops and concentrates, again throwing new masses of superfluous hands on the street. In agriculture, as in ancient Rome, it furthers the extension of large landed estates, with all their consequences. Ireland, the most typical country of Europe in this respect, the land that has been more desolated than any other by the English system of spoliation, possessed in 1876, 884.4 square miles of meadow and pasture land, but only 263.3 square miles of land under the plough, and year by year the conversion of arable land into meadow and pasture land for sheep and cattle, and into hunting grounds for the landlords is making greater strides.* The arable land in Ireland is to a great extent in the hands of a large number of small and even petty farmers, who are unable to carry on its cultivation to any adequate degree. Ireland accordingly presents the aspect of a country that is undergoing a retrograde transformation from an agricultural to a pastural land, *i.e.* it is retracing the steps by which it was developed from a pastural to an agricultural land. Meanwhile the population, which at the beginning of the century amounted to 8,000,000, has now sunk to 5,000,000, and still several millions are superfluous. Scotland presents a similar picture.† And the same thing is being repeated in Hungary, which has

---

* Ferdinand Freiligrath : "Irland."

> So sorgt der Herr, dass Hirsch und Ochs,
> Das heisst : dass ihn sein Bauer mäste,
> Statt auszutrockren seine Bogs—
> Ihr kennt sie ja, Irland's Moräste !
> Er lässt den Boden nutzlos ruh'n,
> D'rauf Halm an Halm sich wiegen könnte ;
> Er lässt ihn schnöd dem Wasserhuhn,
> Dem Kibitz und der wilden Ente.
>> Ja doch, bei Gottes Fluche :—Sumpf
>> Und Wildniss vier Millionen Aecker !

† "Two millions of acres, including the most fertile districts of Scotland, have been laid entirely waste. The native grass of Glen Tilt is regarded as the best in the county of Perth ; the deer forest of Ben Aulder was the best grazing land in the large district of Badenoch ; part of the Black Mount Forest was the most excellent pasturage in Scotland for black-faced sheep. A conception may be formed of the amount of land laid waste for hunting purposes when we learn that it covers a considerably larger area than the county of Perth. The loss of land for cultivation in consequence of this violent spoliation may be estimated by the fact that the deer park of Ben Aulder would support 15,000 sheep, and that it only represents the thirtieth part of the Scotch hunting grounds. . . All this land is entirely unproductive, it might just as well have been sunk in the North Sea."

Karl Marx : " Das Kapital." (Capital). 2nd Ed.

only entered the ranks of modern development within the last few decades. A country, the fertility of whose soil is almost unequalled in Europe, is on the brink of bankruptcy, the population, overwhelmed with debt, at the mercy of usurers, poor and wretched, is emigrating en masse, while the land has become concentrated in the hands of modern magnates of capital, who carry on a ruinous system of cultivation in forest and field, so that Hungary will before long cease to be a grain exporting country. In Italy it is just the same. Here too political unity has afforded a powerful incentive to the development of capital, but the industrious peasants of Piedmont and Lombardy, of Toscana and Romagna are becoming more and more impoverished and are fast approaching ruin. Swamps and moors are already reappearing in districts covered a few years ago by the well cultivated gardens and fields of small proprietors. The terrible malaria is assuming such dimensions that the Government, in alarm, instituted an investigation in 1882, by which the deplorable fact was ascertained, that, among the 69 provinces into which Italy is divided, 32 were hot beds of the disease, 32 were already infected, and only 5 were free. The malady, which formerly only occurred in the country, is penetrating into the towns, where the urban proletariat, increased by the proletariat of the country, is accumulating in larger and larger numbers and forming centres of infection.

These facts in connection with all that has been already said in this book on the effects of the capitalistic mode of production show us that the misery and distress of the masses are not the consequence of an insufficiency in the means of subsistence, but, firstly, of unequal distribution, leading to superfluity on the one hand and starvation on the other, and secondly of the constant destruction and waste of material, and neglect of production and cultivation.

The assertions of Malthus apply therefore only to the capitalistic mode of production, and all who make this standpoint their own, have every inducement to defend him, or they would have no firm ground under their feet.

On the other hand, capitalistic production sets a premium on the production of children, inasmuch as it requires their cheap labour in factories. A large family represents a certain amount of profit to the working man ; it costs him little or nothing to support children who at an early age earn enough to support themselves. Indeed he is obliged to have a large

R

family, as it places him in a better position for competing with others, for example, in house industries. Truly an abominable system, which encourages the pauperization of the workman, and forces his own children, who can attend to machines as well as himself, to turn him out of doors.

Precisely because the immorality and abuses of this system are so apparent, and increase with the extension of capitalism, it is easy to understand that bourgeois ideologists—a term that applies to all bourgeois economists—should take up the Malthusian idea so readily, and especially that the doctrine of over-population should gain more and more ground among the middle-classes in Germany. Capital, the innocent defendant, is acquitted, and the workman himself proved to be the criminal.

Unfortunately, Germany has already not only a superfluity of proletarians, but also a superfluity of intelligence. Capital does not only create an over-production of soil, goods, labourers, women and children, but also of scholars and officials, as I shall shew further on. Only one thing is not superfluous in the capitalistic world, and that is capital, and its owner, the capitalist.

If, then, bourgeois economists are Malthusians, it is because they cannot help being so; but they must not apply their bourgeois notions to a communistic community. For instance, John Stuart Mill says: "Communism is precisely the state of things in which opinion might be expected to declare itself with the greatest intensity against this kind of selfish intemperance. Any augmentation of numbers which diminished the comfort or increased the toil of the mass, would then cause (which now it does not) immediate and unmistakable inconvenience to every individual in the association; inconvenience which could not then be imputed to the avarice of employers or the unjust privileges of the rich. In such altered circumstances opinion could not fail to reprobate, and if reprobation did not suffice, to repress by penalties of some description this or any other culpable self-indulgence at the expense of the community. The communistic scheme, instead of being peculiarly open to the objection drawn from danger of over-population, has the recommendation of tending in an especial degree to the prevention of that evil." And on page 376 of Rau's "Handbook of Political Economy," Professor Adolph Wagner says: "A socialistic community would, as a matter of principle, be less able to grant freedom of marriage or freedom in the procreation of children than any other."

Both these authors assume that the tendency towards over-population is common to all states of society. But both allow that Socialism is better able to preserve the equilibrium between population and means of subsistence than any other form of community.

In this radically wrong conception of the relations between population and food on the one hand, and Socialism on the other, they have recently received a reinforcement from the socialistic camp, which helps to support their views. I refer to the already quoted book of Karl Kautsky's: "Der Einfluss der Volksvermehrung auf den Fortschritt der Gesellschaft" (The Influence of Increasing Population on the Progress of Society). Kautsky attacks Malthus, and yet agrees with him in principle. He speaks just as Malthus does of a Law of Diminishing Returns, without formulating it distinctly; indeed he partly refutes it himself, by citing numerous examples to prove how high a degree of development not only agriculture, but its kindred department, the production of meat and the utilization of domestic animals might attain under scientific treatment. He does not fail to recognize that the present want is caused by the irrational system of property that determines distribution, and he is aware that an exaggerated fear of over-population is common to all declining societies. Nevertheless, he comes to the conclusion that Socialism would do well to begin where other societies have left off, with a limitation of population. The position is a most contradictory one.

According to Kautsky, regard to the laws of population is the indispensable condition for any satisfactory discussion of the Social question. In this he follows F. A. Lange, who possessed an exaggerated admiration for John Stuart Mill, and was powerfully influenced by him. To Kautsky the period of over-population appears so imminent and so alarming, that he asks in consternation : " Shall we fold our hands in despair ? Is it really a crime against humanity to seek to make men happy ? Are prostitution, celibacy, disease, misery, war, murder, and all the other factors in the unspeakable wretchedness that devours the race at the present day, unavoidable ? " And he answers the question himself, by exclaiming : "they are, unless the law of population is recognized in all its terrors."

Hitherto every law that was once recognized was thereby robbed of its terrors — in this case, it would seem, the terrors increase with recognition. And accordingly, in the

2

face of this awful danger, Kautsky advises—not abstinence from women, like Malthus, Paul, and the Fathers of the Church—but intercourse with preventive measures, as he fully allows the necessity of satisfying the sexual impulse.

Our Malthusians believe, that as soon as the condition of the people is improved, society will be transformed into a rabbit-hutch, and its members have no higher aim in existence than the most unlimited sexual enjoyment, and the equally unlimited procreation of children, This is a low conception of man at a higher stage of civilization. Kautsky quotes the following passage from Virchow: " The English workman in his deepest depravity, in the most utter emptiness of mind, at length only knows two sources of enjoyment, drunkenness and sexual intercourse, and similarly to within the last few years the population of Upper Silesia concentrated every desire, every endeavour upon these two things. Brandy and the gratification of sexual feeling had become completely sovereign, and it is therefore easy to understand that the population increased as rapidly in numbers as it declined in physical strength and moral character." In my opinion this points very clearly to the direction which development will receive under higher culture, and a manner of life in harmony with natural laws.

Another quotation of Kautsky's, taken from Karl Marx, expresses an equally true and generally applicable view of the circumstances in question. " As a matter of fact, not only the number of births and deaths but the absolute size of families is in inverse ratio to the height of wages, *i.e.*, to the means of subsistence which the various categories of workmen have at their disposal. This law of capitalistic society would sound absurd among savages or even civilized colonists. It reminds us of the enormous power of reproduction among animals that are individually weak and hunted down." And a note on the subject in Marx, taken from Laing, runs: " If all the world were in comfortable circumstances, the earth would soon be depopulated." We see the view taken by Laing is exactly the opposite of that taken by Malthus.

Kautsky himself is not of opinion that an improved manner of life and higher culture would act as checks on the birth of children, on the contrary he believes that they would have the very opposite effect, and prescribes the use of preventive measures as the only means of obviating the Law of Diminishing Returns.

Let us examine the so-called Law of Diminishing Returns,

and enquire what physiology and experience teach us with regard to the generation of children. A man, who was at the same time a first rate agriculturist on a large scale, and a scholarly national economist, in both which directions he far excelled Malthus, says with regard to agricultural production: " The productivity of raw materials and especially of food will in the future not be exceeded by the productivity of manufacturing and transportation. . . . In our days agricultural chemistry is beginning for the first time to open out prospects, which, though they will doubtless lead to many a mistaken path, in all probability *will eventually place the provision of food in the power of society to the same extent as it is already in the power of society to provide an unlimited quantity of cloth*, if only the necessary amount of wool is to be had."[*]

Liebig also, another authority on the same subject, is of opinion, that as long as human labour and manure are present in sufficient quantities, the soil is inexhaustible, and will permanently yield the most plentiful harvests. We see, the Law of Diminishing Returns is a fancy of Malthus', which was to a certain extent justified at a time when agricultural development was at an extremely low stage, but which has since been refuted by science and experience. The Law ought to be expressed thus: *The returns of a field are directly proportionate to the amount of labour* (including science and technical appliances) *expended on it*, and to the amount of suitable manure employed. I have already pointed out what an enormous increase of returns might be achieved, in the present state of science, if agriculture were carried out on a large scale. If France with its small peasant proprietors was able to quadruple its harvests within the last ninety years, during which time it did not even double its population, very different results might be expected from a community working on socialistic principles. And apart from this, our Malthusians entirely overlook the fact, that we have not only to reckon with our own soil but with the soil of the whole world, in other words, to a large extent with countries whose fertility, properly utilized, would exceed that of our own twenty and thirty-fold, and even more. Large areas of the earth's surface are already covered with inhabitants, *but with absurdly small exceptions, the land is nowhere cultivated and turned to account as it might be.* Not only could Great Britain, as already shown,

---

[*] Rodbertus: " Zur Beleuchtung der Socialen Frage" (Enquiry into the Social Question), 1850.

produce a very considerably larger amount of food than at present, but also France, Germany, Austria, and still more the remaining countries of Europe.

European Russia, estimated by the present population of Germany, could support 475 millions, instead of the 78 millions which it actually contains. Russia has about 750 inhabitants to the square mile, Saxony 10,140. If Russia were as closely populated as Saxony it would contain over 1,000 million inhabitants, but the whole earth at the present day does not number more than 1,430 million inhabitants.

The objection that Russia possesses large tracts of land, the climate of which excludes any high degree of fertility is not valid, inasmuch as it possesses on the other hand, especially in the south, a climate and a fertility infinitely superior to anything in Germany. Moreover a denser population, combined with the corresponding cultivation of the land, thinning of forests, drainage of bogs, &c., would modify the climate to an extent that cannot even be estimated beforehand. Wherever large numbers of men congregate together, the climate becomes materially changed. We pay very little attention to these phenomena at present, and are unable to grasp their whole importance, because we have no occasion, and under existing circumstances no possibility of making experiments on a large scale. Further, all travellers agree, that even in the far north of Siberia, where spring, summer, and autumn follow each other in quick succession, and are limited to a few months only, suddenly a luxuriance of vegetation appears, astonishing to behold. Then again Norway and Sweden, thinly populated as they are, with their endless forests, their well-nigh inexhaustible wealth in metals, their numerous rivers and extensive seacoast would afford ample means of subsistence for a dense population. At present there is a deficiency of labour, because the means and appliances requisite for opening up the riches of these countries are unattainable under the given conditions.

And if these remarks apply to the North how much more do they apply to the South of Europe,—Portugal, Spain, Italy, Greece, the countries on the Danube, Hungary, Turkey, &c. These countries possess a climate of unrivalled excellence, a soil more fertile and luxuriant than the best soil of the United States, and could afford abundant nourishment for vast numbers of inhabitants, but in consequence of their corrupt political and social conditions, many hundred thousands of our countrymen prefer to cross the ocean than to settle in districts so much nearer home and so much easier of access. As soon as a rational social and international state of things has been established there, many millions of men will be required to bring these large and fruitful lands into a new state of cultivation.

We have at present, and for a considerable time shall have an insufficiency instead of a superfluity of men in Europe to carry out the high cultural aims that lie before us, and under such circumstances it is absurd to entertain the slightest fear of overpopulation.

If we turn from Europe to the other countries of the earth, we find a much greater deficiency of men and an over-abundance of land. The most fruitful and luxuriant countries of the world are lying entirely or almost entirely waste, because they cannot be made arable and cultivated by a few hundreds or thousands; *nothing short of an en masse colonization of many millions can avail to carry the day against the extravagant exuberance of nature.* Such countries are for instance, South and Central America, an area covering many hundred square miles.* Carey asserts that the Orinoco valley alone, 360 miles in length is capable of yielding a sufficient amount of food to sustain the entire present population of the globe. If we assume that the district in question would support half this number we have allowed an unnecessarily wide margin for mistakes of calculation. Certainly South America alone could support many times as many human beings as are at present scattered over the earth. The nutritive worth of ground planted with banana trees and of an equal extent of ground planted with wheat are as 133 : 1. While our wheat in a good soil bears 20 fold,† rice bears 80 to 100 fold in its

---

* 1 square mile equals 7.4² kilometres.

† The extent to which the returns of crops might be raised in our own country may be seen from the following remark in Liebig's Letters. " The Dresden Journal " of the 16th September, 1858, writes :—" We learn that in Eibenstock (Erzgebirge) the Inspector of Forests, Thiersch, has for years been making the most successful experiments in transplanting winter corn in the autumn. In the middle of October he removed the plants reserved for the purpose, covering a hundred square rods with 5·4 litres of seed. The returns were exceedingly high. Some plants had as many as fifty-one stalks with ears of corn containing a hundred grains." Liebig, who ascertained the accuracy of the information, adds that without doubt the process would amply repay itself in countries in which labour was abundant and the soil good. Give us, therefore, men and manure and exemption from capitalistic exploitation, and our harvests will increase in a manner which seems fabulous to us at present.

native country, maize 250 to 300 fold, and in some districts, for instance in the Philippine Isles, the reproductive power of rice is estimated to be 400 fold. A further task is so to prepare all these articles of food, as to preserve and utilize their nutritive properties. Chemistry will find an inexhaustible field in all these questions of nourishment; for instance, Liebig proved the advantageous effects on the nutritive value of bread gained by baking it with chalk water.

Central and South America, and especially Brazil, which is alone nearly as large as all Europe, (Brazil has 152,000 square miles with about 11,000,000 inhabitants, and Europe 178,000 square miles with about 310,000,000 inhabitants) overflows with a luxuriant fertility that rouses the wonder and admiration of all travellers and these countries are equally rich in untold stores of ores and metals. But these stores have hitherto been as good as inaccesible to the world owing to the indolence of the inhabitants, as well as to the smallness of their number and the low state of their civilisation, which made it impossible for them to grapple with such gigantic natural problems. The condition of the interior of Africa has been shown by the discoveries of the last few years. And not only are there in Asia large and fruitful countries capable of supporting further millions; we know from the past that in districts at present uncultivated and almost in a state of desert, the mild climate summons a plentiful and valuable vegetation from the soil, as soon as man learns to supply it with beneficent water. Owing to the annihilation of the inhabitants in desolating wars of conquest, and their insane oppression by the victors, the aqueducts and systems of irrigation fell into decay, and thousands of square miles were transformed into sandy wastes. Millions of civilized men may here find the task of unlocking inexhaustible sources of nourishment. The fruit of the date palm prospers in almost incredible abundance, and the tree requires so little space that 200 palms only cover 3·917 hectares of land. The Durrha in Egypt bears more than 3,000 fold, and yet the country is poor and starving. The cause is not over-population, but a ruinous system of exploitation, thanks to which the desert is encroaching on the cultivated ground from one decade to another. It is impossible to calculate the enormous results that might be attained in all these countries by the agriculture and horticulture of middle Europe.

Measured by the present standard of agricultural produc

tion, the United States of North America could with ease support twenty fold their present population, *i.e.*, 1,000,000,000 instead of 50,000,000. Canada could support 500,000,000 instead of the four and a-half million which it actually contains, and there still remains Australia, and the numerous partly large and mostly extremely fertile islands of the Pacific and Indian Oceans. Do not diminish the population but increase it, that is the message of civilization to man.

Wherever we turn, we find, not that the number of the inhabitants, but institutions, and the mode of obtaining and distributing products are at the root of all want and misery. Who does not know that a few good harvests in succession send down the price of food to such an extent that a considerable number of our small and middle-sized farmers are ruined in consequence. Abundance, instead of improving the condition of the producers, makes it worse. And this state of things is supposed to be a rational one. Speculating corn dealers often let the grain rot, when the crop is plentiful, because they know that the price rises in proportion as the supply fails, and in the face of such facts as this, we are told to fear over-population. In Russia and Southern Europe many thousand of cwts. of grain are scandalously wasted every year, for want of suitable storehouses and proper means of conveyance. Many million cwts. of food are annually thrown away in Europe, owing to deficient means of harvesting or the want of the necessary labourers at a given moment. Many a stack of corn, and many a well filled barn, and entire farms are burnt down, because the insurance money enhances the profits, for the same reason as that which induces ship owners to sink whole cargoes and crews in the sea. During our military operations crops are annually destroyed to a very considerable amount. In the year 1876 the cost of a manœuvre between Leipzig and Chemnitz, lasting only a few days was 300,000 marks (£15,000) for cornfields that had been trodden down, and we know that such estimates are apt to be extremely moderate. A large number of such manœuvres take place every year and extensive districts are withdrawn from cultivation of every kind for similar purposes.*

---

* As early as the time of St. Basil similar conditions must have existed, for he apostrophizes the rich as follows : " Wretches that ye are, how will ye answer the divine judge? Ye cover the nakedness of your walls with carpets, but not the nakedness of man with raiment. Ye adorn your houses with soft coverings of great price, and despise your brother who is clothed

Finally if we remember that to these sources of increase of food the sea has still to be added, the entire surface of which is to the surface of the earth as 18 to 7, or two and a half times as large, and which still awaits the utilization of its enormous supplies of nourishment, future prospects are opened to us that do not bear the faintest resemblance to the sombre picture presented by Malthusianism.

Who can predict the limits of our advance in chemistry, physics, physiology and other sciences ? Who would venture to foretell the, to us, giant undertakings, which men of later centuries will achieve, for the purpose of materially modifying the climatic conditions of countries, and of utilizing their natural resources in every possible direction ?

We already see capitalistic society accomplishing tasks which, fifty years ago, were regarded as impracticable. Broad isthmuses are severed and seas united. Tunnels, miles in length, are dug into the bowels of the earth, and join separate countries beneath the highest mountains, or they are built under the bottom of the sea, for the sake of shortening distances and obviating dangers and inconveniences of communication between two countries divided by water. And the question has been already ventilated and answered in the affirmative as to the possibility of converting part of the Sahara into a sea, and thus transforming many thousand square miles of desert into blooming, fruitful land. The execution of such projects is for the bourgeois world like everything else a question of "paying." Where then is the point at which anyone could say "So far and no further."

We must therefore not only deny the applicability of the Law of Diminishing Returns to our existing circumstances, but discover that we possess a superabundance of land capable of cultivation, awaiting the labour of fresh hundreds of millions.

If all these aims of civilization were to be pursued at once, the population would be too small instead of too large. Human beings may still multiply to a considerable extent, before they will be able to accomplish all that lies before them. Not only is the ground at present under cultivation

---

in rags. Ye let your grain perish and be eaten up in the barns and lofts, and do not deign to cast a glance at those who have no bread." Preaching morality to rulers has always been of extremely little use, nor will it be of any use to the end of time We must so alter our institutions that no one has the power of acting unjustly towards his neighbour, if we wish to assure the welfare of man.

far from being utilized as it might be, three quarters of the surface of the land cannot be cultivated at all for want of the necessary labour. Our relative over-population, which the capitalistic system of to-day is continually increasing, to the detriment of the workman and of society, will prove to be the very opposite at a higher stage of civilization. It is a means of progress, exactly as the existing possibility of over production in goods, the depreciation of land, the dissolution of bourgeois marriage, the enrolment of women and children in factories, the expropriation of small handicraftsmen and peasant proprietors are the forerunners of further advance for humanity.

When Kautsky says that men, once placed in comfortable circumstances, would take good care not to expose themselves to the dangers of tropical colonization, he misunderstands human nature. No daring enterprise has yet failed to find supporters. It is deeply implanted in the character of man to prove his own worth by fresh deeds of prowess, firstly for his own satisfaction and secondly for the sake of excelling others, *i.e.*, from ambition. There has never been any lack of volunteers in war, nor of volunteers of all ranks and classes for the dangerous expeditions to the North and South Pole, to the Interior of Africa, etc. The civilizing undertakings required in tropical countries, Central and Southern America, Africa, India, Central Asia, etc., are not of a nature to be carried out by individuals, but only by the combined forces of great masses, completely fitted out in every respect, and conducted on the largest scale ; for such purposes millions of voluntary workers can be had, if needed, and the dangers will not be excessive.

We now come to the second half of the question. Can mankind increase unlimitedly, and is their any danger of such an increase ?

To prove the enormous reproductive power of man, the Malthusians are fond of quoting abnormal cases of single familes and small races. Such cases prove nothing. They can be met by parallel cases in which, under favourable conditions of life. in a short time complete sterility or a low degree of reproductivity developed itself. It is often surprising how quickly wealthy families die out. Although the United States offer more favourable conditions for the increase of the population than any other country and many hundred thousand in the prime of life emigrate thither annually, the number of the inhabitants is only doubled in thirty years. The cycle of 12 or 20 years, which has been affirmed to be the normal one is nowhere to be found on a scale of any importance.

Experience has shown hitherto, as was pointed out in the passages quoted from Marx and Virchow, that the population tends to increase the most rapidly in the poorest districts, because as Virchow affirms, sexual enjoyment is the only pleasure such a population has besides drinking. It was mentioned in the early part of this book, that when Gregory VII. imposed celibacy upon the clergy, those occupying inferior posts in the diocese of Mainz complained that they had not all manner of enjoyments like the prelates, but that their only source of pleasure was a wife. Lack of varied occupation and recreation is perhaps the reason why the unions of country clergymen are blessed with so many children.

However that may be, it is incontestable that the poorest districts of Germany, such as the Silesian Eulengebirge, the Lausitz, the Erzgebirge, and Fichtelgebirge, the Thuringian Forest, the Harz, etc., are the seat of the densest population, that is to say, populations whose chief article of food is the potato. Again, it is a fact, that the sexual instinct is especially developed in cases of consumption, and that these patients often beget children at a stage of decline at which such a thing would seem impossible.

It appears to be a law of nature that, on an average, what is lost in quality is replaced in quantity. For instance, the most intelligent and strongest animals, such as the lion, elephant, camel, etc., our domestic animals, the horse, the cow, as a rule bring very few young into the world, while all less highly organized creatures increase enormously, in inverse ratio to their development, for instance, all kinds of insects, most fishes, the smaller mammals, such as hares, rats, mice, etc.

On the other hand, Darwin has proved that certain animals, when they are withdrawn from their wild state and brought under the discipline of man, lose their power of reproduction, for instance, the elephant. This seems to show that a change in the manner of life is the chief factor in determining a greater or less degree of fecundity.

But it is precisely the Darwinians who share the fear of over-population, and on whose authority the modern Malthusians take their stand. I have already shown that our Darwinians invariably get on a wrong track, when they apply their theories to man, because their mode of procedure in this case is generally roughly empirical; laws that hold good with regard to lower animals, they indiscriminately transfer to human beings, without considering that man, as the most highly organized animal, having once recognized the laws of nature, is capable of adapting and utilizing them.

The theory of the struggle for existence, the doctrine that the germs of new life exist in numbers altogether disproportionate to the possibility of their development and maintenance, would be perfectly applicable to the world of human beings, if men, instead of using their brains and turning to account the means within their reach for subduing air, land and water, spent their lives in grazing like oxen or in gratifying sexual lusts with the immoderation and shamelessness of apes, in other words, if they were oxen or apes instead of men. We may remark in passing that the fact that men and apes are the only beings in whose case the sexual impulse is not fixed to certain periods, as it is in the rest of the animal world, is a striking proof of the close relationship between the two. But though nearly related, they are not the same, and therefore they cannot be placed on the same level or measured by the same standard.

It is of course perfectly true that under the conditions of possessing and producing which have held good hitherto, the struggle for existence has been waged among men as well as among beasts, and that many were unable to find the necessary conditions of life. But it would be false to conclude that this state of things is unalterable and must eternally remain the same. This is the point at which the Darwinians get upon an inclined plane, because they have studied zoology and anthropology but not sociology; on the contrary, with regard to the latter science they have accepted the theories of our bourgeois ideologists second hand. Thus they arrived at incorrect deductions.

We have agreed that the sexual impulse in man is permanent, that it is his strongest impulse, and claims satisfaction, if the health is not to suffer. Further, this impulse in indisputably the stronger, the healthier and more normally developed man is, precisely as a good appetite and a good digestion are the signs of a healthy stomach and the first conditions of a healthy body.

But gratification of the sexual impulse is very far from being the same the same thing as generation or conception. Only the latter are of importance in the question of over-population. The most various theories have been evolved with regard to the fractifying qualities of male sperma, and the conditions that influence conception. *The principal reason why we are for the most part still groping in the dark on a field of such importance is, that for two thousand years man has been possessed by the most insane aversion to concern himself frankly, freely and naturally with the laws governing his own origin and development, and to study scientifically the conditions of generation and conception in the human race.* A change is beginning to become apparent in these things, and must extend to a radical reform.

On one side the theory has been propagated that higher mental development and strenuous mental exertion, in fact high nervous activity altogether, has the effect of repressing the sexual impulse and of weakening the reproductive power. On the other side this is disputed. The adherents of the first view seek to prove it by pointing to the fact that the wealthy classes have on an average fewer children than workmen, and that this is not to be attributed alone to the use of preventive checks. It is certain that intense mental labour has a repressing influence on the sexual impulse, but it is more than doubtful whether the majority of our wealthy classes are accustomed to mental labour of this description. On the other hand intense physical labour is also a repressing influence. But every excessive exertion is injurious, and therefore to be avoided.

Others affirm that the manner of life, and especially the nature of the food, combined with certain physical conditions on the part of the woman determines the power of generation and conception. The nature of the food, according to them, as proved in the case of certain animals, has more influence than any other factor, on the result of the sexual act. Possibly this is really the decisive point.

The effect of different kinds of nourishment on the organism of certain animals is shown to a surprising degree in the case of bees, *who, by a change of food, can breed a queen at will.* The bees seem to be further advanced in the knowledge of their sexual development than men. At least, they have not been preached to for two thousand years that to concern oneself with questions of sex is indecent and immoral.

An example of the influence of food on men in this respect was given me by an informant, who is intimately acquainted with the country and the people in Old Bavaria. According to his assurance, it is no common occurrence there, for the marriages of rich peasants, that is to say, a race of men that is perhaps the healthiest, strongest and finest in all Germany, to remain childless, and these peasants are therefore often induced to adopt the children of poor people. On inquiring as to the cause, I received the answer that it was because of the fat and nourishing food of the Old Bavarian peasants. As is well known this food consists chiefly in meal puddings, cooked with a considerable quantity of lard. The Bavarian population is famous for its skill in making these puddings. Similar results may often be observed in the case of plants, that grow luxuriantly in good soil, richly manured, but bear neither fruit nor seed.

I was told by a second informant, also intimately acquainted with the Bavarians and their customs that another cause doubtless contributed to the sterility mentioned above. This cause is premature sexual intercourse between unmarried persons, which is extremely common in these districts, and which no one thinks of regarding as objectionable. Now premature sexual intercourse is doubly exciting, when, as is customary in Bavaria, it is not limited to one couple, but takes place indiscriminately. The consequence of this undue stimulation is indifference, which acts as a check on conception. This is supposed to be one of the principal reasons why prostitutes so rarely have children.* We see, a wide field is here opened to conjecture and hypothesis.

There can be no doubt that the character of the male semen and the capacity for fructification of the female ovulum are modified by the nature of the food habitually consumed; and it is therefore not impossible that *the increase of the population may materially depend on the kind of nourishment eaten.* If this were once ascertained with certainty the number of the inhabitants might be more or less exclusively regulated by the manner of feeding. Moreover at certain periods the receptivity of the woman is at an exceedingly low ebb; indeed it seems probable that conception only takes place a few days before and after menstruation.† We must finally take into account that woman will occupy a totally different position in the society of the future, and will have no inclination to bring a large number of children, as "gifts of God" into the world; that she will desire to enjoy her freedom and independence, and not to spend half or three-

---

* The principal reason is chronic congestion and catarrh of the uterus, caused by immoderate intercourse. Trans.

† Recent investigations tend to show that conception is possible at any time during the intermenstrual period. Trans

quarters of the best years of her life in a state of pregnancy, or with a child at her breast. Certainly there are few women who do not wish to have a child, but still fewer who wish to have more than a limited number. All these things will work together in regulating the numbers of human beings, without there being any need for our Malthusians to rack their brains at present. The question will be solved at last, without any injurious abstinence or any repellant preventive measures.

We conclude therefore that in all probability the number of the population will be regulated in the future not by unfounded fears of starvation, but simply by regard to the personal welfare of those most immediately concerned. Karl Marx is right, when he says in "Capital" that every economic period in human development has its own law of population.

In the Socialistic community in which man will for the first time be placed under free and natural conditions, he will consciously direct his entire development in accordance with natural laws.

In all previous periods man has acted unconsciously, without knowledge of law, in everything that concerned production and distribution and the increase of the population; in the new community after he has acquired knowledge of law he will act consciously and methodically.

Socialism is science, applied with knowledge and understanding to all branches of human activity.

Conclusion.

————

The foregoing exposition has shown us that Socialism is not arbitrary destruction and reconstruction, but a natural process of development, that all the elements of dissolution on the one hand and of growth on the other, are factors which act because they cannot do otherwise, that neither " statesmen of genius " nor " demagogues who stir up revolt," can guide the course of events according to their will. They believe that they direct the current, and are borne along by it themselves. At the same time no thinking person who considers the arguments brought forward can doubt that we are at length approaching the " fulness of time."

We must still briefly refer to one peculiar phase of development, which especially characterizes Germany, in order to show that *Germany more than any other country will have the task of undertaking the leadership at the next stage of advance.*

Gluts, arising from overproduction have been frequently mentioned in this book. We explained that overproduction was a result of the bourgeois system under which more wares are produced than the purchasing power of the people, in other words the general market, can digest. This is a pheno·menon peculiar to the bourgeois world and has been observed in no other period of human development. The bourgeois system, however, produces not only an over-supply of wares and men, but also an over-supply of intelligence, and thus enhances the acuteness of the crisis which is destined to put an end to the bourgeoisie altogether.

Germany is the typical land in which this overproduction of intelligence and culture, which the bourgeois world can no longer turn to any account, is going on on a scale of great magnitude. One circumstance, which for centuries has been regarded as a misfortune for German progress, has largely contributed to this condition of things. I refer to the number of small States and the check which these political bodies exercised upon capitalistic development. The consequence of these small States was a decentralization of the mental life of the nation ; small centres were formed all over the country and made their mark on their surroundings. The numerous courts and governments required an extremely numerous body of officials in proportion to that which a large central government would have required, and of all these officials a certain degree of culture was demanded. Thus a number of academies and universities arose, such as no other country in Europe possessed. The envy and emulation of the various governments also played their part in the matter. The same thing repeated itself when some governments began to introduce compulsory education for the people. The desire not to remain behind a neighbouring state had a good effect in this case also. The demand for intelligence grew, as the spread of education and knowledge, hand in hand with the material development of the bourgeoisie, roused the claim for political rights, for national representation and for the local administration of communes. The cultured few formed small bodies in small countries and circles, but they helped to train the mass, and incited the young men of the bourgeoisie to strive for a position among them by acquiring the culture necessary for this purpose.

The same thing applied to art as to general culture. No country in Europe has in proportion to its size so many painting academies, technical schools of all kinds, museums and art collections as Germany. Other lands may have larger galleries in their capital cities, but none, except perhaps Italy, has such a distribution over the length and breadth of the empire.

This process of development gave a certain depth to the German mind ; the absence of great political struggles gave opportunity for a contemplative life. While other nations were contending for supremacy in the market of the world, were dividing the earth among them, and waging great internal wars in politics, the Germans sat quietly at home and dreamed and thought. But this dreaming, meditation and reflection, favoured by a climate which encourages domestic life and necessitates exertion, created German philosophy and formed the critical, observant mind by which the Germans began to distinguish themselves when they at at length awoke from sleep.

The year 1848 was the birth year of the German bourgeoisie, as a class conscious of its own existence, that now came upon the stage as an independant political party, represented by Liberalism. Here the above mentioned peculiarity of German development became apparent. It was not the manufacturers, merchants, men of commerce and finance who assumed the lead, but professors, aristocrats tainted with Liberalism, authors, lawyers, and doctors of all the faculties. These were the German ideologists, and their work was like unto them. The bourgeoisie had received a temporary check on political ground, but it redeemed the time, and furthered its own interests elsewhere. The out-break of the Austro-Italian war, the commencement of the Regency in Prussia roused the bourgeoisie afresh to stretch out its hand towards political power. The National Society (National-Verein) movement began. The bourgeoisie was already too developed to brook any longer the many barriers that restrained its activity, barriers that were economic as well as political, barriers of taxation, of communication and of locomotion. It assumed a revolutionary air. Herr *v.* Bismarck recognised the situation and made use of it in his own way, by uniting the interests of the bourgeoisie with those of the monarchy, whose enemy the bourgeoisie had never been, for fear of revolution and of the people. The barriers that had checked its greater material development were broken down. Thanks to the great wealth of Germany in coal and ore, and to the intelligence and frugality of its working classes, the development of the bourgeoisie during the ensuing twenty years was truly gigantic, and, with the exception of the United States, altogether unparalleled in so short a time and to such an extent. It thus came about that Germany already occupies the second place in Europe as an industrial and commercial State, and is striving to attain the first.

But this enormous material development had its reverse. The system of blockade which had existed in nearly all German States up to the foundation of a united Germany, had enabled an extremely numerous class of artisans and peasant proprietors to maintain a struggling existence. When all protective barriers were suddenly removed and the lower middle class found itself face to face with an unbridled process of capitalistic production, its position speedily became a desperate one. The period of prosperity im-mediately after the war of 1870-71 made the danger at first appear smaller than it was, but it became all the more apparent when the crisis broke out. The bourgeoisie had made use of this period of prosperity to develop on a gigantic scale and now made the pressure felt tenfold, through its production en masse and its accumulation of riches. The gulf between property and destitution widened rapidly.

This process of dissolution and absorption which is taking place more speedily from day to day, the growth of material power on the one hand and the lessening power of resistance on the other, have reduced entire classes of the population to a condition of the utmost distress. They see their position threatened, the comfortable circumstances in which they lived suddenly changed for the worse, and can calculate with mathematical certainty the approach of the day that will strip them of everything.

In this forlorn struggle each one seeks to save himself as best he may, by changing his vocation. The old people can make no such change; only in the rarest cases do they possess independent property to bequeath to their children ; they therefore make the utmost exertions, leaving no stone unturned, to procure for sons and daughters appointments with fixed salaries, which require no capital for carrying on. Such appointments are, firstly, all official posts in the civil or communal service, the entire field of instruction, post office and railway service, the higher posts in the service of the bourgeoisie, in offices, depots and factories, as managers, chemists, technical directors, engineers, &c. ; then the so-called liberal professions, law, medicine, theology, literature, art in all its branches, architecture, &c.

Thousands and thousands, who would formerly have entered trade, seeing that it can now offer them neither a chance of independence nor sufficient means of subsistence, look about them for a position in one of the vocations mentioned. Everyone presses towards the academies, scientific, classical and polytechnical schools spring up like mushrooms, and those already in existence are overcrowded ; the number of students at the universities,* the number of pupils in the chemical and physical laboratories, in trading

---

* 14,676 students studied in the German Universities in the year 1871-2, 16,191 in 1875-6, and no fewer than 22,038 in 1881. That is to say, the students have increased at the rate of 50 per cent. in ten years, while the population has increased at the rate of 10 per cent. during the same period. In Prussia, in the year 1859, there were 20 scholars in the Gymnasia (classical schools) and 9 scholars in the Realschulen (science schools) to every 10,000 inhabitants. In 1876 there were 31 of the former and 22 of the latter to the same number of inhabitants ; in this case also an increase of over 50 per cent.

and commercial schools, in all kinds of schools and colleges for girls increases proportionately. Already well-nigh every branch is overstocked, and still a stronger and stronger current sets in the same direction. Continually new gymnasia and academies are being demanded, to receive the increasing number of candidates. Both the heads of departments and private persons are in despair, and issue warning upon warning against the choice of one profession after another. Even theology, which ten years ago threatened to dry up altogether for want of candidates, profits by the superfluity, and sees its benefices filling again.* " I am ready to teach belief in ten thousand gods and devils, if required, only give me a place that will support me," is echoed from all sides. Prussian ministers refuse to sanction the founding of new upper class schools, " because those already existing more than supply the present demand for candidates of every description."

This state of affairs is further intensified by the exterminating competitive struggle of the bourgeoisie within its own ranks ; numbers of its young men are thus compelled to seek positions and means of support elsewhere. Again our large standing army with its host of officers, whose advancement gets into a serious state of stagnation after a lengthened period of peace, leads to the pensioning of a considerable number of men in the prime of life, who are favoured by the State and appointed to all kinds of official posts. The swarms of subaltern officers who have served their time are also appointed to posts in the civil service, and thus takes the bread out of other people's mouths. In addition to this the innumerable imperial, state and communal officials of all ranks more often than not educate their children for similar vocations, and have no choice but to do so. For it is precisely among these officials that the want of means is greatest, while on the other hand, social position, a certain degree of culture, and the tastes of these circles necessarily exclude the so-called lower occupations, even if they were not already overstocked in consequence of the capitalistic system.

The institution of One Year Volunteers, which permits candidates who have attained a certain standard of education to reduce their term of military service from three years to one, in return for a specified payment, further increases the

---

* In 18 German Universities there were in 1863-64, 236 protestant students of divinity to 1,000 mixed students; in 1870-71, 179; in 1876-77, 109. After this the number gradually increased, till it reached 142 in 1881.

number of applicants for all vacant posts and appointments. This is especially the case with many rich peasants' sons, who, at the end of their year, have but little inclination to return to their village and to the calling of their fathers.

The consequence of all this is that Germany has a more numerous proletariat of scholars and artists than any other country, and a large proletariat among the so-called liberal professions. This proletariat is constantly increasing and carrying fermentation and discontent with the existing state of affairs into the highest ranks of society.

The idealistic spirit in these circles is thereby roused to criticism of actual conditions and helps to accelerate the universal dissolution. Thus is the present system being attacked and undermined from all sides at once.

There can be no doubt that Germany must take the lead in the great giant-struggle of the future ; its whole previous development and its geographical position as the "heart of Europe" have predestined it to do so. It was no accident that the motor laws of modern society were discovered and Socialism scientifically demonstrated to be the social form of the future by Germans. First came Karl Marx, supported by Friedrich Engels while Ferdinand Lassalle followed in their steps and cast the sparks among the masses. Neither is it an accident that the German Socialistic movement is the greatest and most important in the world, surpassing that of all other nations, especially that of France which came to a standstill at a half-bourgeois stage of development. It is no accident that German Socialists are the pioneers who are spreading the Socialistic idea among the other nations of the world.

A quarter of a century ago Buckle wrote as the result of his study of the German mind and German culture, that although Germany possessed a large number of the greatest thinkers, there was no country in which the contrast between the class of scholars and the mass of the people was so great as in Germany. This is no longer true at the present day. It was only true as long as German science remained almost exclusively deductive, and limited to scholars who had little contact with practical life. As soon as Germany was economically revolutionized, the deductive method in science was to a considerable extent replaced by the inductive method. Science became practical. People learned that its value consisted in its applicability to human life. Consequently all the branches of knowledge have become to a large extent democratic during the last twenty years in Germany.

The number of young men who have been trained for higher callings has contributed to this result, while on the other hand the general schooling of the masses, which is in Germany better than in any other European country, facilitates the reception of a large amount of mental impressions of all kinds. And finally, and most of all the Socialistic movement has raised the mental level of the people, by its literature, its press, its societies and meetings, its parliamentary representation and its criticism of all departments of public life.

The Socialist law has altered nothing in this respect. It has to a certain extent prevented the movement from spreading broadly, and checked its too rapid development, and has thus given other countries time to come up with Germany. But it has intensified it, and created an immense amount of bitterness, that is ready to explode, and that claims atonement and victims. Meanwhile the whole social development, the dissolution of society is advancing daily with greater strides.

Thus, in the last quarter of the nineteenth century we see on all sides the great battle of spirits breaking out and being waged with fiery vehemence. Not social science alone, but the wide field of natural science, of hygiene, the history of civilization, and even philosophy are the arsenals from which the weapons are supplied. From all sides* the foundations of existing society are being undermined; the weightiest blows are being dealt against the props of the old régime; the revolutionary idea is penetrating into the most conservative circles, and carrying confusion into the ranks of the enemies of light. Artisans and scholars, agriculturists and artists, in short men of every rank and calling are joining the working classes, which compose the bulk of the army that is to fight the last fight, and mutually support and supplement each other.

Women too are summoned not to remain behind in a struggle in which their own freedom and deliverance is at stake. It is now their part to show that they have comprehended their true position in the movement, and that they are resolved to take their share in the present contest for a better future. It is the part of the men to assist them in freeing themselves from all prejudices, and to support them in the fight. Let no one underrate his own power, or imagine that one more or less makes no difference. No one not even

* Especially in Mainländer's " Philosophie der Erlösung " (Philosophy of Redemption) 1st and 2nd vol.

the weakest can be dispensed with for furthering the advance of humanity. A continual dropping hollows out the hardest stone. And many drops make the brook, and brooks make the stream, and streams the great river, whose majestic course can be stopped by no obstacle in nature. Precisely the same thing applies to the life of civilized humanity. Nature is everywhere our instructress, and if we abide by her teaching, the final victory must be ours.

This final victory will be all the more decisive, the greater the zeal and energy with which each individual pursues the path before him. No one has a right to consider whether he himself, after all his trouble and labour, will live to see a fairer epoch of civilization, and still less has he the right to let such a consideration deter him from the course on which he has entered. Although we cannot predict the duration of the single phases of development, nor the form which they will assume, just as little as we can with any certainty foresee the length of our own lives, in a century such as ours we have no cause to relinquish all hope of witnessing the victory. We struggle and strive onwards, unconcerned as to when or where the boundary posts of new and better times for humanity shall be erected. If we fall in fight, the rearguard will take our place; we shall fall with the consciousness of having done our duty as men, and with the conviction that the goal will be reached, in spite of all opposition from the enemies of humanity and progress.

THE END.